"Stern is famous for confronting our 'Hard Questi[...] meanings before they were worded, and how is tha[...] quent words? Almost every question in psychoanaly[...] book indispensable for the practitioner, who will gain a reassuring[...] of their daily work from Stern's picture of the relationship between words, life, and the expressive states in between. And Stern's account of his progressive revisions is a virtual education in how to think about the human condition."

**Lawrence Friedman, M.D.**, Clinical Professor of Psychiatry, Weill-Cornell Medical College, USA

"Don Stern is a theoretician's theorizer and a clinician's right-hand. He writes of realms that elude our grasp yet are where we need to go—the space between words, that ineffable sense that 'vibrates' with the spoken word. He is a poet of the nonverbal, unformulated, unsaid—the real—and writes in a conversational yet highly sophisticated style. Talking therapy has thus expanded as Stern takes his rightful place among the leading psychoanalytic thinkers of today, depolarizing their global reach. Read this book, it will help you."

**Andrea Celenza, Ph.D.**, Boston Psychoanalytic Society and Institute, USA, author of *Erotic Revelations: Clinical Applications and Perverse Scenarios*

"In this exciting new book Donnel Stern extends his earlier creative and courageous inquiries into the nature of meaning and meaning-making. Meaning is not contained simply in what is or can be put into words or symbolized, Stern teaches. Rather, meaning is like the air we breathe, we are immersed in it without being able to point to it. As his title promises, Stern guides us to appreciate the 'infinity' of our potential experience, the limits of what we can know at any moment, and the awe we feel when we glimpse what might have been understood but never will be. The book is a guide not only for psychoanalysts and other therapists, but for anybody who can appreciate the richness and complexity of what it is to be human."

**Jay Greenberg, Ph.D.**, Editor, *The Psychoanalytic Quarterly*

"The imaginativeness and depth of Donnel Stern's contribution to contemporary psychoanalysis is fully on display in this book. We have the extraordinary opportunity to join Stern in returning to his groundbreaking conceptualization of unformulated experience. This journey is one filled with nuance and depth regarding verbal and nonverbal experience and how translating unformulated experience can lead to spontaneous creative living. Stern displays great subtlety in putting our experiences as patients and analysts into words. Through his considerable capacity for syncretic thinking, he invites us to consider his contributions in relation to a number of theorists. This is a book not just to read but to study."

**Steven H. Cooper, Ph.D.**, Associate Professor in Psychiatry, Harvard Medical School, USA

# The Infinity of the Unsaid

The theory of unformulated experience is an interpersonal/relational conception of unconscious process. The idea is that unconscious content is not fully formed, merely awaiting discovery, but is instead better understood as potential experience—a vaguely organized, primitive, global, non-ideational, affective state.

In the past, the formulation of experience was most commonly understood as verbal articulation. That was the perspective Donnel B. Stern took in 1997 in his first book, *Unformulated Experience: From Dissociation to Imagination in Psychoanalysis*. In this new book, Stern recognizes that we need to theorize the formulation of nonverbal experience, as well. Using new concepts of the "acceptance" and "use" of experience that "feels like me," Stern argues for a wider conception of "meaningfulness." Some formulated experience is verbal ("articulation"), but other formulations are nonverbal ("realization"). Demonstrating how this can be so is at the heart of this book. Stern then goes on to house this entire set of ideas in the commodious conception of language offered by Charles Taylor, Gadamer, and Merleau-Ponty.

*The Infinity of the Unsaid* offers an expansion of the theory of unformulated experience that has important implications for clinical thinking and practice; it will be of great interest to relational/interpersonal psychoanalysts and psychoanalytic psychotherapists.

**Donnel B. Stern** is Training and Supervising Analyst, William Alanson White Institute, New York City and Adjunct Clinical Professor of Psychology and Clinical Consultant, New York University Postdoctoral Program in Psychotherapy and Psychoanalysis. He is the founder and editor of the Routledge Psychoanalysis in a New Key Book Series and author and editor of many articles and books. His most recent authored book is *Relational Freedom: Emergent Properties of the Interpersonal Field* (2015).

# Psychoanalysis in a New Key Book Series
Donnel B. Stern
*Series Editor*

When music is played in a new key, the melody does not change, but the notes that make up the composition do: change in the context of continuity, continuity that perseveres through change. Psychoanalysis in a New Key publishes books that share the aims psychoanalysts have always had, but that approach them differently. The books in the series are not expected to advance any particular theoretical agenda, although to this date most have been written by analysts from the Interpersonal and Relational orientations.

The most important contribution of a psychoanalytic book is the communication of something that nudges the reader's grasp of clinical theory and practice in an unexpected direction. Psychoanalysis in a New Key creates a deliberate focus on innovative and unsettling clinical thinking. Because that kind of thinking is encouraged by exploration of the sometimes surprising contributions to psychoanalysis of ideas and findings from other fields, Psychoanalysis in a New Key particularly encourages interdisciplinary studies. Books in the series have married psychoanalysis with dissociation, trauma theory, sociology, and criminology. The series is open to the consideration of studies examining the relationship between psychoanalysis and any other field—for instance, biology, literary and art criticism, philosophy, systems theory, anthropology, and political theory.

But innovation also takes place within the boundaries of psychoanalysis, and Psychoanalysis in a New Key therefore also presents work that reformulates thought and practice without leaving the precincts of the field. Books in the series focus, for example, on the significance of personal values in psychoanalytic practice, on the complex interrelationship between the analyst's clinical work and personal life, on the consequences for the clinical situation when patient and analyst are from different cultures, and on the need for psychoanalysts to accept the degree to which they knowingly satisfy their own wishes during treatment hours, often to the patient's detriment. A full list of all titles in this series is available at: https://www.routledge.com/series/LEAPNKBS

**Titles in this series include:**

Vol. 44  **The Infinity of the Unsaid**
Unformulated Experience, Language, and the Nonverbal
*Donnel B. Stern*

Vol. 43  **The Mindbrain and Dreams**
An Exploration of Dreaming, Thinking, and Artistic Creation
*Mark J. Blechner*

# The Infinity of the Unsaid

## Unformulated Experience, Language, and the Nonverbal

Donnel B. Stern

Routledge
Taylor & Francis Group

LONDON AND NEW YORK

First published 2019
by Routledge
2 Park Square, Milton Park, Abingdon, Oxon OX14 4RN

and by Routledge
711 Third Avenue, New York, NY 10017

*Routledge is an imprint of the Taylor & Francis Group, an informa business*

© 2019 Donnel B. Stern

*British Library Cataloguing in Publication Data*
A catalogue record for this book is available from the British Library

*Library of Congress Cataloging in Publication Data*
Names: Stern, Donnel B., author.
Title: The infinity of the unsaid : unformulated experience, language,
and the nonverbal / Donnel B. Stern.
Description: Abingdon, Oxon ; New York, NY : Routledge, 2019. |
Series: Psychoanalysis in a new key book series ; 44 |
Includes bibliographical references and index.
Identifiers: LCCN 2018009028 (print) | LCCN 2018012470 (ebook) |
ISBN 9780429468087 (Master) | ISBN 9780429886577 (Web PDF) |
ISBN 9780429886560 (ePub) | ISBN 9780429886553 (Mobipocket/Kindle) |
ISBN 9781138605008 (hardback : alk. paper) | ISBN 9781138604995
(pbk. : alk. paper)
Subjects: LCSH: Psychoanalysis. | Meaning (Psychology) | Experience.
Classification: LCC BF175 (ebook) | LCC BF175 .S6649 2019 (print) |
DDC 150.19/5—dc23LC
record available at https://lccn.loc.gov/2018009028

ISBN: 978-1-138-60500-8 (hbk)
ISBN: 978-1-138-60499-5 (pbk)
ISBN: 978-0-429-46808-7 (ebk)

Typeset in Times New Roman and Gill Sans
by Florence Production Ltd, Stoodleigh, Devon, UK

For it was not the case that language cloaked reality in its moods, but vice versa, reality arose from them.

Karl Ove Knausgaard, *My Struggle, Book 1*.
New York: Farrar, Straus and Giroux, p. 33

# Contents

# Acknowledgments

I would never have written this book, or any other, without the love, patience, and support of my wife, Kathe Hift, who, like me, is a psychologist and psychoanalyst. I spend a lot of time thinking, teaching, reading, and writing. Kathe understands what these activities mean to me, and she gives me the time and clear sailing it takes to do them. I am grateful for the same reasons to our children, Lexi, Babette, and Michael, who grew up with the same acceptance of my work, and even pride in it. My parents, Thomas Lee Stern and Gladys Crawford Stern, had enough faith in me that I am left with the confidence, most of the time, that I have something worthwhile to say.

I owe a special debt of gratitude to my close friends and colleagues at the William Alanson White Institute of Psychiatry, Psychology, and Psychoanalysis, and the New York University Postdoctoral Program in Psychotherapy and Psychoanalysis. I have taught and supervised in these training centers for decades, and they have each nurtured me in many ways. Just living within such a thoroughly psychoanalytic world has been not only formative, but also has kept me focused on the issues of the day in my chosen field. It is natural in such a world to think, to challenge yourself to formulate what you believe. One might even say that, for people who are so inclined, such a life is called for by these circumstances. Conversations, some in the real world and others in my head, with people who are my friends, some of whom are gone now, have inspired me and encouraged new thoughts. I appreciate my partners in these conversations: Lew Aron, Tony Bass, Jessica Benjamin, Phillip Blumberg, Philip Bromberg, Philip Cushman, Muriel Dimen, Darlene Ehrenberg, Jack Foehl, Lou Fourcher, Jay Greenberg, Adrienne Harris, Irwin Hirsch, Irwin Hoffman, Mannie Kaftal, Edgar Levenson, Steve Mitchell, Spyros Orfanos, Jim Phillips, Barbara Pizer, Stuart Pizer, Sophia Richman, Neil Skolnick, Steve Tublin, and Joyce Slochower.

I am grateful, too, to the members of the study groups I lead, which have long been such an important part of my professional life. As might be expected from my orientation in psychoanalysis, we learn together in these groups about interpersonal and relational psychoanalytic theory and practice; but, actually, more often the ideas we study are unfamiliar to us when we begin to read them: Bion, Ferro, Green, Lacan, Laplanche, and others. Few of us would tackle these writings by ourselves. But because we are together, we are emboldened to push beyond the limits of our understanding. Members of these groups become more than fellow students; they become friends and colleagues, and their thoughts come to be influential on my own: Lisa Director, Robert Grossmark, Orna Guralnik, Arthur Heiserman, Katherine Leddick, James Ogilvie, and Debbie Rothschild; Jill Howard, Shelly Itzkowitz, Peter Lessem, Robert Millner, Jean Petrucelli, Sarah Stemp, and Don Troise; Rachel Altstein, Kim Bernstein, Alexandra Eitel, Philip Gardner, Rebecca Posner, Lissa Schaupp, Alan Sirote, Alan Slomowitz; Debra Farbman, Navah Kaplan, Luis Ripoll, and Nick Singman.

I thank my supervisees. As I get older, I notice that consultation offers me, more than it did when I was younger, the opportunity to formulate what it is that I think is going on in psychoanalytic work. As an analyst, I am focused on learning about my patients via the movements of my own emotional life. That same attitude remains important in consultation, of course. But in consultation, because of the didactic intention, I am freer to reflect on questions about the nature of clinical process and therapeutic action than I am when I am doing treatment.

I thank my patients. I have always felt moved and privileged by their willingness to include me in the struggle between fulfilling and obstructing their desire to tell me what is on their minds. I listen with reciprocal desire to know my own mind, and theirs, as thoroughly as the analytic relatedness in that moment allows me. My work gives me the opportunity to know, to feel with, to understand, to grope my way into the role I am playing in my patients' lives, and they in mine. No other kind of work offers that kind of reward.

As always, Phillip Blumberg deserves special thanks. Phil's willingness to read what I write and to tell me what he thinks of it remains undiluted after all this time. A different form of the chapters in this book was originally intended to be the second half of my book, *Partners in Thought* (Stern, 2010a). Phil counseled me to remove this material from its original context and consider it separately. The outcome of that good advice was much revision and elaboration, resulting eventually in the book you are reading now.

An earlier version of a portion of Chapter 1 was originally written for an issue of *Psychoanalytic inquiry* edited by Daniel Goldin and entitled "The Relational Turn: Why?" (in press). I thank Taylor and Francis, LLC for permission to publish a revised version of that excerpt.

An earlier version of a portion of Chapter 2 was previously published by Sage as:

Stern, D.B (2001). Words and wordlessness in the psychoanalytic situation. *Journal of the American Psychoanalytic Association*, 50: 221–247.

I also thank SAGE Publications for permission to reproduce an excerpt from the following article:

Stern, DB. (2013). Relational freedom and therapeutic action. *Journal of the American Psychoanalytic Association*, 61: 227–255.

Archipelago Books and Farrar, Straus & Giroux granted permission to reprint excerpts from:

Knausgaard, K.O (2009). *My Struggle, Book 1*, translated by Don Bartlett. English translation copyright © 2012 by Don Bartlett.

Taylor and Francis Group, LLC granted permission to quote excerpts from:

Merleau-Ponty, M. (1945/1962). *The Phenomenology of Perception*. Translated by Colin Smith. London: Routledge and Kegan Paul.

Harvard University Press granted permission to quote excerpts from two sources:

Langer, S. (1942). *Philosophy in a New Key; A Study in the Symbolism of Reason, Rite, and Art*. Cambridge, MA: Harvard University Press.

Taylor, C. (1989). *Sources of the Self: The Making of the Modern Identity*. Cambridge, MA: Harvard University Press.

Cambridge University Press gave permission to quote excerpts from the following source:

Taylor, C. (1985). Language and human nature. In: *Human Agency and Language: Philosophical Papers, Volume 1*. Cambridge, UK: Cambridge University Press.

# Chapter 1

# Introduction
## Meaningfulness: more than just words

> The phenomenological world is not the bringing to explicit attention of a pre-existing being, but the laying down of being. Philosophy is not the reflection of a pre-existing truth, but, like art, the act of bringing truth into being.
>
> Maurice Merleau-Ponty (1945/1962), p. xx

I undertook this revision and elaboration of the theory of unformulated experience (Stern, 1983, 1997, 2010a, 2015) to take account of the role of nonverbal experience more explicitly and thoroughly than my earlier writings have done. A second goal was to reconsider, through the lens of hermeneutics, the relation of the verbal and the nonverbal in psychoanalysis. Through that lens, the verbal and the nonverbal have more in common than they do in the information processing metaphor that has been so influential in cognitive psychology, and to some extent within psychoanalysis, over the last decades.

The book has been a long time coming. The first draft was written in 2007–2008, as the second half of another book, *Partners in Thought: Working with Unformulated Experience, Dissociation, and Enactment* (Stern, 2010a), that was eventually published without it—although I did promise in the beginning of that book to come back to the themes taken up here. This book is the fulfillment of that promise.

I set the chapters aside at that time, though, and although I always meant to come back to them, other matters attracted my attention, and it has taken this long to return to them. (A third book, *Relational Freedom: Emergent Properties of the Interpersonal Field* [Stern, 2015], intervened.) I have revised, updated, and elaborated the original chapters in many significant respects, but the bones of the project remain what they were ten years ago. The reason this material languished certainly has nothing to do with the significance it holds for me: these ideas have been in the center of my interest since I began writing in the field of psychoanalysis.

In this introductory chapter, I lay out the argument of the book and the plan of the chapters, and situate that argument within certain relevant and growing parts of the psychoanalytic literature (the study of procedural meaning, and the broader subject of unrepresented states); but first, as the context within which the expansion and revision offered in the following chapters find their meaning, I offer a summary of the theory of unformulated experience as it has existed up to this point.

## A brief summary of the theory of unformulated experience

In the late 1970s and early 1980s, when I began to give shape to my thoughts about the unconscious, I found great value in Harry Stack Sullivan's (1940/1953, 1953) developmental theory of cognition. Sullivan proposed three modes of thought and experience, each of which he conceptualized to be more "mature" than the one that came before it; and like the developmental conceptions of a number of other theorists (Bion's reworking of Klein's paranoid-schizoid and depressive positions, for instance), Sullivan's idea was that each of these cognitive stages was also preserved, as life went on, as one of several ways of organizing experience. *Prototaxis*, the most primitive mode, bears some similarity to the "blooming, buzzing confusion" that William James (1890, p. 462) imagined was the state of mind of the youngest infants. Everything is all mixed up together in something like a primordial, cognitive/affective soup. There is no before and after, no differentiation of one thing from another. Sullivan thought prototaxis was rarely observed after infancy, except in psychotic states. We might compare prototaxis to Freud's (1914b) primary narcissism, Loewald's (1978/2000) primary unity, or Matte-Blanco's (1988) indivisible mode of being.

It was Sullivan's (1940/1953, 1953) next two modes of experience, the *parataxic* and the *syntaxic*, that interested me most. In parataxis, experience does have a before and after, but the meanings of this experience cannot be specified. The meanings are what Sullivan described as "private" or "autistic." This is a profound kind of privacy, because the meanings are private even to oneself. That is, one cannot articulate the meanings, even in one's own mind. For all intents and purposes, then, parataxis is

Sullivan's way of conceptualizing unconscious meaning. But, as we shall see, this conceptualization differs from Freud's in important respects.

For Sullivan (1940/1953, 1953), parataxic experience is the form in which the hidden meanings of interpersonal relations exist. Sullivan did not use the term "transference." He preferred "parataxic distortion," by which he meant the attribution of meanings in the here-and-now to another person, meanings that cannot be specified and that are, in fact, not even suspected by the person who creates them. Sullivan created this neologism for the reason he usually had when he invented words, which he did frequently: he wanted to mark the differentiation of his own ideas from traditional psychoanalytic conceptions.

Let me explain the substance of the differentiation in this case. Sullivan (1940, 1953) did not accept the Freudian view that interpersonal life is a compromise expression of the conflict between drive and defense. Even more important to his understanding of the unconscious parts of relatedness was his emphasis on transference as the unconscious aspect of present-day relatedness—in contrast to Freud, whose theory of transference emphasized historical antecedents. It is not that Sullivan ignored history. Quite the contrary. He was insistent on the significance of interpersonal history, especially with the significant people of early life. But his clinical interest in interpersonal relations—that is, in the observable aspects of interaction in the here-and-now—led him to take the position that clinicians' efforts should not be directed at the interpretation of the past, but instead at the observation and description to the patient of the present-day outcomes of those historical events. How does the dissociation of aspects of interpersonal life, whenever they began, affect interpersonal relations *now*? What is distorted, obscured or "mystified" (Levenson, 1972/2005, 1983/2005) in interpersonal life *now*, and why? Sullivan certainly agreed that the clinician must learn what happened in early, important relationships; but therapeutic action, for him, emerges not from the recall or reconstruction of that history, as Freud and the Freudians of Sullivan's day claimed, but from a clinical focus on the present-day outcomes of those events. Sullivan wanted to encourage the formulation of distortions in current relationships, including the therapeutic one, on the basis of whatever the patient's interpersonal history had been; but he did not believe that reconstructing the patient's history, in and of itself, led to change. This position made good sense to me, and I embraced it.

It is only with the *syntaxic mode of experience*, though, the most "mature" form of experience in Sullivan's scheme of things, that we arrive at the idea that most deeply inspired the concept of unformulated experience. The syntaxic mode is *consensually validated* experience—experience that is either explicitly public, or could be public if one chose to make it so. "Public" in this sense is not limited to the expression to another person of knowledge about one's experience; for experience to become "public" is also for the meanings of one's own experience to become knowable to oneself. That is, one can reflect on one's own experience only to the extent that the experience is organized in the syntaxic mode. The conversion of meaning from parataxic to syntaxic is therefore analogous to the move from unconscious to preconscious. In the case of parataxic distortion, to convert parataxis into syntaxis is to become aware of the previously unformulated meanings of the relatedness between oneself and the other.

One of the keys to this set of ideas is Sullivan's idea of consensual validation, which is the means by which parataxis becomes public and enters the syntaxic mode. Consensual validation is defined by Sullivan as knowing in the special way that verbal language allows. For experience to be "public" is for it to be represented in language, or capable of being represented in language (that is, one could put it into words if one had a reason to do so).

Why did Sullivan feel that he was presenting a new perspective on these questions? After all, Freud (1915b) too gave language a special place in his theory. For meanings to move from the unconscious to the preconscious, they needed to become attached to words. We could never actually create a direct understanding of unconscious contents, which Freud described as "thing-presentations." Rather, thing-presentations needed to be connected to language, becoming "word-presentations"; in the process, they were cathected by the preconscious and could then enter awareness.

At a certain point in the development of his argument about things such as this, Sullivan, referring to the link between self-awareness and language, wrote two sentences that had a great impact on me. These two sentences catalyzed much of the reading and thinking I had been doing about the emergent aspects of experiencing.[1] Things began to fall together in my mind. It was suddenly clear to me that verbal language had a different *kind* of significance in Sullivan's theory than it did in Freud's. Here are the sentences, which I first quoted in reference to unformulated experience in 1983:

> One has information about one's experience only to the extent that one has tended to communicate it to another or thought about it in the manner of communicative speech. Much of that which is ordinarily said to be *repressed* is merely unformulated.
>
> (Sullivan, 1940/1953, p. 185; italics from the original)

It took me years to work out what this meant. I think that even Sullivan, who was onto something very interesting here, did not grasp the implications of his own views. He was implicitly taking issue with a concept that lay at the heart of the Freudian enterprise: the substantive unconscious, the understanding of the unconscious as a container of fully formed unconscious contents, or what Klein later described as unconscious phantasies, the nature of which were largely responsible for how meanings became articulated in consciousness. In this brief passage Sullivan was implying, it seemed to me then (and does still), that for psychic contents to be unconscious was for them to be without explicit meaning in any part of the mind. Unconscious states of mind for him, I thought, were not hard-edged, fully formed bearers of meaning; they were *not* unconscious phantasies. They were instead vague, potential meanings, not yet fully shaped or articulated. Experience in the parataxic mode, I thought, was experience that had not yet been formulated. That is what I took Sullivan to be suggesting, without actually saying it, when he used that evocative word, that word that struck me so forcefully: "unformulated."[2]

I can't be sure that Sullivan intended to say all of what I took him to mean. Whether he did or not, though, what he said in those lines was a source of inspiration to me. For me, he was saying that it was only as psychic contents were converted from parataxis to syntaxis—from pre-linguistic, autistic form into language—that explicit meaning was created. Furthermore, the meaning created in the syntaxic mode did not exist before, at least not in any explicit form; that meaning was created, for the first time, as it was formulated. This stance, I saw right away, implied that language is not just a set of labels; it has what the philosophical literature taught me to call "constitutive properties." (Much more about this point in each of the following chapters.) That is, language is not only a medium for the representation of meaning that already exists; it also actually participates in the creation of meaning. The nature of our thoughts or experiences—whatever one wants to call the products of the activities of the mind—are deeply influenced by language. Here is how I made this point in 1997:

> The unformulated is not yet knowable in the separate and definable terms of language. Unformulated material is composed of vague tendencies; if allowed to develop to the point at which they can be shaped and articulated, these become the more lucid kind of reflective experience we associate with mutually comprehended verbal articulation.
>
> (Stern, 1997, pp. 37–38)

One of the most interesting and significant things that constitutive theories of language suggested to me was a contrast with those theories, like Freud's, in which language is understood as a mere label for meanings that already exist. For Freud (1915b), language is inadequate to unconscious meaning ("thing-presentations"), which are only one step removed from things-in-themselves. Unconscious meanings, that is, cannot be accommodated by words. There is a loss of meaning when "thing-presentations" are linked to language, thereby becoming "word-presentations." Word-presentations, the only form in which meaning can enter consciousness, are a paler version than the form they represent. Language, that is, inevitably presents an impoverished rendition of the nonverbal meanings that it labels. In today's world we see this view of language in the work of (for instance) Daniel Stern (1985; Stern, et al, 1998), Wilma Bucci (1997), and Antonio Damasio (1999).

The constitutive theories of language that are discussed in the chapters to come (e.g., Merleau-Ponty, 1945/1962; Gadamer, 1965/2004; Taylor, 2016) do not portray linguistic representation this way. In these views, the use of language not only does not inevitably sacrifice meaning; language actually *contributes* to meanings. Language gives form to these meanings, allowing us to create meanings that would never come into being without it.

In Freud's work, then, and in theories that treat language in the same way, meaning becomes *less itself* as it moves from unconsciousness to consciousness. The unconscious meaning is the "truer" or more complete form. In the way I put it above, consciousness is the paler form, a dilution of the meaning that exists in the unconscious. But the situation is different in constitutive theories of language. In these theories, which are the accounts of language I have always tapped in writing about unformulated experience (Stern, 1983, 1997), meaning becomes *more itself* as it moves from unconsciousness to consciousness. The linguistic expression may very well be the *more vivid* form of the meaning.

We can go further: we can say that, until the situation is right for meaning to become *more itself* in the special way that language allows, it remains unformulated. The act of formulation, that is, takes place only when meaning is "ready" to become more than it has been; and to be ready it must percolate for as long as it takes. As I wrote in 1983:

> It is not as if the unformulated is leaning against the door, just waiting for a chance to overcome resistance and tumble into the room. The unformulated must organize itself first. It must begin to coalesce. . . . It must send up tendrils, or feelings of tendency.
>
> (p. 87)

And then, when the interpersonal field is configured in a way that allows it, a fully formed meaning can emerge. Clinical psychoanalysis is devoted to the recognition and encouragement of such opportunities.

## Wiggle room and the constraints of reality

The vague, potential tendencies that make up unformulated experience, though, would be no more than conventional stages in the development of a thought or a feeling if the outcome—that is, the eventual form of the articulated experience—were predetermined. In other words, if unformulated experience were "pre-set" to unfold into particular articulated, conscious meanings, just as seeds are "pre-set" to develop into particular plants, then the theory of unformulated experience would be nothing more than a description of how a thoroughly predictable thought comes about. The theory would be merely a history of the predetermined unfolding of thought.

But human life doesn't feel this way. One of the most compelling and mysterious aspects of our experience is its emergent, unbidden quality (Stern, 1990, 2015). We have no idea what we are going to think or feel next. We are observers of our own continuous acts of psychic creation, and these acts of our minds have an undeniable spontaneity. We do not know, and cannot know, that our sense of spontaneity is "true" (that is, we cannot know for sure that we are right to accept the impression that experience really is emergent)—because we are locked out of the nonconscious parts of the operations of our own minds. It is at least hypothetically possible that our sense of spontaneity—that emergent, antic, unbidden quality that our experience has—is illusory, and that if we knew the invisible workings of our minds we would see that every thought and feeling is predetermined.

But that seems highly unlikely. Such a characterization contradicts not only our sense of ourselves, but also denies the significance of context. Can it be that, without being affected by context, our experience just unfolds from within, like widgets being stamped out on an assembly line? I think that today no one would make such a claim, despite claims in the Freudian literature of the past that all experience is predetermined. Nor does such a view allow for novelty. Yes, it is true that psychoanalysis teaches us that we re-create the same meanings over and over again; but of course we also create new meanings. Our psychoanalytic observation of the most conservative parts of our functioning is important, because these observations allow us to see the ways we trap ourselves in old, self-destructive ways; but our observations of the temptations of our own conservative casts of mind are also significant because it is only against their background that we see that we can sometimes transcend them. *Thanatos* takes its meaning from its relation to *Eros*, and vice versa.

And so we arrive at another important aspect of the theory of unformulated experience: when I refer to unformulated experience as potential experience, what I mean is that *the final form of the articulated experience always remains to be determined.* There is always "wiggle room." This perspective has often been called "constructivism" in psychoanalysis, especially by analysts generally identified as relational (Stern, 1983, 1992, 1997; Mitchell, 1993; Hoffman, 1998). The core of this idea is that experience always begins with ambiguity that is resolved into a particular meaning via an interpretive, hermeneutic process.

I take this opportunity to rebut a common misconception about unformulated experience that I have tried to correct ever since I began to field reactions to the very first presentation of the idea (Stern, 1983). The theory of unformulated experience is not relativistic; one is not free to simply offer any formulation. To say that experience begins in ambiguity is *not* equivalent to saying, that is, that the process of formulating experience is the creation of something from nothing. It is not correct to say that the theory of unformulated experience holds that there is nothing "there" prior to formulation.

Perhaps the most important way I can put this point is this: the theory of unformulated experience does not hold that there is no unconscious. As far as I am concerned, such a position would contradict clinical reality—everything we know. It would be ludicrous. And yet, for decades now, I have heard and read claims like these made about my work.

Why are these positions inaccurate? How do I answer the claims I have just described? I answer, very simply, that the unformulated is defined by inherent constraints on what it can become. Reality exists in this view, although it can never be directly perceived. Instead, according to hermeneutic philosopher Hans-Georg Gadamer (1965/2004), whose work has had a significant influence on the theory of unformulated experience, reality can be known only via the mediation of culture—or, in terms closer to the consulting room, via that tiny node in the culture that comprises the analytic relationship.

Reality is not directly received, that is, but interpreted. The farther removed from the senses is the reality to be grasped, the less we simply allow the world into our minds, and the more thoroughly our interpretations determine what we experience—and the more thoroughly our experience is therefore mediated by culture. Our interpretive attitude is usually so deeply taken for granted that it is not itself taken, or even cannot *be* taken, as the object of our attention. That is what makes ideology so insidious and compelling: it is invisible (e.g., Foucault, 1980). Heidegger wrote somewhere that the known, simply because it is the known, is the unknown.

We can say, then, that it is axiomatic in contemporary hermeneutic philosophy that the continuous interpretive attitude, ceaselessly exercised by all of us, almost always without awareness of what we are doing, is what makes experience possible at all. But it is just as important and characteristic of these hermeneutic views that, no matter how much we depend on our own interpretive powers in creating our experience, we cannot simply violate the constraints contributed by reality. Or rather, if we do, we are recognized, by others but also (sometimes) by ourselves, to be either lying or crazy. Hermeneutics is not relativistic. This point, which is as just as basic to modern hermeneutic philosophy as the assertion that all experience is interpretation, separates hermeneutics from the stance of much of the poststructuralist philosophy often described as postmodern, which has been more accepting of relativism.

I often use the following example to convey the idea of the constraints on what unformulated experience can become: Imagine a backlighted figure seen through a dense fog. The figure is a dark form, maybe six feet high and a couple of feet wide. It could be a human being; it could be a dancing bear; it could even be the end of a rack of clothes being pushed lengthwise toward you. But it could not be an elephant or an automobile, and to claim that it is would be either a lie or craziness; such an interpretation would violate the reality constraints that limit the range of valid understanding.[3]

### Why one formulation rather than another? The role of the interpersonal field in the process of formulation.

Now we arrive at the real crux of the theory of unformulated experience. If unformulated experience is potential experience that might be given any one of the multiple formulations toward which it tends (sometimes few, sometimes many, depending on whether the reality constraints in any particular instance are tight or loose), then the key question is what it is that determines which of these potential formulations comes to final form in awareness.

Let us return to Sullivan here. How would he answer this question? He never actually formulated the question, since he did not create a theory of unformulated experience; but if he had, I think I know what he would have said. He would answer in the same way I do: The factor that determines which potential experience comes to be articulated in consciousness is the interpersonal field, especially its unconscious aspects. That is, it is the immediate human context between patient and analyst that determines what they can experience in one another's presence.

The interpersonal field is the pattern of shifting and interactive states of being of patient and analyst. I have offered illustrations elsewhere (Stern, 1997, 2003, 2004, 2010a, 2015). The concept of a shifting field is important for a number of reasons, the most significant of which has to do with the role played by states of being or self in the constitution or creation of experience. Consider that, in Freudian and Kleinian theory, that formative role is played by unconscious fantasy. Unconscious fantasy, that is, routinely lends its shape to conscious experience—not necessarily as a simple template, but always as a significant formative influence (e.g., Blass, 2017, who, because she is Kleinian, spells the word with a "ph," of course). In an analogous way, in the theory of unformulated experience, the state of being or self that one occupies at any particular moment significantly influences which unformulated experience can be given an explicit shape, and what those shapes might be.

States of being—the interpersonal field—are no less inherently nonrational than unconscious fantasy, and they can therefore supply the same kind of shaping influence in relational theory that unconscious fantasy supplies in Freudian, and especially Kleinian, theories. The primary source of formative influence—the theory's center of gravity, we might say—therefore shifts from the internal world (unconscious fantasy) to the interpersonal field—the unconscious aspects of relatedness (states of being, or self-states).[4]

The result is a relational/interpersonal theory that I hope preserves, in its emphasis on the unbidden properties of experience, the power of Freud's conception, while also giving significantly more emphasis to the immediate context of the interpersonal field. Even without relying on a theory of substantive unconscious content, in other words, the theory of unformulated experience is a dynamic conception of unconsciousness and, more broadly, the mind.

## Dissociation

In the theory of unformulated experience, repression is replaced by dissociation. Sullivan used the concept of dissociation to represent the process resulting in that experience that he described in those two sentences I have already quoted: dissociation, he thought, kept unformulated experience out of the range of consensually validated thought. In later years, he referred to such experience as "not-me," a term taken up by Bromberg (1998, 2006, 2011) and me (1983, 1997, 2010a, 2015).

Dissociation means something particular in Sullivan's hands, and that meaning is not the one typically assigned to the word by most current students of dissociation. Especially in his earlier work, dissociation for Sullivan is not the process that takes over when one is overwhelmed by trauma; rather, it is the primary defensive process, and it results in that experience that Sullivan (1940/1953) described as unknown to oneself because "one has [not] tended to communicate it to another or thought about it in the manner of communicative speech" (p. 178). Bromberg (2011), to differentiate his model from conventional trauma theory while emphasizing the role of interpersonal events in the creation of mind, writes that dissociation is the consequence of "developmental trauma."

This concept of dissociation is intended to be contrasted with repression. Repression for Freud (1915a) is a defensive process by which existing meaning is distorted or hidden away in the mind: *"the essence of repression lies simply in turning something away, and keeping it at a distance, from the conscious"* (p. 146; italics from the original). It is set in motion by the conflict of drive and defense, and the resulting necessity to move instinctual representations into the unconscious. Sullivan (1940, 1953) built his theory on different grounds. Dissociation is the mind's response to the parts of life—thoughts, feelings, patterns of interaction, etc.—that would lead to intolerable anxiety. Anxiety, and the dissociations that guard against it, come about via "emotional linkage," which is Sullivan's term for the process by which children (and others) "pick up" the anxiety of significant others (often parents, but of course many others, as well). Thereafter, awareness of the parts of one's own experience that have been linked to the other's anxiety are sources of one's own anxiety, and so this part of experience goes unobserved and unthought, prevented, compromised—dissociated.[5]

Sullivan was not entirely clear about the status of these dissociated psychic contents. But if we take our cue from the passage I have already quoted ("Much of that which is ordinarily said to be *repressed* is merely unformulated" [Sullivan, 1940/1953, p. 185; italics from the original]), we can imagine that those contents are unformulated. In any case, whatever Sullivan might say, my own view is that dynamically significant, dissociated psychic contents are maintained as unformulated experience—that is, they are maintained as *potential* experience in the form of vaguely organized, primitive, global, nonideational, affective states.

In my elaboration of Sullivan's view of dissociation (Stern, 1983, 1992, 1996, 1997, 2003, 2004, 2010a, 2013c, 2015, 2017), influenced by the work of Schachtel (1959), defense is a matter of avoiding the deployment of one's own curiosity and imagination, so that one simply does not have the requisite motivation to create the relevant meanings. Not all unformulated experience is dissociated, of course, since in this frame of reference all conscious experience develops from a previous, unformulated state. But all dissociated experience is unformulated.

I am often asked whether, in my frame of reference, repression can co-exist with dissociation. I say no. The understanding of dissociation that has its source in the theory of unformulated experience grows from a conception of the mind that is contradicted by the concept of repression—because repression has to do with an understanding of the unconscious as a repository of representations—that is, fully formed contents.

## Reflection

In *Unformulated Experience* (Stern, 1997), while my conception of the nature of unconsciousness diverged from the widely accepted psycho-analytic model of the day, in some statements I took the more or less typical position that the aim of psychoanalysis is reflective awareness in verbal language. One of the book's key arguments was that language, and therefore what is spoken by patient and analyst, is hardly the dry or impoverished expression of a vibrant inner world, as some important psychoanalytic writers tend to characterize it.[6] Quite the contrary. The book's message was that language needs to be liberated in psychoanalysis to do what it does naturally. When it is not obstructed by dissociative influences, when it is given its head, when it is allowed to create new meanings that seem to have a life of their own, language lets us know that *this* is something we really *mean*.

In *Unformulated Experience*, I often did accompany statements about the significance of reflective awareness with an attempt to contextualize the matter in a wider semiotic context (see especially Chapter 1 of that book, which was written for the express purpose of taking a broad, semiotic approach to language); and I not only frequently cited the significance of nonverbal meanings, but also indicated respect for, and fascination with, those meanings. Nevertheless, it is true that that book was intended to be a study of reflection in psychoanalysis; and that very choice indicates the significance that verbal-reflective awareness in psychoanalysis held in my mind at the time. Here is one statement of that kind, which I think illustrates both the centrality I attributed to verbal-reflective awareness in clinical practice and my acceptance that nonverbal meanings were nevertheless critical.

For the most part, what we and our patients are trying to do is to bring into words experience that has existed before that time in a different, inarticulate form. And often, the meanings we work with are less than fully expressed until they reach such a stage—until they can be said. We and our patients are not aiming at the unnameable bliss of mysticism, nor are we trying to create art. What we do bears the same relation to nonverbal experience that the work of the critic bears to a play or a piece of sculpture. Like the critic, we would not be drawn to our work unless we had a greater appreciation and love of the subject matter than most people do. Psychoanalysts love the forms experience can take as critics love art. And it is true that to become and remain good analysts, we must retain that direct and unmediated appreciation. But our relation to our subject of study—to experience— does not remain merely appreciative. We are driven to understand. Creating experience, by itself, does not satisfy what we want from our work; we must say things about what we create. We acknowledge how often the important parts of psychoanalytic treatment occurs in the shadow of the interpretive task, spontaneously and apart from verbal representation; we hope, and even pray, that we and the patient will find our way to that kind of authentic experience. But we do not know how to make authenticity happen. So, while we are grateful for the unexpected and inexpressible benefits along the way, we focus our conscious attention on trying to say things.

(pp. 89–90)

I believed when I wrote this passage, and still do, that reflection requires words. We can explicitly consider only those parts of our experience that we can symbolize in verbal language. Words, that is, are what makes it possible to turn back reflexively on experience, whether the content of that reflexive thought is our own experience or someone else's. Verbal language allows us to take the critical distance required to disembed ourselves from the immediacy of the moment.

The link between words and reflection is very often obscured, however, by what Merleau-Ponty (1945/1962) calls "the wonderful thing about language," which is

that it promotes its own oblivion: my eyes follow the lines on the paper, and from the moment I am caught up in their meaning, I lose sight of them. The paper, the letters on it, my eyes and body are there only as the minimum setting of some invisible operation. Expression fades out before what is expressed, and this why its mediating role may pass unnoticed . . .

(p. 401)

The same thing is true of our reflections on ourselves and our lives: the language that brings us to these thoughts often disappears, leaving us feeling that we just *know*. It is as if we have been deposited at the airport by a taxi that has now vanished: we cease thinking about the taxi; we are simply *there*.

I know (because they have told me) that many people disagree with the position that reflection requires words. I can only imagine that those who disagree with me on this point mean something different by reflection than I do. I mean something very specific. I do *not* mean to claim, and have never meant to claim, as sometimes I have been read to say, that verbally-mediated reflection is the only form of knowing. There are many forms of knowing—a point that I will take up in some detail later in this chapter, and in even greater detail throughout the book. For instance, we can indeed have what we might call a sense of familiarity with experience, a sense that we cannot put into words but that nevertheless guides us; and that sense of familiarity is certainly a kind of knowing. We find it in procedural knowing, for instance—"implicit relational knowing" in the wording of the Boston Change Process Study Group (2010). (More on this topic later.) But reflection is different than that: it is the kind of knowing that allows direct consideration and internal manipulation of experience, what we call explicit thought.

For me, only verbal language allows the flexibility that reflection requires; only verbal language allows us to shape our own nascent meanings into thoughts that come into our view, our capacity to know, in the very same moment we create them. And so I simply cannot see my way around the view that thought requires, as Marie Cardinal (1984) formulates the matter in the title of her powerful novel about psychoanalysis, *The Words to Say It*. Merleau-Ponty (1945/1962, p. 178) puts it this way: "[A]uthentic speech" (and, we can say, "authentic thought" as well), "which formulates for the first time, . . . is identical with thought."

*But*—and this "but" is a kind of hologram for the present book, containing within it the book's entire content—I also believe, as I have said already, that explicit reflection does not constitute the only means by which therapeutic action is accomplished. I can state this point more strongly, and perhaps, given what I have just said, more strangely: I believe that nonverbal events are, in a certain sense, primary in the creation of therapeutic action.

In saying this, I would certainly not want to be understood to be diminishing the significance of new verbal-reflective understanding in therapeutic action. New reflective understanding is often crucial in provoking other new experiences, or in creating a new awareness of old ones; and reflective understanding, when it is successful in bringing the nonverbal into the realm of reflective thought, often plays the central role in consolidating the new freedom in the field that allowed the understanding to emerge in the first place. (We shall see, as the book progresses, that the verbal can only sometimes express, or represent, the nonverbal; often nonverbal meaning is inexpressible in words.) New reflective understanding may also contribute to the creation of a new configuration of the field, a configuration that then has everything to do with forming the next generation of clinical events. I maintain the same interest in verbal-reflective understanding that I have always had.

What I mean when I say that the nonverbal is in some ways primary is this: in the sequence of clinical events that eventuates in therapeutic action, what comes first is the shift in the field that allows new understanding to come about. (For a fuller presentation of this view, see Stern, 2009.) And so I can say quite explicitly that I no longer believe, and haven't for decades, that in psychoanalysis the first stage is understanding in words, which then leads to change in experience and behavior (although I do think I harbored a version of this belief when I started out in the field five decades ago). Change is an unplanned, affectively charged, transactional event (Stern, 2009). We may (or may not) symbolize it sometime after it takes place. But in the moments in which it happens, if we see it or sense it at all, it is out of the corners of our eyes. I have long agreed with writers as disparate as Edgar Levenson (1972/2005, 1983/2005, 1991/2016, 2017) and Jean Laplanche (2011) that the task of psychoanalysis is to destabilize the status quo and thereby open the mind to novel possibilities. The new meanings that come about as a result of this destabilization happen by themselves and are unpredictable. We do not attempt to insert new content into the patient's mind. Instead, we hope to loosen up the rigid and stereotyped parts of the analytic interaction, which tend to lock the minds of both participants into constricted patterns of experiencing. The new meanings that come about as a result of this destabilization are the patient's to create—although inevitably in partnership with the analyst—a process that begins to happen as soon as it becomes possible.

## Reassessing the role of language

One of the primary factors that provoked me in *Partners in Thought* (2010a), the book that followed *Unformulated Experience* (1997), to reconsider how we should conceptualize the nature of unformulated experience, and how we ought to understand its formulation, was the process of dissociative enactment, the study of which was the heart of *Partners*. I became convinced that therapeutic action relied on the kind of work with clinical process that releases the grip of unconscious enactments on patient and analyst, thereby allowing the resumption of relatively greater freedom to experience and to think in the interpersonal field and in both minds; and in the course of thinking through this point I became convinced that what eventually broke up, melted, or breached these unconscious enactments was not any kind of verbal reflection at all. The crucial clinical ingredient in resolving enactments, that is, seldom, if ever, seemed to me to be words. It was instead something nonverbal. The mutative event was a procedural meaning, not a symbolic one, a *new perception* of the other and oneself, and the relationship between the two; and this new perception unmistakably arose outside the realm of words—although it seemed to me that frequently it could be verbally symbolized sometime after it took place.

I have already expressed my conviction, held from the beginning of my life as a psychoanalyst, that the contents of consciousness depend on the nature of the interpersonal field, especially its unconscious aspects; and I have held for 35 years that the appearance of new conscious experience on the part of either patient or analyst requires some kind of prior shift in the field between them (Stern, 1983, 1989, 1990, 1997, 2009, 2010a, 2013c, 2015). My focus on enactment, from its earliest forms (Stern, 1989, 1990, 1991) through *Partners in Thought* (2010a) and then *Relational Freedom* (2015), is a specification of the changes in the field that were most relevant to therapeutic action.

In the end, though, even with these changes and additions, my attitude about the nonverbal did not really change very much from *Unformulated Experience* in 1997 to *Partners in Thought* in 2010. While it had always seemed to me, even when I was emphasizing the curative role of broadened and deepened verbal self-reflection, that the nonverbal events of clinical process—many of which did not seem to be undertaken with conscious purpose by either the patient or the myself—were crucial, I did not conceptualize these nonverbal events with the same degree of specificity that I conceptualized the verbal ones. It was harder to think through the nonverbal; I even wondered if it could really be done. I knew perfectly well that nonverbal, relational (procedural) events were crucial to thera-peutic action, for instance, but I did not imagine how I could explicitly conceptualize these parts of clinical process. With a mixture of amusement and resignation about my own apparent helplessness in this regard, over several decades I used to tweak myself with the thought that the reason my patients and I told ourselves we were trying to understand things in words was to give ourselves a reason to sit down together and let the *really* important things happen by themselves.

And so, despite emphasizing verbal self-reflection, I have also always been interested in thinking through the nonverbal, relational part of clinical process. In other words, in order to begin to explicitly conceptualize the nonverbal in clinical practice, it was not my *interest* in the nonverbal that had to change; it was my confidence that the project could be accomplished. Over the years, I felt my way into a deeper sense of what "nonverbal" means in life, and in clinical process.

A new understanding began to dawn on me when I found myself thinking repeatedly about what I have just referred to as the "new per-ception." Under that rubric, I mean to include the analyst's new perception of the patient, the patient's new perception of the analyst, and both participants' new perception of the relatedness between them. That was when I began to see that when dissociative enactment dissolves, it is not because the enactment is understood in verbal-reflective terms, but because something shifts in field, freeing analyst and patient to see one another differently (e.g., Bromberg, 1998, 2006, 2011; Stern 2010a, 2015). These enactments, I began to grasp (Stern, 1989, 1990, 1991), may not even have been observable or knowable by the participants until the appearance of the new perception, which meant that enactments often functioned invisibly as "the grip of the field" (Stern, 1989) on both participants.

As I observed the clinical process between my patients and me from this new vantage point, I came to believe two things: the new perception must happen spontaneously, it must occur "by itself"; and the participants must "mean it." The new perception, that is, could not be the calculated outcome of a decision made by the analyst on a rational, theoretical, or technical basis. It had to grow out of the analyst's unconscious involvement with the patient.[7]

I was excited to find my way to what seemed to be the clinical significance of the new perception; but this new understanding was also disturbing. If therapeutic action relies heavily on the spontaneous appearance of new, nonverbal perception, how could I continue to maintain that the process of formulation must be verbal? I couldn't very well maintain that therapeutic action required some kind of verbal reflection while simultaneously claiming that the primary clinical event was the emergence of something apart from words.

I have already reported that, even before dissociation and enactment took center stage for me, I had always known, as all psychoanalysts do, that many of the most significant clinical events take place outside verbal language. I had also considered the possibility that I assigned too exclusive a role to verbal language in my earliest work. After the publication of *Unformulated Experience* (Stern, 1997), some of my colleagues criticized me for doing just that, and I could understand why they felt that way. With the "new perception" serving as the straw that broke the camel's back, I felt it was time to see if I could redefine the process of formulating meaning in a way that would make it possible to conceptualize the formulation of nonverbal meanings. Just as formulated verbal-reflective meaning emerges from an unformulated state, I reasoned, perhaps there is a way to think about how nonverbal meaning (that is, whatever it is that we experience when the "new perception" appears in clinical process) emerges, in similar fashion, from a similarly unformulated state. From these thoughts emerged this book.

## A broader sense of "linguistic"

Looking back at the concept of unformulated experience, I think that if there was a problem, it was not so much that I privileged verbal language; it was, instead, that I had not fully grasped the relationship between verbal language and language as it is more broadly defined—words as one kind of signifying system: verbal expression, that is, as one kind of semiotic. I began to see that I still had work to do to grasp language as semiotic. In *Unformulated Experience* (Stern, 1997, Chapter 1), I had addressed explicitly the relation of the verbal and the nonverbal, basing my argument in semiotics (i.e., verbal language as one symbol system among many), but I now see that I did not present the issues with sufficient clarity or subtlety; and as I began to find my way into them (an exploration I will describe here in Chapters 2–4), I found that what I learned was the key to expanding the formulation of experience into the nonverbal realm.

## A vexing problem: the relation of the verbal and the nonverbal

I am not alone in finding the relation of the verbal and the nonverbal a vexing problem. It is, in fact, one of the more vexing problems in psychoanalysis, past and present. Psychoanalysis was devised as "the talking cure," of course; and verbal interpretation, verbal reflection, and verbal insight were the guiding lights of theories of technique and therapeutic action for generations. More recently, the nonverbal has become at least equally important in many psychoanalytic theories and accounts; and in some contemporary accounts of treatment, especially those contributed by Daniel Stern (1985) and the Boston Change Process Study Group (2010), the nonverbal has actually overtaken and surpassed the verbal. The verbal, meanwhile, has not lacked for recent defenders of its own (e.g., Loewald, 1978; Ogden 1997, 1998, 1999, 2016; Vivona 2003, 2006, 2009a, 2012, 2013, 2014; Litowitz 2011, 2014; Harris 2014; Kirshner 2014; Spivak 2014).

The position I take in this book is an elaboration of the position I have always taken. I can offer this statement as a first approach to it: To understand the verbal and the nonverbal as essentially different and therefore conflicting, as if we must choose which form of representation is more basic, is to misconceive the problem in an important respect. If we conceive the problem differently, in the way I propose here, especially in Chapter 4, some of the most significant difficulties in the relation of the verbal and the nonverbal disappear, or are least attenuated. The reconceptualization I suggest is to recognize that the verbal and the nonverbal are our two ways of establishing meaning; and furthermore, that these two forms of meaning are united under the broad conception of language contributed by hermeneutic philosophers. These two factors constitute a common ground of such significance that it may actually outweigh their differences.

I do still believe, as I always have, that language is first among equals, the single most important form of symbolization. And for all of us, because we are practitioners of the talking cure, verbal reflection will always hold a special and honored place in our clinical theory and practice.

But even if we grant verbal language this special status, it is nevertheless, from the wider perspective of semiotics, one among many systems of symbolization. Culture, we are told by hermeneuticists such as Heidegger and Gadamer, is the sum total of all those signifying systems; and the limits of what can be meaningful for human beings coincide with the limits of these means of representation. Outside these limits there exists Being that we cannot contain in symbolic form, what Lacan called the real. Working from a Lacanian perspective, Dyess and Dean (2000), in a phrase I particularly like, referred to what lies outside the range of the symbolic as "the impossibility of meaning."

I am implying a point that I now state explicitly: In psychoanalysis, I believe that the most important question we can ask about psychic phenomena is not whether they are symbolized in verbal or nonverbal terms, or even whether they are conscious or unconscious, but instead whether they are *meaningful*. The question in psychoanalytic treatment is whether psychic phenomena are transformed from their initial, non-meaningful state into *either* a verbal or a nonverbal meaning. For me, that initial state is unformulated experience; for Bion, as a point of comparison, it is beta elements. For Bion (1962), I think, meaningfulness (a term he never used) would be defined by our capacity to employ psychic material in the composition of waking dream thoughts. For me, the critical thing is whether the material can be used in the construction of spontaneous, creative living. I will have a good deal more to say about what I mean by this.

The subject of meaningfulness leads into this book's central proposals. Before those ideas are introduced, though, I need to turn to a more detailed consideration of procedural knowing and meaning, and the literature of unrepresented states. Procedural phenomena demand attention because they complicate the question of what it means for psychic life to be meaningful; the wide literature on unmentalized and unrepresented states compels my attention because the theory of unformulated experience belongs to it, and so needs to be situated within that context.

## Procedural meaning

In the recent past, procedural knowing and meaning have been increasingly acknowledged in psychoanalysis. Procedural knowing has no symbolic form in the mind, and is defined by what it does, like knowing how to ride a bicycle. Examples with psychoanalytic relevance include various affective, prosodic, visual and auditory sensory-perceptual, kinesthetic, motor, and social-interactive phenomena—the stuff of somatic experience, and social and interactive living. Much of what is meaningful in day-to-day dealings with others is coded procedurally. Procedural knowledge, despite not being symbolically represented in the mind, is generally accepted today, inside and outside psychoanalysis, as a significant portion of psychic life.

This new recognition of the procedural has been spurred by a number of significant bodies of work. Bucci (1997) proposes a model of clinical process according to which much of what is most significant in clinical work, phenomena that are generally affective in nature, takes place without symbolic representation, in the "subsymbolic" mode of information processing (which we can also describe as procedural). Bromberg (1998, 2006, 2011; see especially 2008, 2009) vividly describes dissociative clinical process in which meaning grows from what is revealed to be transpiring between patient and analyst outside the reach of the symbolic. Change derives from this work with the unconscious, procedurally-organized (Bromberg, 2003/2006) aspects of relatedness, and not from the interpretation of unconscious, symbolic content already present within the mind.[8]

Observers of the early communication and attunement of babies and mothers, and the analogous interaction of patients and analysts, have drawn our attention over and over again to the crucial role of procedural meaning and procedural interaction in both development and psychoanalytic treatment. Some of these writers are developmentalists, some of them clinical psychoanalysts, and some of them both (Trevarthen, 1979; D.N. Stern, 1985; Beebe & Lachmann, 2002, 2013; Tronick, 2007; Benjamin, 2017). Among these writers, Winnicott certainly deserves special mention, although exactly where to focus in his work is less than obvious, because much of what he wrote is distinguished by its poetic, verbal expression of procedural matters in both development and clinical practice. As a matter of fact, Winnicott's capacity to convey in words what actually never could have occurred in words might even be a way of describing the defining quality of both his charm and his genius.

Benjamin (2017) is another crossover figure, having addressed both development and clinical practice (and sociopolitical matters, as well). She describes how "the Third," the part of relatedness that makes intersubjectivity possible, develops from the thoroughly procedural rhythmicity of the earliest mother-infant relationship, first described by Sander (2002); and she goes on to describe certain kinds of clinical interaction in which rhythmicity is significant in adulthood. She calls this phenomenon "the rhythmic Third," and she says, "It is present in the earliest exchange of gestures between mother and child, in the relationship that has been called *oneness*." It is "the principle of affective attunement and accommodation to share patterning that informs such exchanges" (2004/2017, p. 30).

Fonagy and his colleagues (Fonagy, 1991, 1995; Fonagy & Moran, 1991; Fonagy, Moran & Target, 1993; Fonagy & Target, 1995, 1996, 2000, 2007; Target & Fonagy, 1996; Fonagy et al, 2002) in their extensive study of "mentalization," or the capacity for reflection, focus often on the conversion of pre-reflective experience, much of which qualifies as procedural meaning, into a symbolic form that can be thought.

Among writers who have contributed to the conceptualization of mentalization, we might also include those who have written on unrepresented states (e.g., Bion, 1962; Green, 1975, 1999; Matte-Blanco, 1988; Lecours & Bouchard, 1997; Botella & Botella, 2005; Levine, Reed, & Scarfone, 2013). From the frame of reference of Bion (1962) and Matte-Blanco (1988), Lombardi (2016, 2017) offers a thoroughly illustrated view in which explicit, symbolically represented meaning (Matte-Blanco's "symmetrical logic") is preceded by unarticulated somatic, procedural proto-meanings and an undifferentiated kind of procedural mental process ("symmetrical logic") somewhat reminiscent of Freud's primary narcissism.

Last but certainly not least, the Boston Change Process Study Group (BCPSG, 2010; see also D.N. Stern, 2004) has contributed a widely recognized body of work on psychoanalytic treatment as a conception of relational reorganization. Their conception of "implicit relational knowing" (D.N. Stern, et al., 1998) has perhaps done more than any other single idea to draw attention to procedural knowing and memory. Lyons-Ruth, et al (2001, p. 17) describes the BCPSG perspective:

If clinical process is affect-guided rather than cognition-guided, [then] therapeutic change is a process that leads to the emergence of new forms of relational organization. New experiences emerge but they are not created by the therapist for the benefit of the patient. Instead, they emerge somewhat unpredictably from the mutual searching of patient and therapist for new forms of recognition, or new forms of fitting together of initiatives in the interaction between them.

(p. 17)

In fact, despite my stab at a very brief review in the preceding paragraphs, it is not really feasible to cite all of the immense literature in psychoanalysis that is directly relevant to the procedural varieties of meaning, communication, and memory. Just the citations themselves would fill a book—even without consideration of the research reported. Consider the fact, for instance, that the entire literature on relational effects in therapeutic action and relational aspects of clinical process (and what part of clinical process is not relational?) is rooted in matters that should be described as procedural. And note the indisputable point that almost all of the daily contexts that make up our lives, actually, are procedural in nature, and that what is meaningful to us is not merely contained by these contexts but shaped by them (D.N. Stern, 2004; Wachtel, 2014b, 2017).

We have not discovered something new in describing the procedural, then; rather, in finally recognizing the significance of the fact that the procedural has no symbolic representation we have instead discovered something new and interesting about matters that have long been familiar.

There are two consequences of this acknowledgment of procedural meaning for any conception of thinking, feeling, or experiencing, including the one presented in this book. I take up each separately.

### I. The first consequence of acknowledging procedural meaning: Rethinking the differentiation between verbal and nonverbal.

The differentiation between verbal and nonverbal must be rethought. It used to be taken for granted in psychoanalysis, during the years in which all psychic life was understood to be representational, that the verbal and the nonverbal were simply the two ways that anything could be symbolically represented and known. Since all knowing was representational, these two alternatives, taken together, covered the waterfront. Psychic content was either represented in words, or in imagery of one kind or another: visual, auditory, kinesthetic, etc.

Procedural knowing/meaning breaks the mold: it is a variety of knowing and experiencing, but it is not representational or symbolic. Bucci (1985) addressed this issue by expanding her "dual coding model" of information processing (verbal representation and nonverbal, visual-imagistic representation), adopted from cognitive psychologist Allan Paivio (1971, 1986), into her later "multiple code theory" (Bucci, 1997). In multiple code theory, the verbal and nonverbal symbolic modes of processing information are supplemented by what Bucci refers to as the "subsymbolic" mode. The addition of the subsymbolic mode is meant to accommodate affect, which is not represented symbolically. But the category of the subsymbolic accommodates just as well all the other procedural parts of knowing and experiencing. So Bucci ends up proposing three modes of information coding.

I have not taken the same route to a solution. I have preferred, for reasons that will become clear in Chapter 3, to preserve just two ways that experience can be structured, or formulated: verbal and nonverbal. I have subsumed procedural knowing and procedural experiencing within the nonverbal, so that this category has become, we could say, *all that is not verbal*. For me, then, the nonverbal has two components: the nonverbal symbolic, such as imagery of all kinds; and the procedural.

## 2. The second consequence of acknowledging procedural meaning: Rethinking meaningfulness as symbolic representation.

The second effect of our acknowledgment of the procedural serves as a reminder of a position that has become influential in psychoanalysis in recent years for other reasons. That position derives from the recognition among analysts that what is meaningful is no longer synonymous with what is symbolically represented. For Freud, and for many years after Freud, it was taken for granted that meaningfulness and symbolic representation were synonymous. Perception was understood in the traditional way, as the mental representation of sensory events that, in themselves, were not part of mental life; and other, higher-order events in the mind were understood to be traceable to what happened within and between symbolic representations.

An increasing number of psychoanalysts today, though, hold that psychic events can also be the consequence of certain absences of meaning, or of the process by which meanings are created where there were no meanings before. And so, for these analysts, the most significant differentiation in psychic life is not necessarily our consciousness or lack of consciousness of symbolic representations, but the presence or absence of meaningfulness.

That is certainly the case in my own work, in which the main event in psychic life is understood to be the process by which potential meaning (unformulated experience, which is not yet meaningful) is formulated as meaning of one kind or another. Bion (1962), too, while he did not make a point of acknowledging procedural knowing (the idea was not acknowledged in so many words in his time), recognized, especially in his early work, the significance of the presence or absence of meaningfulness. He reconceptualized the unconscious as a storehouse of (meaningful) symbolic representations, or alpha elements, that could be drawn upon to create experience as circumstances demanded. The dynamic relation of consciousness and the unconscious remained significant to him; but his primary focus of interest in those years, the 1950s and 1960s, was the study of the creation (and destruction) of meaningful psychic elements (alpha elements) from sensory and affective phenomena that remained non-meaningful, or things-in-themselves (beta elements), until they were made meaningful.

I share Bion's intention to anchor the creation of meaningfulness in relatedness. For Bion (1962) this relational process is projective identification; for me it is the breaching of dissociation and the consequent loosening of constriction or stereotypy in the interpersonal field (D.B. Stern, 2010a, 2015). Others whose work recognizes the basic significance of the divide between meaningfulness and its absence have explored topics such as mentalization and unrepresented states (Segal, 1957; Green, 1975, 1999; Lecours & Bouchard, 1997; Fonagy, et al, 2002; Botella & Botella, 2005; Levine, Reed, & Scarfone, 2013;). Perhaps the most widely known of these psychic absences is André Green's (1986) conception of the "dead mother," the image of whose emotional absence is internalized and thenceforth exists at the core of the psyche, an absence where there should be presence.

Such unrepresented states, these writers believe, existing outside the range of any kind of thought or meaning, nevertheless have effects on the psyche. There is a paradox in this, since "nothing" is being understood to have an effect on "something." In all cases, though, these writers have understood unrepresented states to be without meaning; none of them, that is, have tried to take into account the position I adopt in this book: that there exist unrepresented psychic phenomena that are actually meaningful—i.e., procedural meaning.

## The literature of unrepresented states

We reach the literature of unrepresented states via the consideration of procedural meaning. But the subject of unrepresented states is itself, independently, a highly significant part of the scholarly and clinical context for the theory of unformulated experience. This point could always have been made—that is, it was already true when I began to write about unformulated experience in the 1980s. But the literature of unrepresented states has become both much larger and more influential in the years since then. And so, before going on with the introduction of my argument in this book, I shall take a few pages to describe that literature and situate the arguments of this book within it.

In traditional models of technique and therapeutic action, and theories of mind, the emphasis was on the revelation of unconscious mental contents. The interpretation of unconscious mental content, which of course continues today to play a significant role in any analyst's work, was for generations unquestionably *the* primary aim of clinical practice and therapeutic action for just about everyone, at least in North America. Mental contents were understood to be representations, or symbolized experience, that pre-existed their discovery. Their revelation was understood to be a kind of highly skilled clinical labeling of these invisible, fully formed contents. And therapeutic action was understood to rely on that revelation: where id was, ego shall be; or from the interpersonal or relational perspective, the treatment, by revealing what has been selectively inattended or dissociated, clarifies the relational world in a way that makes it possible to negotiate it.

In many models—some of them recent (e.g., Fonagy, Target, and their collaborators), others created decades ago (e.g., Lacan's)—the emphasis has changed. Some of these ideas originate in interpersonal and relational psychoanalysis. The theory of unformulated experience belongs to this tradition; so does Bromberg's (1998, 2006, 2011) work on the multiple self and aspects of Benjamin's (1988, 1995, 1998, 2017) intersubjectivity theory. But many more of them originate outside the United States, in psychoanalytic traditions that are less familiar to many North Americans. I have mentioned some of these just above, in connection with procedural memory and meaning. In Great Britain, I am thinking of writers such as Bion, Winnicott, and Fonagy and Target and their collaborators; in South America, the Barangers; in Italy: Ferro, Civitarese, and Matte Blanco; in France, the Botellas, Lacan, Laplanche, Faimberg, and Green.

While these writers differ in so many highly significant ways from one another that they may seem to challenge the sense of a conceptual category, other than psychoanalysis itself, that contains them all, they do have an important characteristic in common: the emphasis in all of them lies on the growth or repair of mind via creation of a new capacity for symbolization; and in that way their emphasis differs from the content interpretation of the past. We might say that they reach similar destinations by very different paths, or that they reach conclusions that mirror one another in this one respect, but for reasons that are often pointedly divergent.

Pre-existing mental contents in most of these theories continue to exist, of course; but there is an increasing interest in the states of mind that are not symbolically represented in the mind at all (Levine, Reed, & Scarfone, 2013). These states are instead understood to be unrepresented, unmentalized, or unformulated. They remain to be shaped, articulated, created, or given meaning. Furthermore, problems in human living and their treatment are understood in these theories to have at least as much to do with unrepresented states as they do with problematic symbolizations in the repressed unconscious.

And therefore clinical work is focused in these models on the transformation of these unrepresented states into symbolic form and whatever it is that might be standing in the way of the development of that new symbolic capacity. The most significant clinical outcome for all of these writers is the development of mind, a new capacity to think. While interpretation often continues to be important, the transformation of unrepresented states is based less on the content of interpretations and more in the kinds of analytic transactions—described and conceived differently in each theory—that make possible new symbolization and a new capacity to think. These range from Benjamin's (2017) recognition, intersubjectivity, and the Third; to Bromberg's (1998, 2006, 2011) and my own (Stern, 2010, 2015) work with the difficulties in opening ourselves to the patient's dissociated impact on us, and accepting it; to the analyst's immersion, with the patient, in a "second look" at the "bastion," and the consequent liberation of the field, in the work of the Barangers (Baranger, Baranger, & Mom, 1983; Baranger & Baranger, 2009); to Bion's (1963) container/contained model; to the Botellas' (2005) recommendation that analysts allow themselves to become their patients' "doubles," thereby coming to know the patient's mind from the inside and sometimes finding their way to the symbolization the patient's unrepresented experience; and so on.

In all of these theories, and many others, even when interpretation is used, the content it reveals is no longer understood to be what is mutative about the intervention. Instead, the interpretation is a contribution of the analytic relatedness to the growth of mind.

That is, the process of treatment is not defined by the task of revealing hidden or distorted, pre-existing mental contents. Instead, each theory describes the analytic situation as a field of some kind in which certain kinds of analytic transactions have transformational effects on the mind of the patient (and, in the interpersonal/relational models, on the mind of the analyst, as well [Slavin & Kriegman, 1998; see also Benjamin, Bromberg, Ehrenberg, Stern]).

While, as I've said, the members of this group of writers are often quite different from one another, most of them (at least those from Europe and South America) are familiar with one another's work, and many of them, even most, consider their work to be part of a certain broad consensus about the nature of psychoanalysis, a consensus rooted in the belief that their theories stay true to the centrality of the unconscious in psycho-analysis—more true than the theories bred in North America: interpersonal and relational psychoanalysis, self psychology, intersubjectivity theory, and the contemporary Freudian psychoanalysis that grew from ego psychology. Perhaps even more problematic than this claim about the inadequacy of theories of the unconscious in North American psycho-analysis is the position that often follows as a corollary: North American psychoanalytic theories are diluted forms of psychoanalysis.

Lacan and Lacanians, for example, have long held a fine disdain for ego psychology, and therefore, in their view, for much of contemporary North

American Freudian psychoanalysis. Lacan—and many other French analysts, as well, past and present—believe(d) that ego psychologists turned away from any really serious consideration of the unconscious, and gave primacy instead to adaptation to drive demands and the outside world. This attitude, in spades, appears among contemporary French analysts toward relational psychoanalysis. Lacan did not specifically address relational psychoanalysis, since it came about after he wrote; but he would no doubt have been highly critical of it, since he rejected object relations, just as he rejected ego psychology, and in fact tended to think of the former as a form of the latter. Waintrater (2012) tells us that French analysts today are horrified by relational psychoanalysis, which they see as a threat to the existence of psychoanalysis. As a result, none of Stephen Mitchell's work (to take just one example) has been translated into French; and *Psychoanalytic Dialogues* is literally never cited in French journals. Waintrater (2012) writes that,

> French analysts react with perplexity, if not astonishment, to such ideas as the relative nature of interpretation, the primacy of the here-and-now, and the deconstruction of authority, especially the analyst's. In the French view, such ideas reflect an ideological tendency, close to cultural relativism; they mark the end of the specificity of psychoanalysis, reduced to a branch of psychology.
>
> (Waintrater, 2012, p. 296)

It seems quite obviously wrongheaded to me to question the validity of North American psychoanalysis, just as it was wrongheaded for the ego psychologists of North America to take that attitude toward interpersonal psychoanalysis in times past (see Stern, 2015, Chapter 2). A more sensible position is to recognize that all the theories I have cited, North American as well as European and South American, grow from themes of unrepresented or unmentalized states, and unformulated experience; and that, as I have already said, each writer's understanding of therapeutic process and therapeutic action is defined by the kinds of therapeutic transactions believed by that writer to be effective in creating or repairing the capacity to transform unrepresented states into thought, thereby contributing to the growth of mind. If we could agree on these two points—the significance of unrepresented states in the theory of mind, and the significance of therapeutic transactions in expanding the capacity of the mind to symbolize these unrepresented states—then we might have a ground on which to compare the broader theoretical accounts.

In any case, this group of ideas—North American, South American, and European—virtually cries out to be compared with one another, and to the theory of unformulated experience. This book, however, is not the site for such a project, which requires at least one book of its own. For now, I can only cite the need for it, and establish that the theory of unformulated experience belongs in the conversation among theories of unrepresented states.

## A note on Lacan

One of the theories of unrepresented states, Lacan's concept of the real, deserves special mention in the context of the purposes of this book.[9] Lacan, perhaps more than any other major psychoanalytic writer, focused on language, which he understood as the structure of the entire symbolic (cultural) order. And while he certainly was not a hermeneuticist, and would not have identified himself as such, he did share with hermeneutic writers such as Gadamer and Charles Taylor (see the following chapters, especially Chapter 4), the primary inspirations for this book: the understanding that language and culture were coterminous. Although Lacan did not reach these conclusions from philosophical hermeneutics, but instead from structural linguistics (early in his work) and the study of drive and desire (later on), he did understand language to be the source of all meaningfulness in human life, in just the way that hermeneutic writers do (again, see especially Chapter 4). And therefore, Lacan, like the hermeneutic writers whose work will be my focus, understood language to include any system of interconnected meanings, or differential relations among meanings (compare to Taylor's description of language as a web, introduced in Chapter 2); and that means, again in agreement with the hermeneuticists, and with me, that language for Lacan goes far beyond the verbal-reflective mode, and includes any aspect of the nonverbal that is meaningful. I will return to an exploration of this point in all three of the following chapters, but especially Chapter 3.[10]

These points alone make me believe that pursuing the relation of Lacan's ideas and my own would be fruitful. But the connection goes further than that. Lacan's conception of the real bears a significant relation to unformulated experience. The idea of the real changed as Lacan's work developed over time, but in all its forms it is understood as the unknown, that which lies outside the symbolic order and the process of symbolization.

Reality (not to be confused with the real) is for Lacan the symbolic order—i.e., that which falls within the range of language; and language is a social or cultural structure—or rather, *the* social or cultural structure. In Lacan's early work, the real is what has not yet come within the range of the symbolic—but there is no suggestion at this stage of Lacan's thinking that the real *cannot* be symbolized, and in fact, in the clinical process, it is. In this period of his thought, there is therefore a suggestive connection between the real and unformulated experience, and with language as the instrument by which these unknown parts of life are given symbolic form.

Later in Lacan's work, the real is not only unknown, but unknowable, and is identified with trauma. Under some circumstances, unformulated experience, too, is the outcome of trauma (Stern, 1997, 2010, 2015). The relationship to trauma, given the other links via language and unrepresented states, provides yet another suggestive relationship between the real and unformulated experience.

## Meaning and its absence: Drawing the boundary

Now I can return to an introduction to the role of meaningfulness in the theory of unformulated experience, and to the path of this book. The problem of procedural meaning draws that much more attention to the question of meaningfulness, because meaningfulness is what the procedural has in common with symbolically represented meaning. And therefore, if we want to draw a line between what is meaningful in psychic life and what is not, as I intend to do in revising the concept of unformulated experience and its formulation, then we must use a criterion that is something other than the boundary between symbolic representation and its absence.

In my frame of reference, as I have explained, until experience is formulated, and thereby comes into being, it exists only in a state of potential—and this is true, I now want to propose, not only of the states of mind that will become verbal-reflective experience but also of those states that will become nonverbal experience (keep in mind that the nonverbal includes the procedural). *All* of this potential experience, both the verbal and the nonverbal, can be understood to be *unformulated*.

When unformulated experience is formulated, it becomes meaningful, and can thereafter be used in the spontaneous creation of living. Experience becomes meaningful, I will suggest in Chapter 3, because it "feels like me"; it has a quality of "me-ness." I can "own" it; I can tolerate feeling that this experience is part of me. When this is the case, I am able to *accept* the experience in question, and I can comfortably *use* it in the spontaneous creation of living. In Chapter 3, I offer my own definitions of *acceptance* and *use*, and a detailed description of what I mean by the "spontaneous creation of living."

Sometimes parts of subjectivity remain unformulated (unmeaningful) simply because attention has not been drawn to them; and so when attention is paid, there is no reason for this unformulated experience not to "feel like me," and it therefore can be spontaneously and comfortably accepted and used. It can become meaningful. But there are other parts of subjectivity that cannot be formulated in this way, because they feel so alien that to allow them to be "me," or meaningful, would lead to the feeling that one is not recognizable to oneself (Bromberg, 1998, 2006, 2011); and sometimes, *in extremis*, the feeling would be that this is a person one simply cannot *tolerate* being. Anyone's reaction to the quality of alien-ness ranges, depending on the nature of the experience and the interpersonal context of the moment, from mild discomfort to complete intolerance. ("One *will* not, *can*not be this person, because when one was, life was not bearable; and yet, if not-me enters consciousness, one *is* that person" [Stern, 2009, p. 716; italics from the original].) The means by which we "refuse" (I put the word in quotes to signify that this is an unconscious refusal) to accommodate or accept (formulate) what is simply too alien is, in a word, dissociation, the maintenance of experience in its unformulated state for unconscious defensive reasons.

In the following chapters, then, I expand the range of unformulated experience to include both the verbal and the nonverbal, and I simultaneously challenge the everyday view that the verbal and the nonverbal are essentially different. The most important link between the verbal and nonverbal is supplied by the hermeneutic perspective on language that is discussed throughout the book, and then becomes the subject of Chapter 4. But it is also important to preserve a recognition of what is unique about the nonverbal. And so I have tried in this book to walk a line between the hermeneutic position, which advocates the unity of the verbal and the nonverbal under the rubric of language, and the position of cognitive psychology, in which the nonverbal is acknowledged as a separate medium or code of meaning. The best way to do this is to understand that, as empirical research has begun to document (Fonagy, 2012; Vivona, 2012), from the beginning of life

> . . . emergent verbal categories profoundly affect the way [we interact] with the world even as the actions they modulate constantly create refinements to these categories—a truly dynamic system.
>
> (Fonagy, 2012, p. 288)

This is a perspective that applies just as well to the relationship between the verbal and the nonverbal within the hermeneutic perspective I take in this book as it does to the empirical perspective of writers such as Vivona and Fonagy.

I turn now to a description of the chapters to come.

## Articulation, realization, manifestation

Three terms, taken together—*articulation*, *realization*, and *manifestation*—refer to the project I have described in this introductory chapter, and serve as the titles of the three chapters to come. And so a brief introduction to what I mean by these words will, at the same time, introduce the structure of the book.

Chapter 2: *Articulation*. Explicit, verbal-reflective meaning is formulated by a process I have called *articulation*. This chapter describes articulation and goes on to offer initial forays into the relations between the verbal and the nonverbal suggested by an interpretive, hermeneutic perspective.

Chapter 3: *Realization*. A different portion of unformulated experience, when it can be formulated and then used in spontaneous, creative living, naturally assumes a nonverbal form of meaning (symbolic or procedural). I refer to the process of the nonverbal formulation of meaning as *realization*. In Chapter 3 are introduced the key concepts of *acceptance* and *use*, which I describe as the criteria for formulation of both verbal and nonverbal meaning. The presence or absence of acceptance is the criterion of meaningfulness; and that point allows me to conceptualize in this chapter, for the verbal and the nonverbal alike, a common boundary separating unformulated experience from formulated meaning. Two types of unformulated experience are described. One becomes verbally meaningful when it is formulated; the other becomes meaningful in nonverbal terms.

The work of the Boston Change Process Study Group (BCPSG, 2010, 2013) is significantly related to the ideas presented in Chapter 3, especially their understanding of procedural knowledge and implicit relational knowing. In addition (and for a different reason) BCPSG has been critical of my work. A response to the criticism and an appreciative consideration of the points on which BCPSG and I agree each belong in Chapter 3. However, it would be distracting to my argument to introduce such a discussion. For that reason, I present the relation between my work and the work of BCPSG in an appendix. Chapter 3 can be read without this material; or readers, if they prefer, can interrupt Chapter 3 to read the appendix and then return to the thread of the argument.

Chapter 4: *Manifestation*. The hermeneutic theory of *expressivism*, especially in the work of hermeneutic philosopher Charles Taylor, goes a long way toward unifying the verbal and the nonverbal. In expressivist accounts of language, and contrary to theories of information processing, all meaning—the verbal and the nonverbal alike—*manifests* the particular person who creates it. The chapter goes on to show that the way we think about the relation of the verbal and the nonverbal determines our positions not only on matters of theory but also on pragmatic clinical issues with important ethical and moral implications.

## A few words about the title of this book

"The infinity of the unsaid" is a phrase coined by D.E. Linge (1976; see Chapter 2), an interpreter of hermeneutic philosopher Hans-Georg Gadamer. Linge used the phrase to convey something like what Charles Taylor (1985) describes as "the web of language," (see Chapter 4), the whole of which vibrates whenever language is used. However much it may sometimes seem to us that each meaning we create stands alone, we really cannot ever activate only a single meaning, because all meanings derive their significance from the meanings to which they connect—and also, from all those potential meanings that surround them, not yet having been formulated, but nevertheless, even in their nonverbal and/or nascent state, contributing as context, invisible but irreplaceable, to whatever meanings we do formulate. In the passage from which my title is drawn, Linge writes, "It is the infinity of the unsaid—this relation to the whole of being that is disclosed in what is said—into which the one who understands is drawn" (p. xxxii).

The grandeur, eloquence, and truthfulness of this view appeals to me. But grandeur, of course, is hardly a cardinal element of psychoanalytic work. At least not in the present tense—that is, as we are doing it. But as we look back at sessions, sometimes we sense something like that. As we review clinical experience in memory, sometimes we are deeply affected by our awareness of the vastness of the landscapes in which we worked without even recognizing their presence. So many other things could have happened! So many other things could have been known and said!

I don't necessarily mean to say that we recognize unrealized possibilities with regret, though. No, more often we recognize them with a sense of wonder for what might have been. We sense their manifold possibilities, at least in retrospect.

In teaching, I have often used a more pedestrian metaphor: Imagine the possibilities for experience in a single analytic session as the volume of air in a hangar large enough to hold half a dozen jumbo jets. Then imagine the path a housefly takes from one end of that hangar to the other. That tiny path, carved across that immense space, represents the proportion of the possibilities of that session that are actually formulated. We barely touch the vastness of experience.

After I selected the title for this book, having rejected dozens of others, it occurred to me that I am only the latest in a number of psychoanalytic writers to have found inspiration in some notion of the infinite. Two stand out. Bion (1965, 1970) referred to Milton's "deep and formless infinite" as a description of "the face of the deep" in *Genesis*. We can imagine, with Grotstein (2007), that Bion "entered the galactic vastness" to harvest his grasp of concepts such as O. And then there is Matte-Blanco (1988), whose "indivisible mode of being" is defined by *infinitization*, in which all of experience is one, "symmetrical," not broken into the manageable, "asymmetrical" pieces that constitute identifiable meanings. Lombardi (2015) has recently brought the infinities of Bion and Matte-Blanco together in his own work—and in the title he chose for his first book (*Formless Infinity*). I am pleased to acknowledge any links (no pun intended) that might exist between these prior psychoanalytic uses of infinity and my own.

It is not coincidental, I think, that both Bion and Matte-Blanco proposed models in which the unconscious is conceptualized as unformed rather than repressed. That, too, I share with them. All three of us understand the unconscious as potential experience; and it is a short step from that commonality to an agreement among us, whatever our other differences, that the unconscious is infinite.[11]

## Reading this book

Very often, psychoanalytic books, especially in the contemporary era, are composed of chapters previously published as articles. While these articles are often revised for book publication, and while they usually have, or are given, thematic coherence, most of the contents of many books, including my own, have appeared before. That is not the case with this book. Part of Chapter 2, and the portion of Chapter 1 that summarizes the theory of unformulated experience that has existed up to now, are revisions of previously published articles; but the remainder of the material presented here was written expressly for this book. Therefore, while many psychoanalytic books today can be read by dipping into them here and there, that is not true of this book, which, because it was written to develop a particular argument, is probably best grasped by reading it from beginning to end.

## Notes

1 Besides psychoanalysts, these writers were literary critics, philosophers, academic psychologists (experimental, development, and social), sociologists, and linguists. Some of them are cited in Stern, 1997.

2 Sullivan was an empiricist, and as such, he found many psychoanalytic conceptions to be less than useful, especially those that concerned unobservables, such as a substantive, repressed unconscious. "I tried to say nothing about the unconscious except to suggest that it was not phenomenologically describable. I don't use the conception particularly ... It is very useful for theory, but there are some other expressions that are perhaps more communicative" (Sullivan 1950/1971, p. 221). Sauvayre and Hunyadi (2018), who drew my attention to the quotation I have just made from Sullivan, also point out that, in *The Interpersonal Theory of Psychiatry* (Sullivan, 1953), often taken as Sullivan's major theoretical work despite the fact that it was compiled by editors from his lectures and notes after his death, Sullivan does not refer even once to "the unconscious," but, rather, to "covert processes." In thinking this way, Sullivan could focus on active interpersonal processes instead of static content, and could imagine unconsciousness as unformulated

rather than repressed, directions he preferred to the conventional psycho-analytic account. Sullivan never said as much, but it seems consistent with his frame of reference to say that the next moment's experience has yet to be created, and that this creation is the outcome of interpersonal processes.

I do not share Sullivan's interest in limiting theory to an exploration of what is observable; my own interest in an unformulated unconscious has developed for other reasons, which I hope are clear in the text.

3 The metaphor contradicts itself in one respect: it does not really represent the genuine ambiguity of unformulated experience. (Nothing describable could represent this quality, of course, since the point is that unformulated experience cannot be known in words.) In the physical world, though, an object in a fog already has an identity; it already exists as an identifiable object even when its shape appears to be vague, and so as it moves toward you, and its contours become clearer and clearer, what emerges is not being created, as I argue is the case in the articulation of unformulated experience, but was always there. But as long as we limit our consideration to the quality of emergence of the figure coming forward in the fog, the metaphor works as an illustrations of what I mean by the constraints on unformulated experience.

4 I am in the process of writing a formal presentation of this aspect of the theory of unformulated experience. For the moment, only an informal summary of the idea (Stern, 2014) is available.

Note that unconscious fantasy actually *could* not play a formative role in the theory of unformulated experience, because unconscious fantasy is substantive, shaped mental content, and therefore is inconsistent with the position that unconscious content is unformulated. See Stern, 2010b.

5 Levenson (e.g., 1992) rightly points out that Sullivan described dissociation and selective inattention separately. Selective inattention is a much less severe operation: one "sort of" knows what one doesn't know. In dissociation, though, the "unknowing" is more or less complete: one doesn't have an inkling. For my purposes, I combine both processes under the rubric of dissociation, because both differ from repression in having to do with the prevention of formulation, not the distortion or hiding away of meanings that already exist.

6 Examples of such an attitude appear in the following chapters. For the moment, let me just point the reader toward the conceptions of language in the thinking of Daniel Stern (e.g., 1985) and Wilma Bucci (e.g., 1997), to both of whose work I return in Chapters 3 and 4.

7 Of course, the point that the analyst's interventions must grow from a deep, even unconscious affective involvement, not just an intellectual or rational grasp of the patient's experience, is commonplace in a large slice of the psychoanalytic literature, across many theoretical and clinical orientations; but the way I mean the word "involvement" is particular, I think, to the interpersonal and relational literatures. By "involvement," I mean the analyst's unconscious participation in the interpersonal field. In interpersonal and

relational theory, this involvement takes place on a level playing field—that is, the unconscious involvement of the analyst with the patient is *the same in kind* as the patient's with the analyst's. The analyst is not understood to be able to titrate, or control, the depth of his involvement. He has no choice but to observe what he can of the nature of his involvement and then to decide how it is best to proceed. In most other theoretical conceptions of the analyst's involvement, there are usually provisos expressed about the degree of analyst involvement that is advisable or permissible—as if the analyst's control of his involvement is feasible. The analyst's involvement with the patient, in this sense, is not "the same in kind" as the patient's involvement with the analyst. But how can such a thing be done if the phenomena involved are unconscious? One cannot control the unconscious! Here is a typical statement of a proviso of the kind I am referring to:

> . . . [T]he phenomenon of projective identification must have very special characteristics in the analytic couple. It must be allowed be massive on one side (the patient's) but kept very limited on the analyst's. . . .
> (Baranger & Baranger, 1960–61/2008, p. 37)

I have compared the interpersonal/relational conception of the analyst's involvement with the patient with the conception in Bionian field theory (Stern, 2013a, b). There remains much to discuss about this topic.

8 Bromberg does accord interpretation an important place in the clinical work that can be done once dissociative process has been seen and changed. At that point, not-me processes, or dissociation, which can only be enacted, are replaced by the capacity for conflict, and therefore also by the capacity for thought. When that happens, the analyst's interpretations can be meaningful. But "when that happens" should not be taken to mean that there exists a single threshold in the course of the treatment, beyond which interpretation becomes useful all the time. The presence of multiple states of being in Bromberg's (and my own) frame of reference means that the necessities to recognize the existence of this threshold and find a way to cross it are ongoing parts of any treatment from beginning to end.

9 Actually, I have thought for a long time that a comparison of my own thinking with Lacan's would be a good idea, and apparently I wasn't the only one to have that thought. To wit: In about 1990, at the annual meetings of Division 39 (Psychoanalysis) of the American Psychological Association in Chicago, I served as the discussant on a panel composed of papers on constructivism in psychoanalysis by Louis Fourcher, Irwin Hoffman, and Michael Tansey. During the discussion after I spoke, an older man in the audience stood up and said, with great severity but also with what I thought was a gleam in his eye, "Dr. Stern, could you please tell us the relation of your ideas to those of Jacques Lacan?" There was just the faintest note of amusement in the man's delivery, and I imagined that he knew very well the discomfort his question caused me. Only a very few Americans in those days knew Lacan's work, and

I was certainly not one of them. If that's what the man thought—that I would be uncomfortable—he was right. "Dr. Gill," I said with as much authority as I could muster (because I didn't yet know Merton Gill, but I recognized him, a hero and celebrity to me, a man whose work I had read and admired ever since I began in the field of psychoanalysis), "I don't know whether to thank you or to kill you!" Thankfully, Gill thought this was funny. He sat down, and with the rest of the audience he laughed and laughed. I never answered the question.

10  This brief discussion of Lacan is based on his *Ecrits* (1977/2004) and on numerous secondary sources, which non-Lacanian readers may want to read both before and during tackling the *Ecrits*. There are many secondary sources, some of them introductory summary presentations; a few others are companions to a close reading of *Ecrits*. In the introductory category, those I have found useful include: Bowie (1991), Fink (1995, 1999), and Homer (2005).

11  What Bion (1962) calls the unconscious is actually the storehouse of *alpha elements*, the symbolic elements of experience that we link together to create dreams (thoughts); in Bion's thought what we usually think of as the dynamic unconscious is more closely related to raw, unsymbolized emotion and sensation, or *beta elements*.

# Articulation

## The formulation of verbal-reflective meaning

Visionary power
Attends the motions of the viewless winds,
Embodied in the mystery of words:
There, darkness makes abode, and all the host
Of shadowy things work endless changes,—there,
As in a mansion like their proper home,
Even forms and substances are circumfused
By that transparent veil with light divine,
And, through the turnings intricate of verse,
Present themselves as objects recognised,
In flashes, and with glory not their own.

Wordsworth, *The Prelude 1850*, Book 5, lines 595–605

We take it for granted that we and our patients know what we are doing when we use words. We feel that we use words in a way we can describe; conversation holds no particular mystery. We call this activity language, talk, speech, conversation, free association, and so on; and we call the corresponding mental processes and experiences by familiar names such as verbal memory, verbal encoding, conceptualization, intellect, thought, cognition, insight, interpretation, and reflection. We believe we know what we mean when we say these things.

And by extension, if anyone were to ask us, we would know without having to be told how to differentiate all these worded processes and experiences from the rest of what transpires in psychoanalytic treatment. We would simply divide the treatment into two portions: "worded" and "wordless," or "verbal" and "nonverbal." We think we know the difference because we take for granted our capacity to define the role language plays in our lives.

But the differences between "verbal" and "nonverbal" and between "worded" and "wordless" do not tell us anything very important about how psychoanalytic treatment is actually different in these two realms—how "verbal" and "nonverbal" describe different ways of being in the clinical setting. Unless we can say *how* these differences make a difference—that is, unless we can say how worded experience differs from experience for which we do not have words—we don't really know as much as we assume we do about what we are up to when we use words. In fact, without elaboration, the distinction between "worded" and "wordless" actually means nothing at all, because we can make two such mutually exclusive categories out of any descriptor we choose: red and non-red, for example, or paved and unpaved. It is certainly true that the floor in my office is unpaved, for example, to say nothing of the ceiling or the books on my shelves—but it doesn't mean much to say so.

Yet we all have the strongest kind of feeling that, in psychoanalytic work, the difference between words and their absence is neither trivial nor arbitrary. We believe, as a matter of fact, that the difference is crucial. It is this feeling about the significance of words—a sense about which we have no doubt but which is not necessarily easy to explain—that lies behind what I have to say in this chapter. I will try to specify what is most clinically important about this difference, at least for me. I will, in the process, arrive at a restatement of the theory of unformulated experience, and I will define the first of the two ways that I believe unformulated experience can be formulated: the articulation of verbal-reflective meaning.

It will become clear as the chapter proceeds that the nonverbal, by serving as the background for verbal meaning and thereby helping to establish the possibilities that exist for words, plays a constitutive role in the construction of verbal-reflective meaning. And that role is just the beginning of the part played by the nonverbal in experiencing. The nonverbal is not only background, of course. It can also become foreground—but without entering the realm of words. In the chapter that follows this one, I present the other way that unformulated experience can be formulated: the realization of nonverbal meaning. That chapter and this one should be read as companion pieces.

## Clinical illustration

As an example to use in tying to the ground the points I want to make about verbal-reflective meaning, I begin with a clinical illustration. To tell the event I have in mind I need first to offer background and context.

I had been seeing a certain 25 year old man, who I will call Robert, for a year or so. We began by meeting twice a week; sometime after the event I will describe we began to meet three times per week. For quite a while, the problem that stood in the way of turning what began as a mostly supportive psychotherapy into the more exploratory psychoanalytic treatment it has become was the patient's ambivalence about taking himself and his experience seriously, and a defensive tendency to deny subtlety and to think in the most concrete terms. Such a person is not usually a prime candidate for an exploratory psychoanalysis of the traditional kind—although today, thankfully, there is once again, as there was in the time of Searles (1965), Fromm-Reichmann (1955), and others, a movement to expand the range of psychoanalytic treatment (e.g., Lombardi, 2015, 2016). The episode I recount here comes from that initial period of treatment and was one of the reasons I began to be optimistic about a more exploratory approach.

Robert was always deeply concerned, and often worried, about interactions with the members of his family of origin, who remained the most significant people in his day-to-day life. He wanted to know how to ensure that any conflict he could detect between himself and his parents or siblings could be swept under the rug. Sometimes, when he was in the right frame of mind, he was willing to set aside his insistence on harmonious family relations long enough to be mildly interested in thinking about them. Even at those times, though, he did not make spontaneous observations. Often enough, however, he did seem to take in my observations, sometimes even extrapolating from them. At certain rare moments he was actually quite gripped by this new, psychological way of thinking, although he was also aware of being afraid of where it might lead: he had flashes of insight (brief stretches that more often than not disappeared quite thoroughly within a few minutes) that he and his parents and siblings had substantial problems that stood in their way of living the lives they all tried to convince one another they were leading—well adjusted, unruffled, progressing steadily forward toward what is good.

Robert wished for a family of his own, and professional success, but he was very far from reaching those goals. He seemed to me younger than his years, with very little self-confidence, little history of accomplishment to build on, and no professional goals to pursue (at the time, he worked in a secretarial position in a company that belonged to his father). He could see, furthermore, that it was true (as I had told him) that he had seldom been curious about himself, and in fact had seldom had a good reason to be curious about himself. To know his own mind would have been dangerous to the status quo in his family, in which any kind of emotional pain went routinely and insistently unacknowledged, and life was supposed to go smoothly. The siblings only rarely developed a clear idea of how they felt about their parents and one another, because there was no recognition of feeling states, at least negative ones. Even positive feelings, which were of course more acceptable, were stereotyped and drained of particularity and intensity in a way that made them difficult to grasp. Robert might say that things had been "good"; that he felt "positive" toward his father this week; and so on. My inquiries generally did not provoke much articulation of such statements.

And yet Robert also said, during the brief episodes in which his denial relaxed, that he had many more observations inside him than he had ever let anyone know. He recognized at those moments that no one had ever known him very well. He would not let them. He would see, briefly, that the reason he had never thought about himself is that he had had no one with whom to think, what I have elsewhere called a partner in thought (Stern, 2010a)—and that now that he was in treatment, he did. He some-times came quite close to understanding why it was that I always made such a "big deal" (his description) of "curiosity," which was the word I used in my attempts to explain to him how it was that he and I could set out to talk about unpleasant things without our purpose being to trash his family. Most of the time, though, Robert fell back on understanding things about himself by means of explanations like "that's just the way I am," or on good days, "I'm just like my father in every-thing"; but once in a while he began to grasp what I meant when, in my frustration in the face of his insistent superficiality, I resorted to educational efforts and told him that the reason I was always asking him just to tell me what was on his mind is that there is this thing called "the unconscious," and that when you really know you have an unconscious you have no choice but to observe your conscious experience and try to understand the role you unwittingly play in its construction. Once he even understood what I meant when I suggested, on the occasion of our observation of his resentment of his father's control over him, that we both should be on the lookout for the rise of that issue in the relationship we were beginning to construct between us. Robert was able to observe, again once or twice, that his emotionally impoverished upbringing had left him with the

feeling that he was incapable of handling his own feelings, so that knowing about them did not offer him a richer life, or a way of understanding
himself, but merely the threat of being overwhelmed. And the outcome of
all this, he saw on those rare occasions, was that he had come to feel
unable to make it on his own, to take care of himself in the outside world
("outside" relative to his family), and that he therefore was now fearful
that he was condemned to a career in the sheltered atmosphere of the
family business. Robert was probably bright enough to have done reasonably well in school, and he did finish a second-rate college, but he did it
only by the skin of his teeth. He had thought about going on to earn a
teaching credential—he admires teachers—but he just could not bring
himself to take the risk of failing. At the time of the episode I will recount,
he had not yet made a real life for himself.

After his moments of clarity, however encouraging they had been, the
next session would almost always take place as if those insightful few
minutes hadn't happened at all. In nine sessions out of ten, as a matter of
fact, Robert would insist that all was well and that he was "nothing but
happy." He would say that there was absolutely nothing to talk about.
At these times, if I were to remind Robert of the angry outbursts at work
that had led his father to insist that Robert come to treatment (the father
apparently believed that his son would be sanitized of rage by psychoanalysis, so that life could be smooth once more), Robert would tell me
that he no longer had those outbursts. Everything was *fine*—and to this
extent, and for the time being, no doubt his father was delighted by
Robert's progress in treatment.

It is true, actually, that Robert's outbursts disappeared soon after
treatment began. One might think that a person like him—someone not
particularly psychologically-minded, someone who finds conflict, and
even most affect, aversive—would drift out of treatment at this point, a
transference cure in the purest sense, a passenger on the next flight into
health. But he did not want to stop coming to see me. Quite the contrary.
He was usually twenty minutes early, and he never missed a session; he
was actually quite eager to come, feeling that it was safe to have nothing
to say, and knowing that, even in his wordlessness, something interesting
might happen, even if it was a bit distressing. He could not make these
interesting moments happen, and he found it most natural to avoid them—
but he was nevertheless simultaneously intrigued by them. If you combine
Robert's developing attachment to me with his flashes of genuine capacity

to be intrigued and to think about himself, you can see, I think, why I felt optimistic about the treatment becoming an analysis.

In the session I will discuss in more detail, Robert (who had just begun to use the couch, at my suggestion) was talking about his sister, who had left her job working with Robert at the father's company and had then "blown off" two family occasions in a row. In each case, she had promised to attend, but did not show up, offering excuses (later) that Robert could not swallow. Mind you, one just does not behave this way in this family. Evidently the sister was having her own separation struggle. I commented that Robert's sister seemed not to want to come, but that she seemed equally unwilling to say so. Robert said that if she had let them know she wasn't coming, he and his brother would have made life difficult for her. They would not have accepted her decision and would have argued with her, so that she would have had a much harder time not coming than if she just didn't turn up. Robert was angry at his sister, but also recognized that at least she was making an effort to live a life of her own. It wasn't the best way to do it, he said, but at least she was trying. "It's more than I've been able to do," he said, and lapsed into silence.

Robert knew that I was interested in dreams, but he had said more than once that he had none to report, and that he never remembered them. Now, though, after about twenty seconds, he told me excitedly that he had just remembered a dream he had had repeatedly since he was a child. He said he recognized this dream, but that it was as if he had never *really* realized before that he had had it. He had never described it to anyone, and had never made it the explicit object of his own attention; it was as if, up to this moment, it had just "happened to him" (my description, but one with which he agreed). I was interested in the dream, of course, but I also found myself wondering whether Robert's excitement was due to the dream itself or to the suddenly available opportunity to give me what he had reason to believe I wanted.

It is difficult to reproduce the wording Robert used in telling me the dream, because I had to ask dozens of questions (literally dozens) just to understand the nature of the image. Robert simply could not describe the spatial relations and sensory qualities of the dream in a way that I could grasp them. He was actually quite inarticulate. In the end, once I got it, the image was fairly simple. The fact that the object in the dream was nothing identifiable, and the fact that he had never tried to tell anyone about it before, or even thought about it in words, probably made conveying it a complicated communicative task.

The object was some kind of cube that Robert was trying to pick up. Its surfaces were smooth (Robert began by saying they were "soft," a mistake he and I have not yet understood thoroughly, though we have come back to it more than once; it confused me at the time); it was smooth "like Formica," the material the kitchen counters were made of in all the houses he lived in growing up. The cube was in front of him, and its size was indeterminate, though it was too big for him to get his arms around. After a few minutes of questioning, he was finally able to say that he was standing at the corner of this cube, stretching his arms down either side. All he knew, therefore, was that he could not reach the far corners of the cube; but he did have the sense that it was an object small enough to be lifted. It was frustrating not to be able to pick it up; the dream was about trying to do so. "Frustrating" once again was my word, not his, though he agreed with it enthusiastically. My offer of the word came about as follows: When I first asked him how he felt in the dream, he said he was "sad." I asked what was sad. He shook his head, seemingly frustrated, and said that "sad" was totally the wrong word (and another meaning to be grasped only at a later time). He fished around for another word, and came up with something quite different, an affect-label I don't remember, but one which didn't satisfy him any more than "sad" did. Finally he asked me in some exasperation, "What is it that you are when you want to do something and you can't?" When I suggested "frustrated," he said that was it exactly, and wondered why he couldn't think of it himself.

Then Robert said with some feeling, "You know, it's just this thing that I wish I could do, but I can't do it. I'm not *able* to do it. There is this thing I want to do and it's just *totally beyond* me. I feel like I have to give up." There was a long silence, during which I felt the force of this metaphor as a representation of Robert's more general impotence. I wonder if I would have interpreted it. I might very well have done so.

I will never know, however, because after perhaps half a minute, Robert whispered, in a tone of awe that I had never heard from him, "Did you hear what I just said?" He lapsed back into a silence, this time what seemed to me a very excited silence. It seemed clear to me that he had had the same thought I had had: his dream was a metaphor for his life. I imagined that he had remembered the dream at that moment because of the feeling he had just expressed that at least his sister was *trying* to live a life of her own.

After a little while, he said, "That's really interesting. But it freaks me out, too." He didn't go on, so I asked him what he meant. "Well," he said, "I had this idea inside me all this time and I didn't know it. That part's really interesting, but it also means I don't know what's inside me, and that part freaks me out." Robert went on to describe how he had taken several psychology courses in college and not gotten anything out of any of them. The theories were all arbitrary; they had meant nothing to him. But now he saw, he said, that you probably have to learn these things from yourself. He ended by saying something rather remarkable— remarkable at least for someone like him, who so recently would never have had the faintest idea about such a thing: "Freud," he said with that same tone of awe and wonder, "must have been his own most important patient."

I made an agreeing noise, some kind of "mm-hm," and said nothing more. Robert was silent for a moment and then said simply, "That's good," and sighed. After a moment he added, "I didn't want you to say anything."

I thought I understood what he meant. He had made this new thought himself. It was his own, as very few of his thoughts really were, and he didn't want me mucking about with it, which might either have ruined it or taken it away from him.

During this session, I turned over in my mind the fact that Robert wanted my approval. I also felt sure he knew about, and probably regretted, the exasperation I had sometimes felt when he had insisted that, because everything was fine, there was nothing to talk about. It seemed likely to me that the positive feelings Robert had for me, along with his desire to avoid arousing negative feelings—in so many words, the transference—helped him remember the dream and had something to do with what he did with it. He wanted to please me, of course, and probably did not want me to be exasperated. And that's fine. Freud (1913) taught, after all, that what makes a treatment an analysis isn't that we *don't* use the transference, but that we use it in the service of the treatment. I believe the positive transference, in combination with Robert's feeling of safety (the feeling of safety actually being part of that transference), was a primary reason that the experience in this session was possible and available to Robert. The experience was no less authentic because Robert hoped it would please me.

Now I turn to the difference between words and wordlessness. I review several ways we might assign significance to the distinction, citing aspects of the case of Robert along the way. Eventually, I choose the difference I think is most useful to us, returning to Robert and me at the end.

The way I characterize the difference between words and their absence is not necessarily the same way someone in another field would do it—a painter or a musician, say, or a philosopher, or a cognitive scientist. We know that how we judge an answer always depends on the question we have posed and our purpose in asking it. Since I will be supplying an answer to a question, I ask you to keep in mind that my question concerns the difference between words and wordlessness in the very specific context of psychoanalysis and psychoanalytic psychotherapy. That means to me that a meaningful way of characterizing the difference also must be compelling in everyday experience. As far as I am concerned, it is insufficient to offer a merely logical explanation in psychoanalysis; to be useful, our theories must be appreciable in phenomenological terms.

Because it is my aim to discuss the difference between words and wordlessness in the clinical situation, I cannot discuss in the detail I would like what is arguably the central ingredient of the *relation* between the two: the analytic relationship. It is only within the context of the transference and countertransference that the relation between what can be said and what cannot be said is meaningful; and the nature of that relational context is what allows the relation of words and wordlessness to change. All understanding is dialogic (e.g., Gadamer, 1965/2004); and that suggests that the nature of the analytic field, conscious and unconscious, interpersonal and intrapsychic, determines what each of its participants can reflect upon and what must remain unarticulated. Understanding is thus a relational event, and words gain their meaning from the relational contexts in which they are used. I must be content for the moment here with this passing reference to the relational aspect of language.

## Word and act

One way to describe the difference between words and wordlessness is to set words against acts: such a position holds that if we have words for experience, we are not compelled to act on it, to act it out; and if we do not have words for it, we cannot avoid enacting it.

Freud's theory of mind was not this simple. It was a core part of Freud's (1900, p. 599–601, 1911, p. 221) conception that words (and thoughts that could be worded) delayed the kind of action motivated purely by impulse and the accompanying desire for hallucinatory wish fulfillment. To this extent, words were inconsistent with acts. But Freud also indicated that when action was realistic (secondary process), words *facilitated* it; words (thought) were "an experimental kind of acting" that postponed direct discharge and allowed an increased tolerance of tension (1911, p. 221; see also 1895, pp. 332–335, 1900, pp. 599–600). The result was that, "Motor discharge was now employed in the appropriate alteration of reality; it was converted into action" (1911, p. 221).

Freud's clinical thinking, on the other hand, contained a more straightforward opposition of word and act. Consider the prohibition of action in the treatment, an intention of which (among other intentions) was to channel psychic life into words and out of enactment. In a well-known passage, Freud describes the treatment as a "struggle between the doctor and the patient, between intellect and instinctual life, between understanding and seeking to act . . ." (1912, p. 108). Here Freud does oppose thought and act—and by "thought," of course, he means words. Perhaps his most famous and unambiguous statement opposing compulsive, repetitive action and verbally specifiable memory comes in "Remembering, repeating, and working through" (1914): ". . . we may say that the patient does not *remember* anything of what he has forgotten and repressed, but acts it out. He reproduces it not as a memory but as an action; he *repeats* it . . ." (p. 150).

Much has changed in this respect (cf. Greenberg, 1996). Today, it is a clinical commonplace that the patient's verbally expressed memories can be just as thoroughly embedded in an enactment of the transference as any more conventionally defined action. Contemporary clinicians also take it granted that every time they speak, *they* are taking some kind of action with and toward the patient; the effect of the analyst's language, like the patient's, is hardly limited to its truth value. The prohibition on acting in the treatment has gone by the wayside. We take the position instead that both we and the patient are always acting, so that the question about technique is not how to manage *not* to act, but rather what action to undertake. As Levenson (1979) put it forty years ago, psychoanalysis may be what is said about what is done; but it is just as much what is done about what is said.

This point is certainly obvious in what I have told you about Robert and me: When Robert speaks to me, he also acts in the transference, does he not? How could it be otherwise? After telling me about Freud and hearing my simple response, does he not make it clear he wished for a certain kind of interaction in words—which in this case, he got? And for my own part, did I not directly participate in the transference—that is, did I not indicate part of my countertransference—in that "mm-hm," or even more clearly, in my various frustrated "teachings" about the unconscious?

The upshot is that it is now routine for us to see language as a kind of action—not only in our theories of mind, as Freud did, but in the treatment setting itself. And action, we can add, is language. We have learned from structuralism and its aftermath that our acts are organized in complex and meaningful ways that are actually linguistic (semiotic), at least in the broadest sense.

This collapse of the difference between word and act in the clinical situation is interesting, of course, and its importance for psychoanalysis is unquestionable; but you might wonder why I have cited it, since in doing away with that distinction, I do not seem to have helped myself along in the attempt to understand what makes words and wordlessness different in the clinical setting. As a matter of fact, it might seem that all I have done is erase the distinction I set out to describe.

But perhaps I have advanced toward my goal more than it first appears. This very brief discussion of word and act reveals something that I will need to acknowledge in any valid and useful way of understanding the difference between words and wordlessness: both must be portrayed as kinds of conduct, as varieties of action (cf. Schafer, 1976). This point will help, and I will return to it.

Now that the divergence of acts and words in the treatment setting has been questioned not only for patients, but for analysts as well, it is that much easier—natural, even—to accept that interpretations routinely have noninterpretive effects. The existence of noninterpretive interventions has become noncontroversial. Today, in any issue of any psychoanalytic journal, one finds references to enactments, transitional phenomena and relating, the holding environment, the analyst's capacity for containment and survival, the empathic acceptance of selfobject transferences, the analyst's receptive function, the rootedness of psychoanalysis in intersubjectivity, the significance of the analyst's authenticity—and even the analyst's love. It can be dizzying to realize how much the conception of the analyst's legitimate activity has changed over the last thirty or forty years.

When I told Robert that I believed he resented his father's control over his life, no doubt I also did several other things, about which I can only speculate: I may have made Robert admire me for daring to say the unsayable; I may have established the beginnings of a "monkey-in-the-middle" relationship with Robert, in which his father was the one who was helpless for once; I may have made Robert wonder whether he now would owe me the allegiance he had always felt he owed his father; and so on. Today it is probably fair to say that virtually all interpersonal and relational analysts, and many others as well, recognize all their interpretations as acts and not just words; interpretations are inevitable participations in the interpersonal field, mutual enactments in which we expect the analyst to be interested, but which we recognize he or she cannot avoid.

In considering noninterpretive interventions we stumble across two other binaries that may be of help: public and private, and thought and feeling. Nonverbal interventions such as attunement, the empathic mode, and affirmation, after all, are more often centered on affect than words; and the unconscious enactments that we cannot verbalize, but that many of us believe are essential to an ongoing psychoanalysis, are private meanings: they cannot be known in communicable terms, at least for a time, and therefore cannot be public meanings for either analytic participant. Could it be that the difference between words and wordlessness in the clinical setting lies in either the difference between public and private, or between affect and intellect?

## Public and private

In has been argued in social science ever since George Herbert Mead (1934), Benjamin Whorf (1956), and Edward Sapir (1941), and in some philosophical circles long before that, that language makes meaning communicable and public, while wordless experience is private and incommunicable. On the basis of such a stance, it could be argued that the difference between worded and wordless is the difference between public and private. The medicalized, normalizing, instrumental attitude of one strand of the mainstream American psychoanalysis of the past is certainly reminiscent of such a distinction. The basic tenet of that attitude is that one's interests are best served by making one's meanings lucid, public, and rational, whereas maintaining meaning as private, unconscious, mysterious, and nonrational is liable to be psychopathological, or at least immature. As a matter of fact, it is probably fair to say that one of my most valued clinical and intellectual forebears, Harry Stack Sullivan, took this very perspective (see Chapter 1).

But there are also many, many writers who see the issue from the other end. I cite just a few of those who have been important to me. Maurice Merleau-Ponty is one who does not idealize rationality, preferring what he calls the "wild-flowering mind" (1964, p. 181), the primary manifestation of which is the use of language in creative and unexpected ways. For Merleau-Ponty, language has its own life, to which we "lend" ourselves when we speak with authenticity and creativity. Neither does Lacan (1953/2004, 1977/2004) believe that what we can say is more valuable than what we cannot. In Lacan's thinking, communicability and mutuality are deceptive covers, suggesting falsely that life is a stable affair, and serving as the false reassurance we crave to protect us against the disturbing truth that our worlds are in continuous flux. For very different reasons, Winnicott, Ogden, Fromm, Bion, Matte-Blanco, and a disparate group of many others also take the view that the truth is not necessarily what is available in the language of publically verifiable discourse. Each of these writers believes that we may have to use words strangely to say something true. Words are not coterminous with consciousness, then: they may be bursting with meanings we do not know we intend, conveying to the right listener a good deal more than what we are aware of saying.

This is already enough testimony, along with my own experience, for me to conclude that I will not find my answer in the difference between public and private meaning. But let me cite just one more point, which for me would be enough by itself to make the case. Perhaps the most telling evidence that the verbal is not only public but private is the existence of poetry. The author of a poem works the words over and over again, until they capture what the poet wants to say in as precise and sparing a way as possible. However free its form, a good poem, while its origins may have arrived unbidden in the poet's mind, is as planful and carefully constructed as an origami sculpture. Yet consider that poetry is nevertheless read differently by different readers. The reason for these multiple interpretations is not simply that readers find their own private meanings in what they read. That is certainly part of what happens, but it is also true that writers never know fully what they write. Anything that is new, that is really worth saying and not just a repetition of what is appropriate, familiar, or conventional, is at least partially private and mysterious. Sometimes we are right to claim that we mean what we say, because it feels right, even when we later discover that we did not explicitly know at the time all of what we meant. This point seems to me to be as true about what is said by patients in psychoanalysis and psychotherapy as it is about the productions of poets. We should be skeptical about the substantiality of a psychoanalysis in which it is always easy to understand what a patient means by the words he or she speaks. Important speech contains private meanings as well as public ones, affective resonances as well as information (Loewald, 1978; Bruner, 1990; Vivona, 2003, 2013).

Remember Robert's initial descriptions of the object in his dream. Why in the world did he say "soft" when he thought he meant "smooth?" And he made this "error" several times before my confusion eventually led him to see that he was not in control of what he was saying. *Is* this just an error? Of course not. *The Psychopathology of Everyday Life* (Freud, 1901) should have answered that question once and for all. Perhaps one day Robert and I will thoroughly understand the significance of Robert's "soft"; but whether we do or not, I strongly suspect that it does has some kind of significance. In any case, though, there is no consensually verifiable meaning in the word "soft," not in this context. Robert spoke it for private and—for the time being—inexpressible reasons.

## Thought and feeling

We tend to associate thought with words, and feeling with their absence. Feeling, while it can be described in words, is clearly not a verbal phenomenon at all, but one of the body. We register affect in the realm of body-life, just as we sense pleasure and pain.

But language is not that simple: intellect alone does not define the domain of words. Intellect by itself, after all, is precisely what is meant by intellectualization and isolation of affect, both of which are caricatures of genuine intellect. Thought that really matters is deeply infused with feeling, so much so that the meaning of the thought *depends* on the feeling (Loewald, 1978; Vivona, 2003). This is true even in the most abstract matters. Most undergraduate textbooks, for example, are exercises in intellectualization, which is probably why it can be so mind-numbing to read them. But the significant original work the textbooks are written to convey, no matter whether that work is literature or physics, was almost always done with the deepest kind of feeling. This point is clear in any first-person account of creative accomplishment, and it is underlined with particular force by the frequency with which, in such accounts, dreams are reported to have provided either creative material or the verbal solutions to seemingly intractable problems (see Chapter 4 of Stern, 1997; Stern, 1990). Here we have not only affect, but intellect, as the expression of body-life, as a representation of one's deepest intentions—intentions so deep, so much of a piece with living itself, that they shape one's thoughts without one's conscious or preconscious participation.

We usually take it for granted that we and our patients select the words we pronounce as straightforwardly as we settle on a china pattern or what to have for dinner. We refer to "choosing our means of expression," as if the meaning is already there and only requires us to find the best way to represent it. This is not the way I think about language; it is obviously not the way language is used in the creative solutions that appear in dreams.

The most important things we say come to us unbidden. Most of the time, we simply find ourselves in possession of the words we use. We just say them, finding them on our tongues as we pronounce them. We certainly don't "select" them in any conscious way. We infrequently even have to cast about for them. Yet we seldom consider the fact that we have absolutely no idea where these words came from, or how we get them; and this makes words more similar to affects than we generally consider them to be.

The most full-bodied and authentic of our thoughts, in treatment and outside it, are not only unbidden; they are also fully imagined (Stern, 1997, Chapter 5). By "fully imagined" I mean that they are closely woven with affect, and deeply embedded in the conflict, pain, and satisfactions of whatever matters most to us. As we speak or write, we seldom have the satisfying feeling that we mean absolutely every word just exactly as we have used it—what a patient of mine used to call "speaking from the heart" (Stern, 1997)—but we always desire to speak this way. We all recognize those among us who speak from the heart with any regularity.

We describe such people as wise, substantial, or profound. There is often something unusually strong and comforting about their presence.

However much we desire to speak from the heart, though, we cannot will it; fully imagined speech occurs on its own schedule. The application of force to language results in aridity, convention, and intellectualization. Paul Valéry's (1952) lovely expression of this point no doubt would have pleased Freud:

> [We] can act only upon the freedom of the mind's processes. We can lessen the degree of that freedom, but as for the rest, I mean as for the changes and substitutions still possible under our constraint, we must simply wait until what we desire appears, because that is all we can do. *We have no means of getting exactly what we wish from ourselves.*
> (p. 102; italics from the original)

Would Robert have known how to get the memory of his dream from himself? Would I? Could I even know with certainty how it came about, after the fact? Do either of us know exactly how Robert's grasp of the message in his dream came to him, or how and why he suddenly understood the point that psychological theories of experience are best understood from one's own perspective?

There is a mystery here about which we can say no more. We can say, though, that the difference between affect and thought is not the difference that distinguishes words and wordlessness in clinical work. Once again, there is a lesson to be had: in any solution to the problem I have set myself, and however diametrically opposed the differences between words and wordlessness may turn out to be in other respects, affect must play a significant role in both terms of the distinction. Words and wordlessness are both affectively charged.

## Reflection and unformulated experience

Hermeneutics is the study of what it is to understand, and hermeneutic theories are theories of the conditions of understanding and how it takes place. It makes sense, then, that most modern hermeneutic views, especially those based in the work of Heidegger and especially Heidegger's student, Hans-Georg Gadamer (1965/2004), who built Heidegger's thoughts about the nature of understanding into a more phenomenologically appreciable theory of what it is to experience at all, maintain a special place for reflection—that is, for the kind of verbally formulated thought that is our sole means of having explicit knowledge of ourselves and our world. For hermeneuticists, consciousness is an "engagement" with the world. It is the active taking up of a perspective on what is given; understanding becomes an *act* in hermeneutic thought, a kind of conduct. It is not just the pronouncing of words that is an action; consciousness itself is an action (Fingarette, 1963, 1969). To reflect is to take an action, and to take an action is to interpret—and here I use "interpret" not in its psychoanalytic sense, but in its much more general hermeneutic one. In that hermeneutic sense, interpretation is the heart of every act of understanding; it is an existential given. Since our reflective experience is made up of *nothing but* understanding, these acts of interpretation are continuous. We perform them in every moment; each moment's reflective experience is shaped anew.

On what, though, does one base the act of understanding? Exactly how *do* we understand? The first thing to realize is that we can never wait to formulate an understanding until everything is crystal clear. Complete clarity is a myth; there is an essential ambiguity in all experience, an ambiguity that only interpretation can dispel, and even then, often only temporarily. And so we must understand on the basis of a grasp that is never more than partial. What do we do? We "read" the situation at hand for its similarities to other situations with which we are familiar, and we then supply an interpretation—or "project" one, to use a word that is employed distinctively in hermeneutics—on the basis of these partial understandings. And then, following this projection of understanding, we try to remain open to the possibility that our understanding may need to be revised. In the ideal case, we try to treat our projection as a hypothesis, not as an assumption, and in this way we do something more than simply find what we expect to find.

But that is more easily said than done, because the understandings we project are often quite precious to us. They are frequently based on pre-existing interpretive commitments we do not even know we have. These commitments may be crucial (for instance) to how we see ourselves—our identities. When we are unaware of our interpretive commitments, we have no way to know we are acting on them, of course, and so we treat anything we understand as "natural" (e.g., Berger & Luckmann, 1966) or "the way of the world," remaining ignorant of our constructive or interpretive role. In such cases, we have no way to "change our mind" and reinterpret what faces us. In the clinical context, good examples of such unconsidered assumptions are transference and countertransference, which after all are nothing more than interpersonal predictions we do not know we make and expectations we do not know we have. By way of summary, we can say that, in hermeneutic terms, we frequently undertake interpretive acts (interpretive in the general, hermeneutic sense, but also frequently enough in the specifically psychoanalytic one) for reasons we cannot specify, reasons that—in psychoanalytic terms—we would refer to as unconscious and dynamically meaningful.

This way of grasping the nature of reflection is different than what we are used to in psychoanalysis, and in a very important way. Psychoanalysts tend to think of consciousness as a symptom of sorts, or a dream. In Freud's frame of reference, consciousness is a deeply ambivalent compromise between the efforts of the id, ego, and superego, or between drive and defense. In Sullivan's interpersonal theory, we have a similar situation: consciousness is an effect of the security operations of the self-system (processes that prevent anxiety and protect security). The self-system allows into awareness only that novel experience that is absolutely essential for living, otherwise maintaining experience in the forms with which we have become familiar. The self-system is a defense of the status quo: we just keep on keeping on. In both Freud's structural theory and Sullivan's interpersonalism, that is, despite their immense differences in other respects, conscious experience is composed of whatever "gets past the gates," so to speak—of whatever we "let in." The implication is that only the effects of defenses or security operations keep us from knowing "everything" (whatever that would be). From these psychoanalytic vantage points, then, consciousness is not so much an activity, as it is a byproduct of other activities, a kind of leftover, the evidence that remains after the activities have taken place. Consciousness is itself less a dynamic process in psychoanalysis than it is the outcome of dynamics.

And thus it is not awareness that qualifies as conduct in most psychoanalytic conceptions, but lack of awareness. Activity is required to block reflective experience, but not necessarily to construct it. Reflective experience is what would happen naturally, and in all cases, if the process of thinking were to occur without the "interference" of the unconscious—if such a thing can be imagined. Consciousness is just not the "main event" in psychoanalysis.[1] I hardly wish to detract from the significance of the unconscious, of course, since the unconscious lies at the heart of psychoanalysis—or rather, *is* the heart of psychoanalysis. Because of that fact, from a psychoanalytic point of view hermeneutics can seem naive to the extent that it conceives understanding without reference to dynamics and unconscious meanings. But we can adopt some aspects of the hermeneutic perspective to the clinical setting without betraying basic psychoanalytic conceptions.

To this point in the argument, in trying to define what is important about the difference between words and wordlessness for psychoanalytic work, I have rejected the dimensions of thought and act, interpretive and noninterpretive interventions, public and private experience, and thought and feeling. The reason these dimensions are inadequate descriptions of the difference between words and wordlessness is the same in every case: each one would force us into too narrow a view of verbal language, which I have claimed is not only thought, but act; not only verbal-interpretive but nonverbal and enactive; not only public or consensually validated, but also mysterious and private, even to oneself; and not only thought but feeling. Through all these points has run a red thread: language is not merely a set of labels; instead, it plays a significant creative or constitutive role in the construction of explicit meaning. Unlike the view of Freud, though, in which the unconscious meaning is the real, true one, the *original* that can only be diluted or degraded as it finds a connection to words, a hermeneutic view leads us to the conclusion that what we formulate in words is not a degraded or diluted or paler version of what it interprets, but a *different meaning*. Words create the particular *kind* of meaning that can exist only in language.

Now, though, I have finally arrived at a description that satisfies me, one that allows me to define the difference between words and wordlessness without slighting the unique aspects of what we do with language. In this hermeneutic perspective on psychoanalytic work, explicit or reflective consciousness is an interpretive *act* that we take on the basis of *affect-laden* conscious and unconscious commitments, commitments that themselves may have never been formulated in words; and the meanings of reflective consciousness, because of those unconscious interpretive commitments, and even though they are contained in words, are sometimes nevertheless *private and mysterious*, not even necessarily known to the person whose meanings they are.

Subjectivity, then, falls on the two sides of a great divide: that which we are capable of reflecting on, and that which we cannot or do not reflect on. We commonly call the latter "unconscious experience," of course— or better, "prereflective" or "nonreflective" experience. For many years (e.g., Stern, 1983, 1997), the term I have preferred for nonreflective experience has been "unformulated experience" (Stern, 1983, 1997). As I said in Chapter 1, while I tried to incorporate a more subtle semiotic, I also held that unformulated experience is that part of our psychic lives that we have not interpreted, or articulated, in verbal-reflective terms. I still believe that reflection requires language, and I still use the term "unformulated experience"; but I no longer accept that verbal-reflective meaning is the sole variety of formulated experience. I now believe that the theory of unformulated experience is more useful in an expanded form, one in which verbal reflection is not the sole criterion of formulation. Nonverbal meaning, too, just like verbal-reflective meaning, can be formulated and dissociated. In the chapter that follows this one, Chapter 3, I take up that problem.

The unformulated can be interpreted in many different verbal-reflective ways, and in clinical work, as in the rest of life, we are all engaged in this interpretive task continuously. I do not mean to say that the dynamic interpretations of psychoanalysis and the everyday interpretations that make up all our experience are the same kind of activities. They are not. On the other hand, from a hermeneutic perspective clinical interpretation is a highly specialized variation on the common theme.

I return now to the case of Robert to illustrate what I have just said. Remember the session in which he reported the repetitive dream of the cubic object he could not pick up. The marvelous thing about that hour was his interpretation: after listening to himself describe that he was incapable of lifting the object, Robert had the sudden and forceful feeling that his description of the task was a metaphor for his life. Now consider the ways we could understand this event. We could posit that the meaning of the dream was always there "inside" Robert (as he put it himself), but that he would not acknowledge it. The meaning of the dream, that is, was "unconscious." That would be the traditional view. Or we could say, instead, that we are better off describing what Robert has never done with his dream as the formulation or construction of a new meaning for it, not as the mere acknowledgment of a meaning that already existed. In this case, we would say that the dream certainly had among its features an *amenability* (to borrow a word Irwin Hoffman used in 1983 in a similar context) to being understood in the way Robert eventually did understand it; but we would also say that, if the interpersonal field between Robert and me had been different at the time the dream came up—if, for example, it had felt less safe to him, or if he and I had been talking about something else at the time of the dream, or if whatever we *were* talking about had had some very different meaning in his psychic life—he would have interpreted his dream differently, or would not have remembered it at all. And keep in mind how much both of us contributed to the construction of his dream itself. The memory of the dream was unclear, remember; Robert had never described it, either to himself or to anyone else. The dream had never been worded. He had trouble finding language that felt to him like a good fit for the experience, and I participated right along with him in finding the words he eventually used. "Frustrated," the description Robert eventually adopted for his emotional state in the dream, was originally my word, after all. How might Robert's explicit experience of this dream have been different in someone else's presence? How might I have influenced its very shape—not only by the words I used, but by the influence I exerted by my very particular personal presence?

If Robert had interpreted his dream differently, how might it have looked? We have no way of knowing, of course. We never do; we never have any more than one chance to construct a moment in time, so that we are never really able to construct the understandings we do not use. But for heuristic purposes—just to make the point that a very different understanding *could* have arisen—I can make something up. If Robert had felt less confident that I was interested in him and curious about his experience, for example, he might have been less willing to make himself vulnerable, and as a consequence he might have said that his feeling of incapacity in the dream had only to do with his worry about schoolwork—which, as far as it went, would probably have been true enough. I have not mentioned it, but a few of his associations focused on geometry, a subject with which he had had a hard time, and one that does have something to do with cubic objects. In my fictional alternative scenario, Robert presents the dream as a metaphor for the feeling that he would never be any good at working with shapes and figures. I have heard interpretations from Robert just as concrete as this one. It rings true. Given Robert's character style, though, the most likely alternatives to saying what he did about his dream would have been remembering it without having the vaguest suspicion that it meant anything more than it appeared, or not remembering it at all.

Perhaps a better example of unformulated experience and reflection is what Robert said next about understanding that Freud's own psychic life must have been the most important source of inspiration for his ideas. Can we say that this thought was somehow already "there" inside Robert, "in" his unconscious, just waiting for him to acknowledge it? Of course not. Robert formulated this thought in the moment he spoke it. It was an unbidden construction, a very particular interpretation created in the context of a very particular time and set of circumstances; and it surprised him. His own capacity to think startled him. Whatever the thought was created from—whatever the raw materials of this very creative moment may have been—they were vague and unformulated until, despite himself, Robert somehow selected the words that brought an explicit meaning into being.

## The circle of the unexpressed

If I were to end the chapter at this point, having described Robert's new meanings only as explicit and verbal, I would be doing an injustice to Robert and to language itself. I would not have addressed the depth and power that we know self-reflection can have, and I might therefore risk leaving you with a superficial impression of what I mean. What I have yet to say is that, in the very same moment that it articulates the present, the formulation of new meaning simultaneously creates an enriching context for those present meanings and new possibilities for the articulation of the future.

As a route of approach to this idea, consider hermeneutic philosopher Charles Taylor's (1995) suggestion that any explicit reflection is con-textualized and made possible by a "vast web of unexpressed and unarticulated meanings, practices, and understandings that remain in the background of explicit awareness and immediate experience" (cited by Zeddies, 2002, p. 17). Taylor (1995) writes:

We can't turn the background against which we think into an object for us. The task of reason has to be conceived quite differently: as that of articulating the background, "disclosing" what it involves. This may open the way to detaching ourselves from or altering part of what has constituted it—may indeed, make such alteration irresistible; but only through our unquestioning reliance on the rest.

(p. 12)

In the same vein, Hans Lipps (quoted and translated by Linge, 1976) writes that each word has around it a "circle of the unexpressed" that is as necessary for its comprehension as the word itself. And compare David Linge (1976), writing about Gadamer, and using the phrase I have adopted as the title of this book:

In every moment of dialogue, the speaker holds together what is said and addressed to the other person with "the infinity of the unsaid." It is the infinity of the unsaid—this relation to the whole of being that is disclosed in what is said—into which the one who understands is drawn.

(p. xxxii)

These points are generic; they each apply to the whole of language. But think of any particular instance of reflection, and consider how we might be able to see it through the lens these writers offer us. Consider, for instance, what Robert thought about his dream. When he whispered to me, "Did you hear what I said?", indicating the dawning of his awareness that his despair about not being able to lift the cube in his dream was also a metaphor for his life, the words he spoke, and the thought they indicated lay behind them, did not simply appear out of nowhere. An enormous number of unthought, unformulated meanings had to come into some kind of new (and equally unthought) relation with one another in Robert's mind in order for him to be able to think what he did. It is the coming together of this "web of unexpressed and unarticulated meanings" (Zeddies, 2002, p. 17) that makes possible the emergence of a new explicit meaning. We never deal with meaning in isolation, as if it were simply there, by itself, right in front of us, a thought to be had. It feels that way often, just as it feels as if we perceive objects one at a time. But our perception of individual objects, Taylor (1985) tells us, occurs only as a result of our capacity to contextualize those perceptions in the backgrounds appropriate to them; and we think and feel in the same way. Each of our thoughts gains its meaning as much from the silent, invisible, and affectively toned background within which it is set as it does from the words of the thought itself.

What we say, then, is only a portion of what we would have to say if we were to account fully for what we mean. The background of a thought, the web of unexpressed and unarticulated meanings that supports any explicit reflection, cannot possibly be formulated, because it is the very unformulated nature of the background that makes an explicitly articulated foreground possible. Articulated foreground and unformulated background define one another, shape one another, serve as the very possibility for one another's existence.

In this sense, words are always inadequate to the task they are set. Something of the context of any of our reflections is always missing, lost, left behind. That is why Robert's dream could not be simply "translated" into words; part of its meaning, as in his use of the word "soft," may be inarticulable for a long time, or even forever. We seldom escape any serious attempt to know our experience without the feeling that some part of what had felt within our grasp has simply vanished in the attempt to give it verbal life.

And yet that unmade meaning, that unknowable remnant or excess that escapes us, is not only, or merely, a loss. Perhaps we can say that, to an extent, it is actually conveyed, recreated, or enacted through its effect on the relationship in which the spoken meaning emerges.[2] The background that accompanies explicit meanings is part of the patterning or emotional atmosphere that underlies the ongoing sense we have of what relationships "feel like" to us. The unarticulated background is "lost," then, only in the sense that it cannot itself be spoken, at least not in the moment during which it contextualizes what *can* be spoken. Thereafter it becomes part of the experience that may (or may not) serve as the source of new reflections in another time. In Taylor's wording, while any new, explicit meaning emerges only because of our "unquestioning reliance" on its background, we may eventually be able to "disclose" some of those background meanings by setting them in contexts of their own.

After we make an explicit new meaning, then, the unformulated meanings that surround it exist in our minds in a different way than they did before. The act of formulation gives these surrounding meanings a new context in language: they now *become* a background to a foreground and therefore exist *in some kind of new relation to something we know*. In that new relation these nonreflective, potential verbal meanings may eventually be more accessible to us than they would have been; and even if we never articulate them in language, they constitute an enrichment of the immediate context within which our explicit meanings are embedded. (We will see, in Chapter 3, that some of this immediate context, while it cannot be articulated, is nevertheless "realized" in nonverbal meanings that deserve to be described as formulated.) The nimbus of the nonverbal around any explicit meaning is part of what gives us the frequent feeling that self-reflection has depth, resonance, nuance, or power.

Much, if not most, of this background is unconscious, at least in the descriptive sense; and no doubt some of it is even dynamically unconscious. It is tempting to speculate that the reorganization of the background that is part of what makes a new reflective meaning possible may also result in the movement of certain other unconscious meanings toward verbal-reflective articulation. It is tempting to speculate that backgrounds tend to become foregrounds and, in the process, to spawn other backgrounds. The free unfolding of such a process is one way to conceive how, as subjectivity moves toward reflective awareness, it is renewed by the events of its own wake.

The obdurate strangeness of dreams has always been reassuring to us: it shows us that the mystery of experience survives all our interpretations, preserving the possibility of meaningful futures we never know to expect, just as neither Robert nor I could have expected the outcome of our thinking together about his dream. We tend to associate mystery and depth with nonverbal experience and the unconscious, and dreams (with their unconscious roots) are often our exemplar here. But poetry, unlike dreams, is a verbal and reflective kind of meaning, and it is certainly composed within conscious states. Yet poetry is just as resolutely strange as dreams are, at least in the sense that its possibilities refuse to dissolve in interpretation. The meanings of poetry are not limited by the ways any of us can imagine them; and that is to say that perhaps verbal language participates in the depth and mystery we usually reserve for the non-verbal (cf. Loewald 1978; Ogden 1997, 1998, 1999; Mitchell 2000; Vivona 2003, 2006, 2013). We should resist the temptation to identify the nonverbal and the unconscious as the one, true source of authentic sub-jectivity, as if linguistic consciousness were nothing more than a pale leftover. Instead, as Ogden (1994) reminds us was Freud's own view, we should locate the source of subjectivity in the *relation* of consciousness and unconsciousness, or perhaps the verbal and the nonverbal. To my mind, the inexhaustibility of both poetry *and* dreams is due to their embeddedness in unusually rich fields of unformulated experience. For that matter, all our reflections, even everyday ones, while they are of course seldom as fertile as poetry, are nevertheless inexhaustible resources, because any act of reflection simultaneously creates a nimbus of the unformulated.

Near the beginning of this chapter I expressed regret that, because I was setting out to think through what separates words and wordlessness, I would not be able to attend to what relates them. I said that the relation of words and wordlessness is mediated by the interpersonal field, that it is the analytic relationship, in all its conscious and unconscious aspects, that has most to do with what experience can be formulated and what experience cannot (Stern, 1997, 2010a, 2015; and see Bromberg [1998, 2006, 2011], whose entire body of work revolves around this center). That point has now gained even greater relevance to what I am trying to say, because in directing attention to the foreground and background of verbal-reflective meaning as a dialectic, I am no longer limiting discussion to the *differences* between words and wordlessness. Somewhat unexpectedly, I find that I have turned to the *significance that words and wordlessness hold for one another*; and that movement, of course, takes us in the direction of the all-important relational factors, a theme I have been exploring for many years.

Language does what it does most eloquently and least destructively when we let go the reins and give it its head. But that doesn't mean that in those moments in which language is crucial we always speak. As a matter of fact, often we don't, as in Robert's thoughtful silence at a certain point during the telling of his dream and my reticence to interrupt his musings. Giving language its head is not passivity, but active discipline: it is a matter of trying hard to feel our way into what language wants to do; it is perhaps a variety of what Ghent (1990), elaborating on Winnicott, calls *surrender*. Especially on the emotional level we generally occupy in doing psychoanalytic work, words are not necessarily what we use in this surrender, at least not to begin with. In our private experience as well as in our work with our patients, our willingness to let fantasy and feeling wash over us, especially the shades and nuances that may be the defining aspects of a moment's context, is not a verbally articulated thing at all, and usually cannot and should not be. Often we must resist the temptation to speak, or even to formulate an experience in the privacy of our own minds (to the extent that we control the process), recognizing that any consciously directed attempt to think would be too pale or ungainly to do justice to the moment; we must be satisfied with the feeling of resonance. To speak at such times hurts the process more than it helps; that recognition is part of the proper use of words. I repeat: it is just as true to say that this kind of reticence is a *use* of language as it is to interpret it as a turning away from language. To use language properly is not only to speak, but also to allow words to sink into the background at appropriate moments.

Language is not only words, then. Language is also all those parts of subjectivity that gather and hover, unformulated, around what we can already say. The most significant part of language is sometimes what it cannot yet speak. Such meanings are nevertheless made possible *by* language, partially created by reverberations of the meanings explicitly available to us. It is true, of course, as Loewald (1978) tells us eloquently, that without the continuous infusion of the nonverbal and the vitality of the unconscious, language would be a dead thing. But it is just as true that, without language, there would be no meaning at all, since even the nonverbal is defined by the possibility of speech and thought. Reflection is more than the words in which it occurs, and the meanings we create in this way have more depth, breadth, and mystery than the phrase "explicit meaning" conveys. To do justice to Robert's budding capacity for self-reflection, we need not only to pay attention to his new words, but also to imagine the fertility of the new wordlessness his words have made possible. In the next chapter, I turn to the problem of how to think about this generative nonverbal background, and how, in the process, background can become foreground.

## Notes

1  A reader of this chapter pointed out that consciousness is not necessarily the "main event" in hermeneutics, either. That is true, and worth emphasizing: prejudices or preconceptions, after all, are neither conscious nor preconscious, which is, of course, why they can be insidious. But in the work of Gadamer the primary emphasis lies on the construction of meanings that were not present prior to the formulation of the interpretations (using the word now in the general, hermeneutic sense) that brought them into being. That constructivist emphasis is significantly different than what is most familiar in psychoanalysis.

2  I am indebted to Tim Zeddies for this point.

# Chapter 3

# Realization

## The formulation of nonverbal meaning

> ... in this physical, space-time world of our experience there are things which do not fit the grammatical scheme of expression. But they are not necessarily blind, inconceivable, mystical affairs; they are simply matters which require to be conceived through some symbolic scheme other than discursive language ... Language is by no means our only articulate product. Our merest sense-experience is a process of *formulation* ...
>
> Susanne Langer, *Philosophy in a New Key* (1942),
> p. 82; italics from the original

In Chapter 2, I suggested that nonverbal meanings, by comprising the inexpressible background of verbal-reflective ones, participate in shaping the meanings that can be articulated in words. That role, by itself, would be enough to make the nonverbal essential to the ceaseless task of interpretation that is living. But more than that is crucial about the nonverbal. The nonverbal has made such inroads on our understanding of clinical process that today it can seem a little quaint to characterize psychoanalysis as the talking cure.

The *Zeitgeist* has seized me, too. The clinical observation that originally ignited my interest in dissociation and enactment, and that therefore lies at the heart of this book, is that enactments are not dissolved by verbal understanding at all, but by the enactor's development of a *new, nonverbal perception* of the other. This point was basic to *Partners in Thought* (Stern, 2010a), in which many chapters concern the ways that the new, nonverbal perceptions that break up enactments come about. In fact, the first (and quite different) versions of Chapters 2, 3, and 4 of the present volume were initially written as part of that earlier book, with the intention of addressing the questions about language and the nonverbal that my work on dissociation and enactment forced me to confront in the theory of unformulated experience.

What we might call the "old perceptions" of the other and oneself—the perceptions, that is, that undergird and contribute to the maintenance of enactments—are rigid, stereotyped, and usually invisible (because they are neither conscious nor symbolically represented in the mind) ways of comprehending the analytic relationship. The old perceptions tend to support the adversarial feeling, or at least discomfort, that is so often the emotional atmosphere of enactments.[1] The "new perceptions" of oneself and the other, on the other hand, are neither rigid nor insistently held, and are drawn from a wider range of the possibilities, resulting in a characterization of the other and oneself that allows a more empathic recognition of the other's participation in the enactment, and a more complete and less angry, shamed, or guilty recognition of one's own part of the relatedness. A new recognition of the other's participation and one's own melts the enactment in the same moment that the new perceptions are finally formulated and emerge into the clinical relatedness. The analyst may see for the first time, for instance, that the patient feels that he (the patient) is being reasonable, and that he is trying to keep the treatment going with an analyst whom he (again, the patient) feels is being quite *un*reasonable. In this example, the important thing is not whether the analyst suddenly changes her view of herself and *agrees* that she has been unreasonable; what makes the difference is that she comes to see through the patient's eyes. She sees the plausibility of this perspective, and she realizes that the patient is just as entitled to this view as she (the analyst) is to her own. In fact, the analyst often goes further than that, not only seeing the patient's perspective as plausible, but "acknowledging" (Benjamin, 2017) that she, the analyst, has indeed been involved in a way she did not grasp before. The communication or "acknowledgment" of this acceptance creates "recognition" and what Benjamin refers to as intersubjectivity, or "the Third" (Benjamin, 2017).[2]

My long acquaintance with Bromberg's work (1998, 2006, 2011) has done more than any other influence to awaken me to the centrality for therapeutic action of the new perception of the other, oneself, and the analytic relationship. In dissociative process, which lies at the heart of Bromberg's work, the primary emphasis is never on interpretation, but instead on the capacity of both participants, no less the analyst than the patient, to find a way to see beyond the stereotyped perceptions of themselves and one another—the hallmarks of dissociative process—and to emerge into new recognition. (But see also Note 7, Chapter 1.)

In psychoanalytic treatment, the power of self-truth remains unchanged unless challenged by perception, which is why enactments hold such powerful therapeutic potential. But for perception to generate an act of meaning (see Bruner, 1990), a relational context must be constructed that includes the realities of both analyst and patient. Unless this takes place, the immediate perceptual context will only be an enactment of the patient's fixed affective memory system that includes some "other" trying helpfully and logically to extract the person's own reality and replace it with a better one—theirs (Bromberg, 2011, p. 160).

Often, although the analyst doesn't necessarily come to agree with the patient, the new perception of what is happening in the relatedness does lead the analyst to the judgment that her own view has been either one-sided or partial. And even when the analyst continues to feel that the patient's perspective is highly selective or skewed, the new perception—a central part of which is the appreciation of what the situation looks like from the patient's point of view—adds to the analyst's capacity and willingness to understand the patient's experience as something more than recalcitrance or opposition.

The new perception may become articulated as a verbal-reflective meaning; but it appears first as a change in one's *nonverbal grasp of what the other is like,* a new and nonverbal *sense* of the other.[3] (In the skeletal example offered just above, for instance, the patient ceases to appear simply unreasonable.) The appearance of the new perception is usually fairly abrupt; often there is little or no sense of gestation, just a sudden difference, as if one had reached a tipping point.[4]

There are often aspects of this new nonverbal sense of the other that are not possible to translate into verbal-reflective terms; something about the new perception, that is, often something tinged with inexpressible affectivity, remains in the realm of the nonverbal. I mentioned in the last chapter the strangeness that poetry and dreams never really shed. One often has some of this same sense of enduring strangeness about these suddenly appearing nonverbal perceptions of the other. At such times, what Hans Lipps (cited by Linge 1976) refers to as "the circle of the unexpressed" (see also Chapter 2) is pressing hard against the boundaries of whatever meaning we can say. We are certain at such moments that we know something new about the other person, but we cannot always say exactly what it is. And we can virtually never say *all* of what it is. The experience comes about in the holistic, global, nonverbal realm that Bucci (1997) describes as *subsymbolic*, a word that she uses in order to contrast it with more traditionally recognized *nonverbal symbolic* ways of representing information, such as imagery.

When I first formulated the observation of the new perception, in the mid- to late 1990s, I was in the process of pulling together my ideas about unformulated experience (Stern, 1997), ideas I had been developing since the early 1980s (Stern, 1983). I did not recognize at that time that this new observation could not be easily described within the frame of reference I had created to that point. Actually, to begin with, I did not formulate very clearly the observation that the new perception of the other is inevitably nonverbal, and that some of it often remains inexpressible in words. In those days I simply had the somewhat disturbing, and only vaguely articulated, feeling that the most important clinical events frequently seemed to go on outside verbal-reflective thought. The disturbing thing, for me, was that the most immediate impetus to therapeutic change, the event that seemed to break up the rigidities of the enactments in which I found myself unconsciously involved, was not a piece of verbal understanding.

Why was that disturbing?

The premise of my first book, *Unformulated Experience* (Stern, 1997) was the centrality of verbal understanding and reflection in psychoanalytic work. I did my best in that book to emphasize the mysteries of language: the unbiddenness of its emergence, its antic quality, the depth of its influence. I wrote with the conviction that we are deluded if we think that language is our servant, as if it merely clothes our meanings and does our bidding. We do influence language, ceaselessly; but language also shapes us, just as ceaselessly and fatefully. Language, I wrote then (and continue to feel) does clothe meanings that pre-exist it; but those meanings are stereotyped, everyday meanings, the kind that Merleau-Ponty (1945/1962) calls "second order." In the case of original meanings—meanings that have not existed before—language formulates, shapes, creates. I wrote that, when we do good psychoanalytic work, it is not because we make sensible or rational choices about how to use words; it is because we manage to climb onto language's broad back and ride.

I was not talking about language as a cognitive process in writing this way. Instead, I was taking the point of view about language that I had absorbed from hermeneutics, in which language is the reason that the world does not remain a thing-in-itself—a view in which language is not only what defines meaning, but the ground of the very *possibility* of meaning. For Hans-Georg Gadamer, it is only through language that the world becomes meaningful for humans. It is language that allows *being*. The following passage from Gadamer (1965/2004) demonstrates that language can be conceptualized as something more, and something other, than the cognitive process it is typically portrayed to be in most descriptions we see in contemporary psychiatry, psychology, and psychoanalysis. I want to warn against what Vivona (2013) criticizes as "a conceptualization of words as abstract, disembodied, emotionally neutral symbols whose connections are primarily with other symbols" (p. 1116), examples of which she finds in the work of writers such as Daniel Stern (1985), the Boston Change Process Study Group (2007), Bucci (1997), and Damasio (1999).[5] Here is Gadamer (1965/2004):

> Language is not just one of man's possessions in the world; rather, on it depends the fact that man has a *world* at all. The world as world exists for man as for no other creature that is in the world. But this world is verbal in nature . . . [L]anguage has no independent life apart from the world that comes to language within it. Not only is the world world only insofar as it comes into language, but language, too, has its real being only in the fact that the world is presented in it. Thus, that language is originarily human means at the same time that man's being-in-the-world is primordially linguistic.
>
> (p. 440; italics from the original)

But despite my commitment to this position, I could not deny, in thinking about enactments, that my new perceptions of the other seemed to be *nonverbal*—and that made me worry that I had it all wrong. For a while after the publication of *Unformulated Experience* (Stern, 1997), as I said in Chapter 1, I flirted with a certain cynicism, or at least wryness, about the issue. More than once I wondered if the very specialized conversation that is the talking cure was merely a pretext for bringing two people together, so that the *real* processes of change, which perhaps were mysterious and had nothing to do with psychoanalytic theories of therapeutic action, or with verbal language, could take place by themselves.

I never doubted the conviction that led me to psychoanalysis in the first place: people can be of profound use to one another. But I did doubt sometimes whether it was really possible to think effectively about how to practice this conviction. At least at the moments when I was most deeply affected by my more wry or cynical sense of verbal reflection, so much of what was most important about the clinical process seemed to occur apart from language.

Even at those moments, though, I did not lose track of the value of words. The question became whether we can know in words what we know outside them. Are the verbal and the nonverbal incommensurable, so that what we do with our patients outside the realm of verbal language is not comprehensible from within it? In the words of novelist Karl Ove Knausgaard (2012),

> It was as if two different forms of reflection rose and fell in my consciousness, one with its thoughts and reasoning, the other with its feelings and impressions, which, even though they were juxtaposed, excluded each other's insights.
>
> (p. 208)

And yet I continued to feel the significance and depth of the reach of words. I continued to find statements like Gadamer's, and this one by Vivona (2013), written from a clinical perspective, compelling, even incontrovertible:

> Because language is always action, psychoanalysis and poetry foster an interpersonal sharing of both meaning and understanding. The experience of hearing a good poem or a good interpretation is of being understood and at the same time seeing something new about oneself that has been articulated by someone else from within that person's own experience. The experience that can happen on hearing such language we call *insight*. Insight is not only knowledge, not only content. It is an experience of resonance with another person's vision of things.
>
> (p. 1129; italics from the original)

"An experience of resonance with another person's vision of things." Yes! In my work as a clinician, *that* is what I am after. That is what we all seek, isn't it? Doesn't language reach beyond the labeling of content in just this way? Doesn't language transcend mere representation, in the process giving shape and meaning to parts of life that have been unspoken and, in fact, unknown in words? Isn't this a good argument that the verbal and the nonverbal are not straightforwardly incommensurable, that their relationship is much more complex than that?

But here once more is novelist Knausgaard (2012), who I was reading at the time I was struggling with these questions. In this passage, he describes what he feels when he returns his visual (i.e., imagistic, nonverbal) attention to a piece of art that he had been thinking about in verbal-reflective terms:

> But the moment I focused my gaze on the painting again all my reasoning vanished in the surge of energy and beauty that arose in me. *Yes, yes, yes,* I heard. *That's where it is. That's where I have to go.* But what was it that I had said yes to? Where was it I had to go?
>
> (p. 208; italics from the original)

And so it went for me, too, back and forth, forth and back, from an appreciation of the interpenetration of the verbal and the nonverbal, their mutual influence, to the compelling experience of the nonverbal on its own terms and the incommensurability between the verbal and the nonverbal that this seemed to imply.

It took time, but eventually I did come to a way of living with this conundrum, if not of solving it. Both verbal language and the nonverbal can be, and should be, accommodated in the theory of unformulated experience. This chapter is my attempt to convey what I have learned and to broaden the ideas that I introduced in *Unformulated Experience* (Stern, 1997). I have preserved the heart of the hermeneutic argument, however, and I will return to it in Chapter 4, showing how it is possible to recognize the significance of the nonverbal within the larger hermeneutic frame of reference.

## An illustration

Let me offer a simple example that I hope will help to illuminate the problem I have begun to discuss. Consider a patient who, during her session, looks at me with an expression on her face dominated by a frown and a downturned mouth. Under some circumstances, this kind of a frown and a downturned mouth suggest sadness; under other circumstances, anger; and under yet others, confusion, doubt, or even a sense of wonder. In life, we generally experience one of these meanings (perhaps you can imagine others) when we see such an expression on someone's face. We supply the meaning to the expression on the basis of context; that is, it is our perception of context that selects which of the meanings we actually create.

One of the themes of the work of interpersonal and relational psychoanalysts in general, and of my work in particular, has always been that the single most significant context of this kind, in life and in psychoanalysis, is the interpersonal field. The field is the sum total of the affects, thoughts, perceptions, fantasies, and bodily sensations that each of two (or more) people have in one another's presence, an immensely complex amalgam that determines how each of us experiences the other, ourselves, and the relationship between us. The field, in other words, has everything to do with *the thoughts and feelings that can be formulated by its participants*. In the case of my small example, one of the many things the field determines is whether I see my patient's facial expression as anger, sadness, confusion, doubt, or wonder.

Let us say, then, that in this case I feel, immediately and naturally, via the influence of the field, that the patient is sad.[6] (To simplify matters, I will eschew the specification of the influences operative in this particular field.) Prior to this perception, if I think about it now, from a distance in time, it appears to me that I did not think of the word "sadness." Instead, this perception of sadness seems to me to have been an affective and visual gestalt, something nonverbal, more immediate and peremptory than a word. Is it fair to say, then, with those who would argue that the nonverbal contains a truth of its own, unrelated to words, that an affective and visual gestalt—in this case, the patient's expression—arose first? Can we say that it is only after such a nonverbal perception is shaped, and the field supplies the influences that nudge us toward the selection, or recognition, of this perception as sadness, that the word for the affect comes into my mind as a label for what lies behind the visual impression— if an affect word does come into my mind at all?

Or is this analysis perhaps too simple? Are we perhaps too quick to leave words out of the equation? Are there grounds for the position that even the parts of our experience that seem obdurately nonverbal, like the visual image of the expression on my patient's face, are more related to verbal representation than we imagine?

Consider the fact that I, the perceiver in this case—and like all of us—live with the recognition that sadness is a possibility in life; and keep in mind that I have a word for that possibility, a word that has an existence in my mind and in my perceptions, even when I am not actively using it.

Of course, I did not say to myself, as I looked at my patient's face, anything as heavy-handed as "Oh, now I see: she is sad." Nevertheless, perhaps it is reasonable to imagine there was some kind of verbal representation here. Perhaps I knew she was sad, but knew it implicitly; that is, perhaps my recognition relied more on verbal representation than I realize. Is it imaginable that some partial verbal mediation of my patient's facial expression played a role in potentiating the unfolding of the nonverbal, affective meaning of this moment?

Let us grant such a possibility for heuristic purposes. Once I interpreted the patient's facial expression with that word "sadness," did resonances of the word from elsewhere in my life, resonances that we would have to call nonverbal, fill in the meaning of the perception? It turns out, for instance, that the patient has a certain way of pursing her lips in making the expression I am calling "sad." This pursing of her lips, I realize when I think about it, puts me in mind of a look my mother sometimes used to have at times in which she was sad—and during which she and I felt particularly close to one another.

Under most circumstances, I feel sure, it would be natural and spontaneous for the resonance to my mother's look to appear in my mind, if it appeared at all, without symbolic representation. That is, if I were not thinking about it in the way that I am at this moment, pursuing the unusual aim of making sense of it, I would never construct a visual image of that facial expression, and would not even explicitly notice its arrival in my mind. I notice it now only because I am writing about these matters and am therefore thinking hard about it in a way that I would not otherwise do. Nevertheless, despite appearing in my mind in a way that I believe would generally go unnoticed, this resonance to my mother's expression awakens me to something in the patient I would not have seen without it.

Is this affective resonance to my mother's expression, and the mood that comes to me as a result (also sad), something we should describe as nonverbal? Yes. Yet might it not have been brought to my mind by my implicit, verbal reflection on my patient's affect? Or, even if the patient's facial expression linked to my mother's on a thoroughly visual-imagistic basis, without any verbal mediation at all, might the stirrings of that emergent perception of similarity not have aroused the word "sad," which might then have consolidated the meaning of the similarity?

And the resonance of the word "sad" with moments of grief and communion with my mother: what about that? Might not my patient's expression have been given additional depth and nuance in my mind by my implicit recognition of that expression as sadness? In other words, might it not be the case that the inarticulate, affect-laden meanings accrued by the word "sad" in my particular life (Loewald, 1978; Vivona, 2003, 2006, 2012, 2013) contributed resonances to an experience that might otherwise appear to be represented in exclusively nonverbal form?

The question is this really: How exactly does the nonverbal connect here with words?

Bucci (1997) would have it that the event I have just described is an example of a relatively simple, more or less mechanical event: the linkage between a verbal representation and a nonverbal one (or perhaps she would prefer to think of the affective resonance as an event taking place in the nonsymbolic mode—but if so, the point about linkage would be the same). The model Bucci is employing here, information theory, has been a dominant paradigm in cognitive psychology for many decades now. Bucci has hardly been its only exponent, although she has been perhaps the most thoughtful and influential contributor in this vein in psychoanalysis.

In the terms of information theory, thought is a more or less computational procedure that can be described as the creation of symbolic representations that stand in for bits of information, followed by the complex linkage of these symbols to create higher-order information structures.

For two reasons, I prefer an alternative orientation, one that grows from certain phenomenological (e.g., Merleau-Ponty, 1945/1962; Gadamer, 1965/2004; Taylor, 2016), and psychoanalytic (e.g., Loewald, 1978; Stern, 1997; Vivona, 2013) theories of mind. The first reason I prefer these latter theories is that they allow us, even encourage us, to think about the creation of meaning, and in particular, the intersubjective or interpersonal creation of meaning (Bruner, 1990). We can, in these terms, make sense of the proposition that mind is not contained in a single skull but "distributed," a phenomenon of the field (Stern 2010a, Chapter 1).

Gadamer (1965/2004), for instance, portrays all understanding as dialogic, a phenomenon that requires the joint participation of the one who understands and the one who is to be understood. Echoing the thinking of those many clinicians who understand therapeutic interventions to grow not from theory or ratiocination, but rather, from the analyst's affective involvement with the patient, Gadamer tells us that all understanding is self-understanding. Why? Because in Gadamer's scheme, one cannot grasp something new simply by labeling it differently; one must instead *become a different person* (see also Slavin and Kriegman, 1998). The person one has been cannot do it. One must become someone who can understand something that has been, until now, outside of one's grasp. And so the fact that all experience is interpretive in this scheme, and that all interpretation requires understanding, means that from Gadamer's perspective one is continuously becoming someone else—or perhaps more oneself.

The second reason I prefer phenomenological and existential theories of mind and language to information theory is that these theories preserve the depth, affective resonance, mystery, and nonrationality of the most expressive and penetrating forms of language. These are qualities that have everything to do with the origins of language in early affective life (Liberman, 1974; Loewald 1978; Bruner, 1990; Vivona 2012), prior to the development of full semantic capacity. Vivona (2012) offers a selective but careful review of the literature on infant speech processing during the first twelve months and concludes that linguistic and verbal-conceptual processes go on in that early period. Among other things, the research she reviews, contrary to prevailing opinion, "raises questions about the view that the nature of infancy is essentially nonverbal" (p. 231).

On the basis of the findings that there exist linguistic processes in early infancy, we ought to cease taking for granted the traditional view that the nonverbal is earlier than the verbal, and thus more basic. This traditional belief has been one of the primary reasons that writers such as Daniel Stern (1985) have felt that the nonverbal is the bedrock of experience, and that the adequacy of verbal language ought to be judged by its capacity to represent it. Writers such as Loewald and Vivona treat language instead as just as surely a source and sustenance of mind as the nonverbal.

Neither poetry, nor dreams, nor good psychoanalytic work is well described by information theory, because the conception of language found there is limited to the use of words as labels for packets of content.

There is nothing in information theory that helps us to grasp the constitutive properties of language, the way language not only represents meanings but creates them. When language shapes new meanings, it is an active participant in worldmaking (Goodman, 1978), sometimes acting through us in ways that make us feel like conduits (Stern, 1990). Language is not simply a tool we use to satisfy purposes we understand; it goes beyond us, so that we are surprised by the most significant of our own thoughts. The most profound expressions of language sometimes rise to the level of the numinous.

Let me see where it leads us, then, to say that the affective resonance to my mother's expression occurred to me not because of a connection between elements of two separate symbol systems, but because such resonances are part of a nimbus of personal affective history that is one of the ingredients of language. These affective-resonance parts of word meaning are actually not symbolic at all, but procedural, or subsymbolic. Loewald (1978) and Vivona (2003, 2006, 2013) tell us that words contain echoes and residues of the emotional contexts in which we first heard and used them, making of them something far more than a collection of publicly understood symbols or packets of information, and preserving their emotional power—the expressiveness we see in fiction, poetry, dreams, and psychoanalysis. Heidegger (1959/1971) puts it this way: "It is just as much a property of language to sound and ring and vibrate, to hover and tremble, as it is for the spoken words of language to carry a meaning" (p. 98).

In my fictional example, when I saw the expression on my patient's face, and then, as the word "sad" occurred to me, I am imagining that an internal presence representing my mother in her own sad moments came into my mind—and maybe not at a level consistent with conscious representation. Maybe not even on a symbolic level, but on a procedural one. Perhaps the word "sad" is permeated, for me, without my recognition (although writing this passage has aroused my curiosity about this), with its origins in that part of my mother's emotional life so many years ago; and so perhaps, in reaction to my patient's facial expression, I am sent along paths of meaning that we might actually want to refer to as verbal.

In Loewald's (1978) moving elaboration of Freud, these nonrational, affectively saturated parts of the verbal represent the crucial contribution of the primary process to the vitality of language. Within Loewald's frame of reference, we can imagine that, once that word "sad" was bound up (in my history) with my mother's sometime state of mind, the visual and affective imagery of sadness actually became imbricated with the word "sad," became part of what the word actually *means* in my very particular psychic world. Language becomes a personal matter. Words do not necessarily mean to me just what they mean to you.

My own takeaway here, and, I hope, one that is also compelling to you, is that it is not tenable to come down hard on either side of questions such as whether my perception of my patient's sadness, or the affective resonance to my mother's sadness, should be described as verbal or nonverbal. My initial experience that my patient's facial expression was purely and uncomplicatedly nonverbal does not necessarily mean that the experience should be described as nonlinguistic. I will return to this issue in more detail in Chapter 4.

For the time being, let me end my consideration of these questions with the claim, inspired by positions such as the one represented in the passage I quoted above from the work of Gadamer, that whatever it is that we *can* say has a great deal to do with our appreciation of the experiences and meanings we *can't* say. The verbal is not only the context within which the nonverbal accrues meaning; the verbal is what makes it possible for the nonverbal to be meaningful at all. Without verbal language to create the possibility of its meaningfulness, the nonverbal could not signify. And yet, despite the complexity of the relation between the verbal and the nonverbal, we must leave room for the undeniable fact that meaningful experience does take both verbal and nonverbal forms.

Let me offer one brief illustration of this point before going on. I recently saw a TV program in which a native Brazilian dweller of the Amazon rainforest, a man who had never before talked to anyone outside his isolated jungle tribe, was interviewed by an anthropologist who spoke enough of the man's language to be understood. The anthropologist played for the man a Viennese waltz on a tape recorder. The man was clearly puzzled. You could see on his face that the sounds were not meaningful to him; they did not signify. Frowning, and grasping for sense, he asked if the waltz was perhaps a way of talking. When he was told that no, the sounds were music, and that they belonged to the same category as his own tribe's organized and expressive ritual sounds, the man was visibly surprised, even amazed. He laughed at the improbability of this thing. But then the anthropologist played the tape again, and the man listened, and you could see the change reflected on his face: he listened to it differently. Now he knew what this nonverbal experience was. He had needed to be able to assign these strange sounds to a linguistic category he knew, and now he could do that. The sounds belonged to a category he could understand, and they thereby became meaningful. Furthermore, we can extrapolate, the more this man learned about Western music (and I do not just mean to refer here to more time spent listening, but to learning in the *verbal* realm, such as what makes a waltz a waltz and not a polka or a samba), the more nuanced and differentiated his *nonverbal* experience of Viennese waltzes would become. Just as verbal-reflective experience can only be meaningful and substantial because of the background of all that is nonverbal and unexpressed, which gives shape to verbal meaning just as surely as the bed of a lake gives a particular form to the volume of water it contains, so is nonverbal experience meaningful only because it is given shape by verbal meanings and categories (see also Zeddies, 2002). Verbal meanings carve up the world into meaningful chunks, as the word for ritual, expressive sound did for the Brazilian man's perception of the Viennese waltz; and thereafter, we experience as nonverbal many of these verbally defined pieces of the world.

Perhaps, then, as I have already suggested, we don't need to make hard and fast decisions about whether each phenomenon in experience should be described as verbal or nonverbal. Perhaps allowing that kind of uncertainty—that kind of recognition that the verbal and the nonverbal are caught up with one another at every turn, even if we cannot deny that psychic phenomena of these two types are represented in separate and different ways—is a more thoughtful way of proceeding than insisting on being able to nail down whether any particular experience or psychic event should be characterized as one or the other.

I have come to think that what matters most is to conceptualize the *possibilities for meaningfulness* (that is, the possibilities for formulating both nonverbal experience and verbal reflection), rather than to take a position about whether each meaning is purely verbal or nonverbal. We don't necessarily need to judge the roles of language and the nonverbal in each particular experience. What we do need is a way to conceptualize how each kind of meaning can become meaningful in a way that also allows them to be related to one another in the complex manner I have only been able to hint at, and will return to in Chapter 4 in presenting Charles Taylor's expressivist conception of language.

## Acceptance and Use: An Introduction

In *Unformulated Experience* (Stern, 1997), I defined the difference between unformulated experience and formulated meaning on the basis of verbal language: the dividing line between formulated and unformulated experience was the boundary between explicit reflection (language) and what comes before it. That idea is not wrong; in fact, it remains crucial. But it is also only half right, or half the story, for the reasons I have already offered. That is, in order to preserve and expand the theory of unformulated experience, I need to find a way to conceptualize unformulated experience as both verbal and nonverbal. I need to find a single way of defining unformulated experience, and formulated experience, too, that applies to both the verbal realm and the nonverbal one. And so I must find a new way to understand the dividing line between formulated and unformulated experience, and I must redraw that boundary. The boundary between verbal-reflective meaning and what comes before it does not suffice for my enlarged purpose.

It seems desirable not to create two different boundaries, one for verbal meanings and the other for nonverbal meanings. It seems desirable, in other words, to think through what it means for experience to be formulated and unformulated in a broader way that applies to both the verbal and the nonverbal.

Our clinical experience often suggests that the meanings that emerge over the course of a treatment were often at least hypothetically available long before they were created. It often seems, in retrospect, that it might very well have been possible to create or formulate them (make them meaningful), but they never came about. We might say that such meanings, prior to our capacity to acknowledge them, were within the pragmatic grasp of our minds, but outside our psychodynamic range. They were cognitive feasible, but emotionally prohibited. They were that part of potential experience maintained in its unformulated state for unconscious defensive reasons (i.e., dissociated [Stern 1997]). For instance, a person might for years have had the information at their disposal that could have led to the conclusion that their mother was narcissistic, but the person in question did not formulate this observation until a particular moment in the treatment.

We are used to thinking of such meanings, prior to their formulation, as dynamically unconscious, and we describe the moment of their new availability as an episode of insight, understanding, or, in the term I use, formulation. I would like to develop now a different vocabulary for these events. In fact, what I will suggest is not just a different vocabulary, but a redefinition of the events themselves—a redefinition of what it means to formulate experience. I undertake this change in conception and vocabulary in the interest of being able to describe, better than before, the dividing line between formulated and unformulated experience, and what creates it. How can we say why a new meaning comes within one's range, and why it happens in one particular moment and not some other? What is the best way to describe how and why it becomes possible to formulate what could not be formulated before?

Another way of asking the question is this: When a shift in the interpersonal field makes it possible for the participants in the field to formulate experience (make experience meaningful) that had been unformulated to that point, how can we understand what mediates the field's influence to the individual mind? What changes in the individual mind, in response to the field, when formulation becomes possible?

Put this way, there is an obvious and simple answer to the question: when a new meaning emerges in one's mind—a new meaning, that is, that one already had the hypothetical ability to formulate—the event takes place because one can tolerate or accept something *now* that one could not tolerate or accept *then*. That is a truism in psychoanalytic work. The field, in other words, changes in a way that makes it possible to accept experience that had to be dissociated prior to that event. In the terms I (Stern, 2003, 2004, 2010a, 2015) have used elsewhere, *not-me* becomes *me*. Subjectivity that had been unformulated, unmeaningful, dissociated, not-me, and non-self becomes formulated, meaningful, me, and part of the self.

Take that observation I just mentioned about a person who could not observe certain aspects of his mother's character. To use the example for this purpose, I will have to complicate it a bit. For the sake of simplicity, I initially constructed it as if what was dissociated was simply the patient's observation about his mother—that she was narcissistic. Generally, in my experience, though, what one dissociates is not really best described as one's observations of others. To be more true to clinical experience, I would prefer to say that one dissociates a *state of one's own self* that would be necessary to occupy if that observation about one's mother were to become possible to formulate. What one dissociates, in other words, is an aspect of identity (Stern, 2010a), a part or piece of oneself. In this case, one *cannot, must not be the person* who sees his mother in this light. It is intolerable to be that person; one cannot accept it.

*Why* can't the patient accept this? Let's say, as is commonly the case with children of narcissistic parents, that he feels he is the good and admirable version of himself only as long as he sees his mother in the same glowing ways she sees herself.

But the mother isn't as simply and thoroughly self-admiring as that, of course. Actually, she is very vulnerable; the glowing version is the only way of seeing herself that keeps at bay the threat of a depressive collapse of her self-regard. It is not surprising that, if the patient formulates any perception that is at all critical of his mother, he is the *bad boy*, mean and selfish—not only to his mother, but eventually in his own eyes, as well. Over many years, one of the patient's primary projects has come to be the continuous occupation of good-boy status and the avoidance (dissociation) of the bad-boy self-states—one of the requirements of which is that he not formulate the observation of his mother's narcissism.

Now let's say that the patient approaches the analyst as if she (the analyst) requires the same kid-glove treatment. This expectation is not formulated in the patient's conscious sense of either the mother or the analyst. Even more significantly, the patient begins to deal with the analyst in ways designed to maintain his desired sense of himself as good, helpful, and admiring.

And now, at some point, let's say that the analyst does something, quite spontaneously, that unintentionally reveals and counters the patient's expectation of the analyst's narcissism—in the same moment that it offers a convincing demonstration that the analyst actually neither needs nor demands the patient's admiration. Perhaps the patient "inadvertently" says something that he immediately (and unconsciously) worries might sound critical of the analyst. The analyst, though, contrary to the patient's (unformulated) expectation, is not thrown; and, in response, the patient is able to see that her feathers seem unruffled. This is vaguely surprising to him, and he begins to grope his way toward a sense of the situation something like, "Huh. That's a surprise. I guess she's not sensitive in that way." (This is a way of trying to describe what happens—but it happens without explicit wording. The patient does not actually say this to himself. Rather, it is *as if* he says such a thing to himself.) It is the contrast with unconscious and unformulated expectation that makes the patient note for one of the first times what he had imagined was about to happen.

The patient now sees the analyst just a little differently. And he sees himself differently, too: maybe he doesn't have to feel so worried about being critical of the analyst; maybe the boy who sees what he isn't supposed to see isn't quite as bad as the patient has always imagined— imagined, that is, without symbolic representation, without ever really knowing he was doing so. (Again, what is happening in the patient's mind is *as if* he were imagining such a thing.) And finally, he sees the relationship differently: there are new possibilities for relatedness, still largely untried and unformulated, but closer to being either tried out and/or thought through.

For the purposes of this little fictional illustration, the patient may start to see his mother differently, too. This incident with the analyst, and many others like it, may nudge him closer to the possibility of grasping his mother's narcissism, perhaps by helping him feel his way a little closer to, and a little less bad about, the wondering and perfidious thought that, "Huh, how about that? That's not what my mother would do."

The point is this: in treatment, we hope the interpersonal field shifts in ways that makes certain dangerous unformulated (dissociated) experiences safer than they were, thereby widening the scope of acceptance and use, and allowing the formulation of new experience. Such mutative processes generally go on in fairly prosaic forms (as in the case of my concocted illustration) over long periods of time, although they may be punctuated by episodes of dissociative enactment that demand attention immediately.[7]

This simple idea can be adapted to my purpose. We can use it to redefine the boundary between experience that is maintained in an unformulated state for defensive reasons and experience that we are dynamically free to formulate if circumstances call for it. The boundary should not be conceived to lie between verbal-reflective meaning and what comes before it, as I drew it in *Unformulated Experience* (Stern, 1997). Rather, we should understand it to lie between experience that can be *accepted* or *tolerated*, and experience that one is afraid, if it were formulated, would be *intolerable*. The boundary lies between experience that *feels like me* and experience that does not. We are much less likely to do the work and feel the pain of formulating experience that does not "feel like me" than we are to formulate experience that feels familiar and acceptable; but we *actively avoid* (i.e., dissociate) the formulation of experience that is so alien that its acceptance would make us unrecognizable to ourselves.[8]

We might say that acceptance is a process of decision; but because it generally takes place without awareness, "decision" may be a misleading word to use. Perhaps it would be better to describe acceptance as an emergent event that takes place when certain tipping points are reached. That is, we accept a meaning when the interpersonal field within which the meaning gains relevance feels safe enough to allow it. The feeling of safety is crucial. In any case, once we can accept a meaning that is within our capacity to create, whether that meaning is verbal or nonverbal, we can *use* it. That is, because it *feels like me*, we can *use* it in the spontaneous construction of creative living. (More about this point to follow.)

Now let us bring acceptance and use together with the thesis I have been exploring that unformulated experience is not unitary, but should be understood to be composed, instead, of two varieties. In the remainder of this chapter, the two kinds of experience, verbal and nonverbal, will be treated as separate phenomena that can be differentiated from one another. But I trust that I have already raised doubts that our capacity to differentiate them necessarily means that they are independent of one another.

One kind of unformulated experience, when it is accepted and put to use, becomes meaningful by becoming articulated in verbal language. But the other kind of unformulated experience does not become articulated in words. The second kind of unformulated experience becomes meaningful in a different way: when it becomes usable, *it does not assume a verbal form, but a nonverbal one.* The nonverbal form may be representational (Bucci's [1997] nonverbal symbolic mode of representation), such as visual imagery or bodily sensations, such as kinesthesia; but it may also be procedural, and therefore nonrepresentational, nonsymbolic (Bucci's [1997] subsymbolic mode). Both varieties of unformulated experience, the verbal and the nonverbal, can exist in an unformulated state for either of two reasons: 1) dissociation; and 2) the simple absence of a reason compelling enough to encourage formulation. And both the verbal and nonverbal can also be *accepted* and *used*. Both the verbal and the nonverbal, that is, can be experienced anywhere in the range between "feels like me" or "feels alien in a way that is intolerable."

To be able to *accept* a certain formulation of experience, in my particular use of the term, is to be free to *use* it. By referring to a new capacity for *use*, I mean to indicate that *acceptance*, and the formulation of meaning that is the consequence of that acceptance, allow the application of this new experience to the spontaneous construction of creative living. If the fictional patient I have discussed were able to *accept* the part of himself, or self-state, in which he grasps his mother's narcissism, he would then also be able to *use* that observation in living. In his case, perhaps he would use it in dealing with his mother, or in understanding and dealing with his own reactions to his mother, or maybe just in feeling his way into a different relationship with her.

Let's say that this patient begins to consider the possibility that his mother is narcissistic. The patient begins to rethink his mother's participation in his life, and begins to feel a little differently than he has before. He begins to perceive her a little differently in the present and to remember her a little differently in the past. I say "a little differently" for a reason: this process is not all-or-nothing. There are circumstances in which he begins to develop more acceptance than he had before, and begins to use this acceptance, perhaps gingerly, in the construction of different responses to his mother, or to other people whose narcissism he may not have perceived before. But there are also circumstances in which he feels, thinks, and behaves in a way quite similar to the way he behaved before.

For these new formulations to become available therefore does not mean that they are available under all circumstances. We must keep in mind the continuous role of the field in selecting and creating what "feels like me" and is therefore acceptable or tolerable at any particular moment. When it comes to human experience, nothing ever changes all at once or forever. What it means to be newly capable of the acceptance and use of a meaning is that the field is no longer as frequently frozen or constricted in the way it had been; and so, when circumstances come about that bring to the fore a meaning that would have been intolerable, or not-me, in the past, the field *may no longer have to remain frozen* in such a way that this meaning can be avoided. Instead, the field now *may be free*, in respect to this particular meaning at this particular time, to react spontaneously to new circumstances.

In this way, the theory of dissociative enactment (Stern 1997, 2010a, 2015; Bromberg, 1998, 2006, 2011) comes together with the subject pursued here: *the breaching of a dissociative enactment frees the interpersonal field and, in so doing, influences not-me to "feel like me" instead, thereby allowing new acceptance and use, or formulation, of meaning*. Over time, the frequency of spontaneity in the relevant part of the field may become greater, so that eventually it could happen that the patient, under virtually all conditions, is able to react spontaneously to events that had to be dissociated in the past. We can describe the process by which the breach of a dissociative enactment takes place repeatedly, resulting in freedom under more and more interpersonal circumstances, as "working through."

To "accept" experience, I have said, means to be able to "tolerate" and "use" it—to allow it to play a part in the ongoing, spontaneous sense and creation of living; it means that one allows a newly formulated experience to participate in shaping the world that one recognizes as one's own. But the capacity to do this is not a conscious choice. It is, rather, something that grows from an intentionality rooted beyond awareness. We can say that to allow experience to become part of living is to *let it be*. The point can also be made by saying that we allow experience to contribute to the spontaneous creation of living only when that experience feels safe, feels as if it is our own. It has a quality we can call "me-ness." To accept and use a meaning is to allow that meaning to become part of what feels like "me."[9]

## Answering criticisms from traditional perspectives

Before going on to a set of theses about the relation of these points to the verbal and the nonverbal, I want to offer a word about the place in psychoanalysis of what feels alien in psychic life. This point is aimed particularly at what I imagine as the concerns of those psychoanalysts who marginalize interpersonal and relational thinking, believing that they represent the unconscious in a superficial and diluted way. I imagine some of these critics feeling just that way about my conceptions of acceptance and use, and especially the boundary defined by "feels like me." The thrust of such criticism would be that taking my perspective is, effectively, to claim that therapeutic action is defined by making sense of, or "making nice" with, the unconscious. If that criticism were so (and it is not), I would be advocating a superficial conception of the unconscious, a view that is not sufficiently "other"—a view of life too deeply influenced by rationality and adaptation to the purposes of the external world and/or the self or ego. I would be giving too little emphasis to the immutability of unconscious meaning and the impossibility of its conscious representation.

My answer to such objections is that those who make them mistake the routing of meaning through the interpersonal field for superficiality, or the absence of depth. (See Wachtel, 2003, 2014a and Foehl, 2014 for an exploration of depth and the social, or in Foehl's term, the "horizontal" frame of reference.) My perspective is based on shifting the center of gravity in psychoanalytic theory and practice from the individual, internal world to the interpersonal field. Continuity is assured; history and character are maintained in this point of view. But the meanings of these relatively stable parts of mind, and their composition in any particular moment, are significantly influenced by context. We can say that the field affects history and character; and so there is a way in which it makes sense to say that the path by which the unconscious shapes consciousness runs through the current state of relatedness. But it would probably be truer to the interpersonal perspective to say that history and character always already belong to, or are part of, the field; and this way of thinking about the problem would lead us to say that the field is itself the unconscious. In either case, the interpersonal field is just as likely to be outside our ken, nonrational, and difficult to understand in reflective terms as the traditional, internal psychoanalytic unconscious.

The field, like the contents of the traditional unconscious, cannot be represented directly in reflective consciousness. All that can be known about either the contents of the traditional unconscious, or the interpersonal field, must be learned via inference. This is important, because the social is often treated in psychoanalysis as if it is continuously open to our conscious, reflective inspection in a way very different from the internal unconscious, hidden away "below" consciousness. This is a position that I and many others dispute (Wachtel, 2003, 2014a; Foehl, 2014).

In the case of the traditional unconscious, the reason we are limited to inference in learning about whatever small portion of the unconscious we can imagine (i.e., the reason we cannot simply observe it) is that unconscious representation (whatever it is) is simply inconsistent, by definition, with conscious symbolization. Unconscious content, Freud (1915b) tells us, must be linked to language before we can even infer it.

But the same is true of the interpersonal field. Because the meanings of the field are nonverbal (procedural), their representation lies outside verbal-reflective knowing. The meanings of interpersonal events, especially their affective meanings, cannot be grasped by reference to their physical appearance. We do not know in any meaningful way the meaning of what someone is doing, or even *what* they are doing, by referring to their movements, gestures, or even their words. And even when the nature of field processes can be represented in words, these words *link* to the meanings, just as they do in Freud's model; field processes and their meanings do not *translate* directly into verbal terms. And so, in the end, we must infer the nature of the interpersonal field in a way analogous to our inference of the contents of the traditional unconscious. Prior to our capacity to infer its nature (such an inference often must await the resolution of a dissociative enactment that makes parts of the field invisible), the field can be just as inaccessible to awareness as the traditional, "vertically" organized unconscious.[10]

Most, perhaps all, psychoanalytic theories of the unconscious today, including those of interpersonal/relational psychoanalysis, reject the idea that the revelation or uncovering of unconscious contents is responsible for therapeutic action. When the point of psychoanalytic treatment was the correction of distortion inside and outside the transference, an idealization of rationality came with the territory, because the therapeutic goal depended on identifying that which was irrational and somehow replacing it with correct perception. In that day, interpersonal psycho-analytic conceptions (relational psychoanalysis had yet to be invented) were as likely as others to be shaped in this way. Today, though, the therapeutic goal for most or all of us, again including interpersonal and relational analysts, is the creation of a wider and deeper range of the capacity to think and feel: the growth of mind. Such growth is not reflected by anything like the "accuracy" or rationality of experience, but rather by flexibility, imagination, maturity, sense of depth, affective responsiveness, and vitality. Most of these goals include the acceptance of the significance of the nonrational in psychic life; and so we no longer believe in any simple way that the nonrational needs to be dissolved. Instead, as in poetry, we imagine the possibility that the nonrational will be generative or expressive, and we try to remain open to those of our internal promptings that might lead us into a fuller appreciation of the next moment.

In my own case, all of this means that the participations and contents of the interpersonal field that have been experienced as "not-me" become experienced instead as "me," or "feels like me," which allows the formulation of experience—the acceptance and use of unformulated experience that could not, prior to the mutative events, be accessed in these ways. It needs to be understood that the nonrational, affect-laden, unconscious parts of the interpersonal field are conceived by interpersonal and relational analysts to be just as difficult to access and represent, and just as generative, as the unconscious aspects of the inner world conceptualized by advocates of traditional psychoanalytic views of the unconscious.

And so, despite other basic differences between my perspective and those of analysts who employ a more traditional, intrapsychic theory of the unconscious, all of us share the points most basic to a psychoanalytic conception of the unconscious: 1) an acceptance that unconscious process and content is alien or other; it is nonrational and inaccessible to direct, conscious, or reflective inspection; and 2) the understanding that therapeutic action, in one way or another, should be defined as the growth of mind: not the uncovering of pre-existing mental contents, or even particular insights (except insofar as these contribute to the growth of mind), but the capacity to accept and tolerate a wider and deeper range of unconsciously mediated psychic content.

## The verbal, the nonverbal, and formulation: Two theses

I now offer a two-point formula that brings together the foregoing notions of acceptance and use with what I have said up to this point about the verbal-reflective and the nonverbal. The first point is largely a restatement of the thesis of *Unformulated Experience* (Stern 1997).

### Thesis I

For that portion of unformulated experience that is most amenable to becoming meaningful as verbal reflection, the meaning that is created in the process of formulation (i.e., the meaning that is *accepted* and *used*) is one of the several or many *verbal articulations* toward which that unformulated experience tends. This variety of unformulated experience, that is, is defined by its amenability to verbal meaningfulness; and so when we formulate it, we articulate it in words and it becomes part of reflective consciousness. The verbal meanings we create on such occasions are not predetermined, but are unconsciously selected from among the available possibilities on the basis of the nature of the current interpersonal field.

With the exception of the addition of acceptance and use as criteria for formulation, the original model of unformulated experience (Stern, 1997) had already taken me most of this way. But it is not far enough. As I have already emphasized, a great deal of what transpires between us and the people around us, as well as what transpires within us, goes on in psychic registers that sometimes cannot be formulated in verbal language. We are unable to attend to this kind of experience in a way that allows it to enter the realm of explicit reflection. The difficulty is not psychodynamically mediated; that is, our incapacity to formulate this material in words is not motivated, consciously or unconsciously. The difficulty is cognitive, as portrayed by Bucci (1997) and BCPSG (2010): such material tends not to be amenable to formulation in verbal symbols.[11] I am thinking of certain aspects of affects, sensations and perceptions (visual, auditory, olfactory, tactile, and kinesthetic), other bodily sensations, small shivers of motives; and I am thinking of imagistic representations, both those that continuously represent experience as it unfolds and those more static, summary images that we construct in memory. I am also thinking of all the procedural, fairly nonspecific social activities and responses that transpire between us and other people in the course of a conversation, or even just in the course of sitting with someone in the same room—i.e., affect, gesture, expression, prosody, and so on; and all the varieties of conduct that go on outside focal awareness, all those procedural meanings that *are* what they *do*, knowing and memory as praxis.

Most meaning, but (and significantly) not all meaning—the procedural or subsymbolic being the exception—attains formulation by a process of symbolization, either verbal or nonverbal. The only criterion of formulation that applies in *all* cases, though (that is, including the procedural)—and therefore the criterion that best serves the purpose of differentiating unformulated and formulated experience—is what I have already described as *what feels like me*: acceptance and use.

As I have said, Thesis 1 is basically a restatement of the claims about language and unformulated experience that I made in earlier work (Stern, 1983, 1997). What must now be added is a second thesis, an application of the same principles to the other kind of unformulated experience—that is, to unformulated experience that, in becoming meaningful, assumes *non*verbal forms.

## Thesis 2

For that portion of unformulated experience that is most amenable to becoming meaningful in the form of nonverbal symbolization or procedural knowing, the meaning that is created in the process of formulation (i.e., the meaning that is *accepted* and *used*) is one of the several or many *nonverbal or nonsymbolic realizations* toward which that unformulated experience tends. This variety of unformulated experience, that is, is defined by its amenability to nonverbal or non-symbolic meaningfulness; and so when we formulate it, it becomes realized in nonverbal symbolic or nonsymbolic forms. Just as is the case within the realm of the verbal, the nonverbal and nonsymbolic meanings we create on such occasions are not predetermined, but are unconsciously selected from among the available possibilities on the basis of the nature of the current interpersonal field.

Let me now make some general comments about the two theses taken together.

First, I repeat, for emphasis, the difference between the two kinds of unformulated experience: the difference lies in the kind of experience that results when the unformulated experience is formulated. In the case of the unformulated experience referred to in Thesis 1, formulation results in the *articulation* of a meaning that is *verbal* or *verbal-reflective*. In the case of the unformulated experience referred to in Thesis 2, formulation results in the *realization* or *actualization* of a meaning that is either *nonverbal-symbolic* (imagistic in one way or another) *or nonsymbolic* (procedural).

Now let me consider the similarities between the two kinds of unformulated experience: 1) Both kinds of unformulated experience are defined as potential meaning that has not, or not yet, come to fruition. 2) In both, the eventual formulated meaning taken by unformulated experience is not predetermined: in each case, it can be realized or articulated in any one of its potential forms. The number of such potential forms varies from few to many, depending on context and the nature of what is to be formulated. 3) The events and configurations of the inter-personal field are key in determining whether and how both kinds of unformulated experience are formulated. The field influences and interacts with the inclinations, preferences, predispositions, and proclivities brought to it by each of its participants, and determines which meanings are formulated in any particular moment, which other possible meanings are not selected, and which experiences remain unformulated.

## Nonverbal meanings in the clinical setting: What do they look like?

As it is articulated, unformulated experience that tends toward verbal meaning undergoes a change in form—or rather, the meaning *takes on* an explicit form for the first time. For that reason, in the case of this kind of formulation—articulation—we usually have no problem seeing that we are able to create an explicit meaning that we could not entertain before. We are suddenly able to think about that meaning in the specific terms of language; it is a new thought, and we are in no doubt about its presence.

This is a simple idea, really. All I mean is this: When we have a new verbal-reflective thought, we know it easily and directly—because it is suddenly *there*, *present*, in our minds. We know an insight when we see it.

But now compare the appearance of a new articulation in one's mind with the appearance of a new *realization*. It is much less immediately or phenomenologically evident what "it is like" to formulate unformulated experience into accepted, useable, *non*verbal meaning. It seems that there must be a kind of transformation involved in the transition; but the nature of such transformation is less than obvious. The transition from unformulated experience to articulation is marked by the appearance of new words, and therefore (to repeat myself) the presence of a new insight is unmistakable.

But what sign marks the transition from unformulated experience to realization? There is no straightforward criterion here. A new formulated nonverbal meaning may make us *feel* differently than we did the moment before; and we may have a sense that the world is different in some way. But it seems to me, on the basis of my own experience, which I presume to be characteristic in this respect, that we cannot necessarily specify the new nonverbal meanings that lead to our feeling that the world has changed. That would require verbal reflective thought; and so we cannot specifically reference new nonverbal meaning in the way that we can usually point to a new verbal articulation.

That is probably why, in fact, psychoanalysts ventured an understanding of the appearance of new verbal meanings in clinical process (insight) so much earlier than we tackled the problem of how new nonverbal meanings emerge and what their roles are. If we do not explicitly think about a nonverbal meaning—and, remember, that kind of explicit reflection requires verbal language—very often we do not even know that it is there. Keep in mind that many nonverbal meanings, and perhaps some portion of most of them, are not even amenable to formulation in verbal language. Often we can say something about such meanings, but the linguistic version, even though it is often useful and even necessary, is routinely inadequate to the wholeness of the nonverbal meaning.

Yes, it is true that the translation between registers is sometimes full and effective. We know that meanings that were originally nonverbal, such as the new perception that comes about in resolving enactments, are sometimes possible to put into words. But at other times some or most of the significance realized in the nonverbal meaning cannot be expressed as reflective meaning. The case can be made that there actually exists considerably less commensurability in the transition from the nonverbal to the verbal than exists between any two verbal languages (English and Chinese, for example) one might select.[12] When we try to force the nonverbal into words, language sometimes (in Nathalie Sarraute's [1939] words) "jumps on" meaning and "crushes it."

There is a great irony here, and a paradox: As I said in Chapter 2, language supplies the very possibility of meaning, including nonverbal meaning; and the nonverbal, part of the "circle of the unexpressed" (Lipps, quoted by Linge, 1976), ceaselessly influences the verbal by serving as the context that surrounds it and thereby gives it not only a significant part of its content, but also contributes to its actual shape, as a corral is given dimension by its fence. Yet despite being so intimately related—despite their continuous mutual influence—verbal and nonverbal meanings are not mutually transmutable. It seems, that is, that the two forms of meaning are seldom capable of simply exchanging places, of being equivalent, of taking one another's forms. What a complex relationship this is!

There remain any number of issues about the representation of unformulated meaning in words; the study of the matter is seriously incomplete. At least, though, we are familiar with the idea that meaning *can* be articulated in words. We take that for granted. It is part of daily life. But our appreciation that meaning can be formulated in *nonverbal* forms, or realized, is not only incomplete, but downright unfamiliar. There remain basic questions about what such a claim even means. For that reason, the remainder of this chapter is devoted to a first look at issues raised by the idea, including some examples of what formulated nonverbal meaning might look and feel like.

## Realization as selection from the possibilities

In the case of unformulated experience that tends toward verbal-reflective formulation, explicit experience is created by accepting some of the available possibilities and articulating them in language. Other possibilities are not selected (again, a decision process taking place without awareness) and remain unformulated. From one standpoint, we can say that the verbal-reflective experience we actually have is the verbal-reflective experience we *want* to have (but this wanting, I must repeat, like desire, derives from an intentionality rooted beyond awareness). We create the reflective experience that we can stand having, or tolerate having—the reflective experience that feels safe enough, that (once again) *feels like me.*

Using the word "tolerate" here helps to make a point I want to stress: to accept a verbal meaning does not necessarily mean that one *likes* that meaning, or feels good about it. Rather, to accept a verbal meaning is to be able to tolerate the relevance of that meaning for the immediate situation in which it arises. In other words, it does not require absolute safety to accept and use a meaning; it requires only that the situation feel safe *enough* (Bromberg, 2000).

A similar process goes on in the case of that part of unformulated experience that tends toward nonverbal realization: Meaning is created by accepting some of the possibilities it offers. But these possibilities are realized in *non*reflective living, and other experiential possibilities go unrealized. As in the case of verbal-reflective meaning, an unconscious selection process takes place; and once again, as in the case of the verbal, we could say that the nonverbal meanings we accept are those that we *want* to accept, or that we can stand, or tolerate. Realized nonverbal meanings, like articulated verbal-reflective meanings, participate in our creation of a sense of agency, because we use them to construct experience that feels like our own.

# The work of the Boston Change Process Study Group

There is a significant degree of relationship between the views I am describing in this chapter and the work of the Boston Change Process Study Group. Their work on implicit relational knowing (BCPSG, 1998) is especially relevant and important, and I want to acknowledge it in this context. But BCPSG has also had critical things to say about my views. These views, too, need to be addressed in this book. Actually, I would have liked to address them in this chapter, since they are particularly relevant to the subject at hand. But doing that, I decided, would distract attention from the argument I am trying to make. For that reason, I have added an appendix to this book in which I take up a comparison of my views with those of BCPSG. The appendix can be read at any point, because it is an independent consideration of the issues it concerns; but it is especially relevant to the themes of this chapter. You can go to that appendix now, if you prefer to compare these views at this point in the presentation, where they are most relevant; but it is not necessary to consult that material to follow the remainder of this chapter.

# A simple illustration

To this point in the argument, the necessity to define the issues I am raising, and to present the thinking that lies behind them, has required that most of my presentation take place on the abstract level. But now that the issues of definition have been engaged, I am eager to offer some examples of what I mean by realized and dissociated nonverbal meaning. What do realized and dissociated nonverbal meanings actually look like? In the first of these illustrations I focus on sexual feelings. That seems like an inherently interesting choice, and appropriate for psychoanalytic readers; but I could have chosen any kind of nonverbal experience.

Let us start by recognizing that the unformulated experience of anyone's sexual encounter contains myriad possibilities, only some of which, in anyone's life, come to fruition as articulated or realized experiences. Now let us imagine someone for whom sexual arousal and sexual feelings are relatively comfortable and enjoyable—that is, someone for whom sexuality is not typically associated with notable anxiety. Such a person, we can say, "accepts" under most circumstances the sexual feelings that come to them; such feelings feel as if they "belong" to them; they "feel like me." They occur within the part of the personality that we describe as the self. This person can allow themselves to formulate (to *realize*, in this case, much more often than to articulate) a fairly substantial proportion of the sensual possibilities inherent in their unformulated experience of sexuality. As in every other situation, shifts in the interpersonal field routinely affect the degree to which this person realizes such experiences and can use them in the spontaneous creation of living; and no doubt we could even imagine some scenario in which formulation of this part of their experience becomes psychically threatening, feels unsafe, and therefore inhibits the experience of sexuality. But most of the time, under most circumstances, this person's sensual and sexual feelings are more or less fully available.

Now consider a different sort of person, someone for whom sexual feelings and arousal are more frequently associated with anxiety and discomfort. This person is less likely than the more comfortable one to find themselves in situations of sexual possibility; and they can realize a much lower proportion of the possibilities that are present in any particular moment of sexual relatedness. Even the relatively few nonverbal sensory and affective experiences of sex that they can allow themselves to realize are probably muted and relatively pale.

Because so much of the range of sensuality goes unformulated in such a person's life, the interpersonal field is even more influential in determining the possibilities for formulation than it is in the case of the person who is generally more comfortable about such things. Of course, the anxious person is less liable than others to find their way into situations in which the question of how they perceive sensual or sexual feelings even comes up. The question of whether they do manage to be in sexual situations is itself an outcome of the field, of course. And when they do, however rare an occurrence it may be, it is the configuration of the interpersonal field that determines whether they feel safe enough to allow (some of) these feelings to be formulated, and with what degree of intensity and vitality.

Because language is frequently not an adequate means of symbolizing the nuances of sensory experience, it is quite frequent that sensory (and sensual) experience cannot be worded. For this reason, both the person who is usually comfortable with sexual feeling and the person who is not are liable to be able to reflect on only a portion of the part of their sexual feelings that is realized. This point can be made, we know, about any realized experience: it may not be possible to articulate it in verbal terms. But the realized meanings that are inaccessible to words nevertheless participate in shaping experience. It is also worth noting in this context that feelings and perceptions that go unrealized because they feel alien (i.e., are dissociated), by their very absence from the meaningful world, also contribute to the nature of the overall sexual experience.

Perhaps the most significant role played by realized nonverbal experience is its part in day-to-day, ongoing interpersonal relatedness. Imagine this same fictional, anxious person in a social situation in which flirtation is a possibility. Flirtation, we imagine, is infected by the person's anxiety about sexuality. This person is therefore hobbled in such a context. They are unlikely to have either verbal or nonverbal access to the experience that they would need in order to make immediate, procedural, intuitive sense of the other person's flirtation, or to participate in a natural way themselves. Their anxiety inhibits their flirtation because, under most circumstances, it prevents them from comprehending much that they would need to know in order to understand the nature of the relatedness in which they find themself. We could say that they are locked out of participating, or even of knowing how to do it.

## Ways of being

Now let us broaden the scope. Instead of focusing just on the perception of one kind of sensory stimulation, let us include an entire relational experience. Each person's realizations of any particular moment of interpersonal life are a selection from among the possibilities. The process is just the same as in the simpler example of the sexual experience, but the level of complexity is much greater. Each possibility for realized meaning, as it is accepted and used, or remains unformulated, feeds back on the possibilities for meaning that remain, altering their relationship to one another and making the realization of some more likely, others less likely.[13]

I face a problem in trying to say something coherent about the nature of nonverbal meaning. The medium I must use limits me: I have no choice but to use words to describe a kind of experience that is defined precisely by the fact that there are often no words for it.

The concepts of acceptance and use come to my aid in tackling this problem. These ideas allow me to imagine both the nature of realized nonverbal meaning and the process by which it emerges from its unformulated state. Here is an outline of what I have in mind: The nonverbal meanings that most interest us as psychoanalysts are what I call "ways of being," a phrase by which I mean to refer to an amalgam of several parts of experience: our unformulated experience of the other's conduct and experience; our unformulated experience of our own experience and conduct; and our unformulated experience of the ongoing relatedness between the other and ourselves. (BCPSG also uses the term "ways of being," but in their own way, which is different than mine in important respects.[14]) Acceptance, an affect state, brings relevance (though not necessarily conscious attention or symbolization) to certain portions of our ways of being; and these parts of nonverbal unformulated experience are then realized and used. Because verbal language is not involved in these processes, we must imagine that they take place without explicit reflection or articulation.

One brings a freshly unformulated way of being into each moment with the other. Ways of being are in continuous flux; they are responsive to changes in context. Among other things, they are therefore unformulated sets of expectations, which become more focused as particular relationships develop. For me, ways of being are *potential* experiences of relatedness with the other (whereas for BCPSG they are *actual* experiences of relatedness, "reasonably accurate sensings of each person's ways of being with an other" [Reis, 2007, p. 378; see footnote 13]). Ways of being (again, for me, not for BCPSG) are a collection of ways the relatedness *might* unfold, a collection of possibilities from which one or more will be (unconsciously) selected by the processes of the interpersonal field in each successive moment.

Note that *the set of unformulated expectations* (that is, not just the experience that is formulated, but the collection of unformulated possibilities from which the formulated experience emerges) changes as context shifts. This raises an interesting point. Up to now, I have emphasized that the *process of formulation* is sensitive to changes in context—that is, I have claimed that the meanings we select from the possibilities offered by unformulated experience are influenced by the nature of the field. Now, though, it seems that *unformulated experience itself*, in the form of ways of being—that is, *the very possibilities for meaning*—are themselves sensitive to context. It is not only the meanings we eventually formulate that change from one situation to another, or from one time to another. The range of potential meanings that might be articulated or realized also changes with context. To recognize this point is to underline the dialectical nature of the formulated and the unformulated: each is context for the other. As new meanings are formulated, the possibilities for future meanings change; and as those possibilities change, different explicit meanings are liable to emerge.

Each person's realizations of each moment's interpersonal life are therefore drawn from the way of being he creates with the other, and each moment's realizations then affect both the constitution of the next moment's way of being and the unformulated possibilities, the ways of being, that emerge from it. This is yet another way to acknowledge a central point for all relational analysts: our experience is deeply influenced, at all times, by the other; or rather, our experience is deeply influenced by the interpersonal field created *with* the other. Mind, as I have said in other contexts (Stern, 2010a, Chapter 1), is much more a phenomenon of the field than we tend to acknowledge. The moment-to-moment relation of two persons' ways of being changes the patterns of realization created by each of them.

I hope that this very brief description of interpersonal life makes clear that a detailed description of experience as it is actually lived would be unimaginably intricate. It is probably not feasible to create a thorough description of even a single moment of actual interpersonal living; the text would go on and on, and we would lose the forest for the trees. And of course the frequent incapacity of language to represent these phenomena fully makes the task even more daunting, since we would have no choice, if we were to try to construct such an account, to do it in words. To the extent that experience is the outcome of myriad nonverbal events, all of which are happening simultaneously and in continuous flux, it is simply beyond our capacity to grasp in reflective awareness. We can only speculate about its details.

We accept some of the meanings of our ways of being and use them to construct our ongoing sense of what is transpiring and how we are feeling about it; and just as consistently, other possibilities stay unformulated in our minds. Prior to being accepted and used, ways of being are always unformulated; we reconstruct our sense of relatedness from one moment to the next. Continuity is assured by the fact that the last moment's realizations exert an influence on which possibilities for meaning are accepted and used (selected and realized) in the next moment. But the ceaselessness of the selection process also means that our sense of ongoing relatedness is also in continuous flux. Relatedness can always be realized in more than one way, and so its course and meaning are always changing despite the conservative influence of history—history as distant as childhood, or even the generations that preceded us, and as recent as a second ago. There is a good deal of latitude in the meanings we assign to our own participation in interpersonal life, in the meaning we take from the relatedness of the other, and in our affective reactions to these things; and continuity from one moment to the next is always under threat of disruption, and relatedness may suddenly turn puzzling.

## The relational repertoire

One of the implications of the fact that realizations are selected from the possibilities offered by our ways of being is that personality, or character, can be meaningfully defined as the patterns of realization that are most characteristic for a particular person. That is, each of us is liable to create characteristic meanings within any given context (interpersonal field), and we are liable to do that on the basis of whatever is familiar and relevant to us in those circumstances. In other words, each of us has a particular *relational repertoire*, a set of characteristic patterns of interpersonal realization that have come about in the course of living, and that are therefore most easily "set off" or catalyzed by the events of the field. Like my way of describing "ways of being," this concept is closely related what Daniel Stern (1985, 1992) and BCPSG (D.N. Stern, et al, 1998) refer to as "ways-of-being-with" (see Chapter 3, Note 13). All these concepts refer to patterns of social living. The trigger for each pattern is the presence of a particular configuration of the inter-personal field. When relatedness *feels* a certain way, we are primed to realize our ways of being in certain characteristic affective and trans-actional forms.

The way that the field "feels" is established by experience with significant others with whom certain highly relevant kinds of experience have taken place in the past (Sullivan, 1940/1953, 1953; Levenson, 1972/2005, 1983/2005, 1991/2016, 2017; Stern, 1997, 2010a, 2015; Bromberg, 1998, 2006, 2011). "Relevance" can be any notable kind of emotional valence, either good (safe, affirming, secure) or bad (insecure, diminishing, unsafe, frightening).

Let me offer a simple example. Let us say that a male student who happens to feel that his father frequently competes with him over intellectual matters seeks out a professor about a research idea. The professor, who often wishes his relationship with his own father had been closer than it was, reacts to the student's interest as if it is a bid for connection, and in an effort to be responsive and protective (he thinks), he mentions some of his own research that he thinks may be relevant to the student's interest.

The professor might have grasped the student's interest in many different ways, each of which would have a certain validity, but this is the one (the attribution to the student of an attempt to connect) on which the professor settles. If it had been sufficiently relevant to him, he might have paid more attention, for instance, to a certain tension in the student's manner, a tension that might have betrayed the student's anxiety that the professor will be threatened by the student and become competitive. The professor, we could say, is identifying with what he imagines as the student's vulnerability in asking him about his research. The professor would say, if he were asked, that he is just trying to be responsive to what the student wants; but certain aspects of the meaning he realizes here are also probably due to the professor's guilt about not having been a good enough son to his own father. He lives with the sense that perhaps the reason he and his father were not closer had to do with his own inadequacies. And so part of what is set off by the student's manner is a need on the professor's part to make sure he cannot reasonably be accused of being unresponsive. In other words, the professor's nonverbal sense that he is trying to be responsive is certainly one of the possibilities of his way of being; and we cannot claim that he is wrong to have this sense. But he does not formulate, verbally or nonverbally, that there is a certain compulsive quality in his responsiveness. He *needs* to be perceived as responsive.

In the meantime, the student, who approached the professor in the first place with a mild trepidation born of his (nonverbal) worry about the professor's competitive feelings, is now sure (also without verbal reflection), on the basis of the professor's mention of his own research, and especially because of the mildly compulsive quality of the professor's attempt to connect, that he has made the professor insecure and competitive; and so he, the student, begins to become anxious and a little irritated. But, not knowing the professor, the student does not feel entitled to these feelings, and certainly not to expressing them, and he reacts by becoming tongue-tied. The professor sees that the student is uncomfortable and, feeling that he has therefore failed to reassure the student of his (the professor's) responsiveness, he retreats to the same kind of self-sufficiency and even coldness with which he is afraid that he met his father—and with which his father often met him.

The awkwardness and artlessness of using so many words to describe this small interaction, which we can imagine took place in only a couple of minutes, or even less, is the reason that writers of fiction are endlessly urged, "Show, don't tell!" Very little of what I have just described would have entered the reflective awareness of either the professor or the student, a fact that makes the use of words even less adequate than it would be otherwise. The events of this vignette, when they did not remain unformulated, were almost exclusively realizations, not articulations. Everyday language often cannot do justice to realization (poetry sometimes does better, because it has the freedom to express more metaphorically and obliquely than conventional language).

But the main reason I offer this example is to illustrate the acceptance and use of the nonverbal possibilities for meaning. You can see how many opportunities were available for each of the players in this vignette to create alternative meanings, and how each of the two influenced the meanings selected by the other; and you can see that the meanings developed and changed significantly as the interaction unfolded. Most of all, you can see that the student and the professor each selected a familiar *pattern* of realizations from the possibilities offered by their respective ways of being—and that these patterns, for each, because of their particular histories, was "set off" with particular ease. It required very little interpersonal influence, that is, to reach a tipping point: for a certain characteristic perception of the other and himself to fall into place, and for the characteristic interpersonal event that was the consequence to play out. If we sum the patterns of realizations that are characteristic for the student and the professor, we would have portions of what I have just referred to as their relational repertoires.

If one's development has only infrequently been marked by trauma, humiliation, terror, or other unbearable insecurity, one's relational repertoire is liable to be reasonably broad and one's dissociations are liable to be touched on only infrequently in the course of living. One's capacity to negotiate interpersonal life is therefore likely to be quite good. These are people who can manage most situations in a relatively unruffled and emotionally responsive fashion; they are people who others find it easy to be around. But for those many less fortunate others whose development has been marked by the kind of feelings that lead them to avoid a much wider array of realizations, and who therefore have relatively small interpersonal repertoires, dissociations are touched on with much higher frequency in everyday life. Life with others is a minefield, and negotiating relatedness is liable to become uncomfortable with a fair degree of regularity. These are people who others experience as "difficult," and they generally suffer a great deal more pain than those in the first group.

Of course, these "types" are the extremes that anchor two ends of a continuum. Most of us fall somewhere between them. I describe them in order to illustrate the impact on living of the breadth of our relational repertoires.

## Realizations, ways of being, and self-states

I am almost ready, in the next chapter, to move on to a further consideration of the relationship between the verbal and the nonverbal. But before I do, there is one last conceptual link I want to emphasize, in order to tie together the thinking in this chapter with my earlier work on dissociation and enactment (Stern, 2010a, 2015). Each characteristic pattern of realization that is called out by a particular configuration of the interpersonal field is neither more nor less than what, in other circumstances, we refer to as a *self-state* or *me-state*—or, when dissociated, a *not-self state* or *not-me state*. A pattern of realization that is characteristic of a particular person in certain interpersonal contexts is a way of being "*me*." When the unconscious necessity is to be *not* that particular person—to be someone *other* than that person—that pattern of realization is denied realization;

it must remain unformulated, dissociated in the strong sense (see Stern, 1997; see also Chapter 2 of this book). Dissociation can be understood, as Bromberg (1998, 2006, 2011) especially has shown us, as the sequestering of states of being from one another. All those self-states that need not be sequestered from one another—that can be experienced together, simultaneously, whenever the interpersonal field makes that appropriate—compose *me*; and all those other states that must not be experienced as *me*, that must be sequestered from *me*, are *not-me*.

When an enactment loses its peremptory quality, when it is no longer so essential to the preservation of one's sense of who one is—when, in other words, a dissociation is breached and a frozen place in the interpersonal field thaws—what has happened is that one has become able to tolerate a wider range of realizations. A state of being that had been *not-me* becomes *me*. The new perception that I wrote about in the beginning of this chapter is, in fact, a nonverbal meaning that has been realized, formulated, for the first time.

Dissociation is part of the operation of the processes of selection in our grasp of relatedness. The parts of our ways of being that remain unrealized for unconscious defensive reasons are dissociated, like those aspects of experience that our sensually/sexually constricted person in my example could not realize. Because the dissociation of meanings, verbal and nonverbal alike, is an outcome of the operations of the interpersonal field, the other person is always involved, in unpredictable ways, in the selection of which meanings we realize and which others we leave behind. Unlike repression, dissociation does not require the expulsion of meanings from awareness; instead, because nonverbal realization, like verbal articulation, requires the expenditure of effort, dissociation of nonverbal meaning merely requires that the effort to realize those meanings (that is, curiosity) not be expended (Stern, 1983, 1990, 1997). The inter-relation of two individuals' ways of being, and the realizations each person derives from them, defines the *interpersonal* or *relational field*.

## Are realizations "more themselves?"

In Chapter 1, in summarizing the theory of unformulated experience as it existed prior to this book, I suggested, as I have written since 1983, that unformulated experience, when it is articulated in words, becomes "more itself"; and I contrasted this view of the transition from unconsciousness to consciousness with views such as Freud's (1915b), Daniel Stern's (1985; Stern, et al,1998), and Bucci's (1997) (and, in fact, with the views of most psychoanalysts, for whom a substantive unconscious is a defining quality of psychoanalytic theory [e.g., LaFarge, 2014]). In all these views, unconscious meaning is the fuller or more complete form, becoming "less itself" as it is linked with words and enters awareness. Words entail a loss of meaning in these theories, and conscious meaning is therefore the paler form, whereas in the theory of unformulated experience, in which language is understood to have constitutive properties, articulation is a process through which meaning is not sacrificed but actually created, and thus comes into its own for the first time.

Now I need to consider whether the same thing should be said about the second kind of unformulated experience, the kind of unformulated experience that when formulated, is accepted and used as nonverbal meaning. Is a new realization "more itself" than the potential experience from which it arose? Can we say that realization, like articulation, is a flowering of meaning?

The question seems to answer itself, because it seems undeniable that the transition from potential to actual is a move from a less meaningful state to a more meaningful one. In that sense, when nonverbal unformulated experience is accepted and used, and thus realized, it seems that the inevitable consequence is that it becomes "more itself," just as articulated experience does.

## Notes

1  Adversarial or interpersonal conflict is often the emotional atmosphere of enactment—at least, when enactment is understood, as I understand it, as "the interpersonalization of dissociation." It will distract from the argument I am creating in this chapter to explain in the text why this is so, but I have done that elsewhere in detail, with extensive clinical illustrations (D.B. Stern, 2004, 2010a). Here, let me offer just a few words of explanation.

"Enactment" is most often defined in the psychoanalytic literature as that part of ongoing interaction that is not available to conscious inspection. That is, enactment is the unconscious part of whatever is taking place. The problem with this definition is that it suggests that the phenomenon in question—enactment—is omnipresent, because every interaction, of course, has unconscious components. If enactment is continuous, the meaning of the concept becomes so diluted that it is virtually meaningless.

I prefer, instead, to limit the definition of the word to those interactions that represent the "interpersonalization of dissociation." This position depends on an application of Harry Stack Sullivan's (1953) conception of "not-me." Not-me is that part of subjectivity that has become intolerable as a result of "developmental trauma" (Bromberg, 2011). Not-me is not part of the self; it is dissociated, and exists only in a defensively maintained, unformulated state. If not-me were to enter awareness—if one were to be the person one must not be—the result would be devastating affect, most often shame, often of catastrophic proportions.

For all of these reasons, when the interpersonal field becomes configured in such a way that not-me threatens to enter awareness, the last-ditch defensive effort to deal with this failure of dissociation is enactment: One treats the other as if *they* were not-me (as if *they* were the dissociated part of one's subjectivity), thereby avoiding the identification of oneself with this unacceptable image. For example, the relatedness may be configured as if one is saying: "I am not greedy—*you're* greedy." The similarity to projective identification is clear; but the differences are equally significant (Stern, 2010a, pp. 17–18).

This is why most enactments, at least as I use the term, are emotionally uncomfortable. Enactments are expressions of those parts of subjectivity that would be intolerable if they were experienced as part of the self, and so if the other is identified with this image, one's relation to the other is liable to take on the same unaccepting emotional tone one would take toward oneself if this same image were shaping one's own sense of identity.

2  In addition to Benjamin (1988, 1995, 1998, 2017), significant contributors to the conceptualization of enactment in the interpersonal and relational literatures include, among others, Atlas & Aron (2017), Bass (e.g., 2003), Black (2003), Bromberg (1998, 2006, 2011), Davies (e.g., 2004), Ehrenberg (1992), Hirsch (2014), Hoffman (1998), Levenson (1972/2005, 1983/2005, 1991/2016, 2017), Mitchell (1988, 1993, 1997, 2000), Pizer (2000), Slavin & Kriegman (1998), Slochower (2006), and Wolstein (e.g., 1959; Bonovitz, 2009).

3  In one sense, the fact that the experience of recognition is a variety of perception, not of understanding, perhaps should not have come as a surprise to me, since I now see that this fact is implied by the phenomenology that has so much appealed to me in the work of Merleau-Ponty (1945/1962): "Perception is not a science of the world, it is not even an act, a deliberate taking up of a position; it is the background from which all acts stand out, and is presupposed by them" (pp. x–xi). And here again: "Now there is indeed one human act which at one stroke cuts through all possible doubts to stand in the full light of truth: this act is perception, in the wide sense of knowledge of existences" (p. 40).

4  That appearance of abruptness is deceptive and should not be taken to suggest that the events in question have no history. I turn to this point in discussing

the work of the Boston Change Process Study Group (BCPSG) in the appendix of this book.

5 Vivona (2013) moderates her criticism of the position taken by the Boston Change Process Study Group by also citing an article (BCPSG, 2008) that she feels places the message of their 2007 article in a broader context.

6 There is interest today, in the literature on mirror neurons, in moving the understanding of how we understand the affective states of others out of psychology and into neuroscience. Although it is probably clear from my presentation of this example that I do not subscribe to this view, I do not intend to take up the issue here. Readers interested in an effective challenge to the mirror neuron thesis should consult Vivona (2009b).

7 Some readers will object that I have not addressed the patient's resistance in this made-up example. If the patient has never made the observation of his mother before, why would he make it now? Such a questioner would wonder if I am advocating some variety of corrective emotional experience, in which the analyst tries to act in a way that counters the patient's transference expectation, or something like Carl Rogers's unconditional positive regard. How am I imagining that the analyst would deal with the patient's unconscious resistance here? My answer would be that I do not use the concept of resistance. I see the patient's reluctance to make the observation as a consequence of the interpersonal field he repeatedly and unconsciously constructs with other people, in which he ends up being treated in such a way that his expectations are confirmed. The analyst's task is to find a way to the grasp of his or her own unconscious participation in that kind of field. The analyst needs to be able to see and feel in other words, how he or she can reasonably be understood, by the patient, to be confirming his expectation. Once the analyst can see that, the field shifts in a way that makes it feasible for the patient to begin to see and feel what he could not see and feel before. I have not laid all of this out in my simple, fictional example.

8 The question that immediately arises is how it is possible to avoid formulating something without having formulated it first. How does one "know" what not to formulate? It would distract attention from the argument to address that question here. Interested readers should consult Chapters 6 and 7 of *Unformulated Experience* (Stern, 1997).

9 William James (1890) describes the quality of "me-ness" thusly:

> If the thinking be *our* thinking, it must be suffused through all its parts with that peculiar warmth and intimacy that make it come as ours. . . . *Whatever* the content of the ego may be, it is habitually felt *with* everything else by us humans . . .
>
> (p. 242; italics from the original)

James's use of "peculiar warmth and intimacy" is not only charming, but also a good observation—although James is referring to the part of *me* that, in my own frame of reference, derived from Harry Stack Sullivan (1953), is *good-me*, not *bad-me* (see Chapter 6). One does not like to be bad-me, although those self-states are tolerable, unlike the intolerable *not-me*.

10 In one sense, I am parting company with Sullivan in saying this, since Sullivan based his entire point of view on the analyst's continuous capacity to observe the interpersonal field of which he was part. I am maintaining, however, Sullivan's emphasis on the interpersonal field as a primary shaping influence on conscious experience. In taking these positions, I am part of the view of Sullivan's work held by contemporary interpersonalists (e.g., Levenson, 1972/2005, 1983/2005, 1991/2015, 2017; Ehrenberg, 1992; Bromberg, 1998, 2006, 2011; Hirsch, 2014).

11 Please note that in making this point, I am *not* ruling out the possibility that this kind of experience can be dissociated. It *can* be dissociated, just as surely as the verbal-reflective kind of experience can be dissociated; it *can* be maintained as unformulated experience for unconscious defensive reasons. That is crucial. My point in the text is only to suggest that the reason that this kind of unformulated experience cannot be articulated in verbal-reflective form is that it is *not amenable* to that kind of formulation. *That* is what I mean when I write that "the difficulty is cognitive."

12 Interestingly, we have even less ability to translate from the verbal to the nonverbal. The apparent exceptions are those realms of art, such as music or painting, in which a verbal thought is given an aural or visual representation. These cross-modal "exceptions," such as onomatopoeia or music composed to inhabit or illustrate a thought or a feeling, prove the rule, though, because they are novelties. Their very capacity to represent the verbal by the nonverbal, or vice versa, is considered remarkable. Or consider the game of "charades," in which the whole point is the difficulty of communicating in nonverbal terms about the verbal. Yet we pay no attention at all to the virtually absolute incommensurability in translation from the verbal to the nonverbal. The existence of this separation, and the reasons for it, deserve their own examination.

13 Tauber and Green (1959) made this point presciently, 50 years ago, sounding very much like the description by the Boston Change Process Study Group (D.N. Stern, et al, 1998) of implicit relational knowing:

> In everyday life the prelogical processes are operative in all interpersonal relationships and form the vast backdrop to every variety of human enterprise and contact. In effect, the most important thing that goes on within man and between man and man is involved with these covert referential processes. A great deal of what we do among one another consists in apprehending nonpropositional emotional responses and reacting to them. Most interpersonal interaction, in fact, goes on in the prelogical mode.

(p. 3)

14  Some time after I had started using the term "ways of being," I learned that
    Daniel Stern (D.N. Stern, 1985, 1992; D.N. Stern et al, 1998), referring to
    "ways-of-being-with," as in "ways-of-being-with-mother," had used the same
    phrase to describe phenomena quite similar to those I mean to draw attention
    to in using the term. Reis (2007) summarizes the BCPSG perspective on this
    subject:

> Although emerging from developmental theory, the idea of implicit
> relational knowing is applied by the Boston Group to analyst-analysand
> interaction. With a similarity to other contemporary intersubjectivists,
> the Boston Group suggests that the implicit relational knowing of patient
> and analyst intersect to create an intersubjective field that includes rea-
> sonably accurate sensings of each person's *ways of being* with an other,
> sensings that they call the "real relationship." This intersubjective field
> becomes more complex and articulated with repeated patient-therapist
> encounters, giving rise to emergent new possibilities for more coherent
> and adaptive forms of interaction.
>
> (p. 378; italics added)

This conceptualization is consistent in many respects with what I have said
in this chapter, although in my frame of reference, unlike that of BCPSG,
ways of being are a kind of unformulated experience. That is not necessarily
because ways of being are dissociated in my frame of reference (although it
is easy to imagine such a possibility—i.e., that certain possibilities for
relatedness do not feel like me, instead feeling alien and dangerous). For me,
ways of being are not descriptions of actual social being, but are instead
*possibilities* for actual relatedness, or social being, as it unfolds in the present
and future. Those possibilities may come to fruition—that is, sooner or later
they may be realized, or formulated in actual relatedness—or they may not
become relevant, and may therefore never be realized. BCPSG does not see
things this way, of course. For them, ways of being are not possibilities, but
actualities—ways that someone actually *is* being.

# Chapter 4

# Manifestation

## The underlying unity of verbal and nonverbal meaning

> ... [T]o talk of "making manifest" doesn't imply that what is so
> revealed was already fully formulated beforehand ... I am taking
> something, a vision, a sense of things, which was inchoate and only
> partly formed, and giving it a specific shape.
>
> Charles Taylor, 1989, p. 374

In the last chapter I revised the privileging of verbal meanings in the
theory of unformulated experience by recognizing the formulation of
nonverbal meaning. In this chapter, I return to language, contrasting two
views: 1) language is a set of labels that designate pre-existing meaning;
2) language is an expressive act by which we create new meaning.
Ultimately, this path will lead to a new unity of verbal meaning and
nonverbal meaning under the rubric of what philosopher Charles Taylor
(1991/1995, 1992/1995, 2016) calls *expressivism* or *manifestation*. On the
most general level, we can in this way ground psychoanalysis as an
interpretive discipline devoted to making meaning. But more specifically,
we can even more clearly do away with the privileging of words in the
theory of unformulated experience—while simultaneously preserving the
position I have held throughout that language has significant constitutive
properties.

The question of whether we discover meanings that already exist or
create them in a way that deserves to be called an expression of our
natures is no purely academic controversy. On our answer to this question
hinge many of the most important questions in contemporary psychoanalysis: Is psychoanalysis a natural science or are we more closely
allied to the humanities and the interpretive social sciences? Should
quantitative empirical research answer questions about the content and
nature of unconscious meaning, and about the value of the ways we

understand it? Should quantitative research be the arbiter of clinical technique? Must we come to terms with the necessity of manualized treatments, or are there alternatives we can believe in and defend? By the end of this chapter, the questions I bring up about the nature of meaning lead to two different kinds of answers to these questions. And so, while this chapter will take up philosophical questions, make no mistake: these are philosophical questions with the most practical implications in the world.

That is where the argument will take us. But it begins once again with words.

## The tip of the tongue phenomenon

We are all familiar with that feeling that we are very close to a meaning, but that we cannot find exactly the right words for it. We have the feeling that we "know" something, but that we cannot say it; it is on the tips of our tongues. What is happening at such a moment?

There are at least two possibilities:

1) Words are inadequate to a meaning that already exists in our minds. The meaning is there; we just can't express it. In this explanation of the difficulty, the problem is the reach or the flexibility of language; or perhaps, as Bucci (2003, 2007a, b) tells us, the problem is the dissociation of information coded in divergent modes of representation: that is, we have access to a nonverbal symbolic meaning, or a "subsymbolic" meaning, but we can't link that meaning to a verbal representation. We feel that the meaning is there, tantalizingly close, but we are frustrated: it remains just beyond our grasp. Some variety of this interpretation is the explanation we usually adopt for the "tip of the tongue" phenomenon, and we adopt it so automatically that we do not consider the possibility of an alternative.

2) But there is another way of thinking about the problem: The meaning that we are groping toward would not be on the tips of our tongues *without* language. The meaning feels so close *because* of language, not in spite of it. Language has created whatever part of the meaning we can sense, but language has not yet finished. The lack of clarity in the meaning is the consequence of our straining creative powers, not of the absence of a link between registers of representation.

The meaning toward which we grope remains vague precisely because it actually is not yet fully there; it does not fully exist. What does exist is the *possibility* of a meaning, maybe even the partial coherence or concrescence of a meaning. An analogy might be the birth of a star —a cloud of gas in the process of falling together into matter. Furthermore, from this perspective the meaning toward which we grope is *our* meaning; it belongs to *us*; it issues from the unique configuration of mental processes that we are. And so it bears our stamp, it is an expression of our particular, unique being. In a sense, if we cannot quite form the meaning, it is because we cannot quite yet be the person who would be expressed through that meaning. In this alternative, then, the unformulated meaning is a good deal more than a bit of coded information that may or may not link to a verbal representation. From this point of view, the process of creating meaning is emergent, and it may be interrupted at any point in its trajectory. And in the end we may be disappointed: the meaning we feel so sure is "there" in our minds may never emerge in an explicit form at all. From the perspective of this second way of understanding the tip of the tongue phenomenon, when we sense that we know something we cannot say, we are counting our chickens before they hatch. The meaning is not fully formulated and hidden away, and it is not merely unavailable to representation in words; it is actually absent.

This description of language has been called the *expressive-constitutive* account of language and the human person by hermeneutic philosopher Charles Taylor (1992/1995), or in a more economical expression adopted from Isaiah Berlin (Taylor, 1975, p. 13), the *expressivist* view of language (Taylor, 1985, 1989, 1991/1995, 2016).

## The designative view of language

The first interpretation of the tip of the tongue phenomenon, the one in which the meaning is already there and we are merely lacking the right words for it, is an example of what Taylor (1985) calls the *designative* account of language, the view that language is a set of representations for meanings that already exist. In the designative view, the activity of thinking in words is the activity of coupling language with pre-existing meanings. When we cannot find the words but have a sense that a meaning is present, the meaning may very well actually be there—but the language is not. Perhaps the words that would cover the meaning have yet to be invented; or perhaps the words exist, but are not available to us; or perhaps the words we do have are not subtle enough to represent the meaning. Words are labels in the designative view, and labels tend to be categorical. We call the object beneath my computer "a table"; only under special circumstances (e.g., while trying to decide whether to buy this particular table from a furniture store) do we refer to it in a way that expresses what it means to us or the part it plays in our lives. Labels are useful precisely because they are categorical; and so we have fewer of them than there are phenomena to be described (the number of potentially describable phenomena is virtually infinite, since there is really no limit on the number of ways we can invent to break up the world into perceptible pieces). Every perception of our world is unique, and so we need verbal labels if we are ever to transcend the continuous rush of unique perceptions and break them into the groups or categories that we need in order to think. Categorical relations make thought and communication possible. It is only because of categorization that we are not provoked into endless study by everything we encounter; we know what categories most of the things in our world belong to, and because of that we can assign them places in our experience quickly and efficiently.

What follows is Taylor's (1985) description of the designative approach. At the end of the passage, when he mentions sentences and their truth conditions, Taylor is linking the designative function of language to analytic philosophy. We shall see that the alternative to the designative account, the expressivist approach, has been the view of philosophers identified with other traditions, primarily Romantic, existential, and hermeneutic.

> Designative theories, those which make designation fundamental, make meaning something relatively unpuzzling, unmysterious. That is a great part of their appeal. The meaning of words or sentences is explained by their relation to things or states of affairs in the world. There need be nothing more mysterious about meaning than there is about these things or states of affairs themselves. Of course, there is the relation of meaning itself, between word and thing, whereby one signifies or points to the other. But this can be made to seem

unmysterious enough. At the limit, if talk about signifying makes us nervous, we can just think of this as a set of correlations which have been set up between noises that we utter and certain world events or states. . . .

But if we are not all that metaphysically fastidious, we can simply take the designating relation as primitive and hope to illuminate meaning by tracing the correlations between words and things—or, in more contemporary guise, between sentences and their truth conditions.

(Taylor, 1985, pp. 220–221)

Designative theories of language can be traced back beyond the Enlightenment, but it was really Locke and Descartes who began to objectify mental contents, beginning the process by which "the furniture of the mind was accorded a thing-like existence" (Taylor, 1991/1995, p. 90). The reader is right to read this last sentence from Taylor as critical of objectification; but despite my sympathies with it, I also keep in mind it was this selfsame reification of mental contents that spurred the Enlightenment and eventually produced contemporary science, accomplishments about which we may be ambivalent, but which of course we cannot fail to profit from in our daily lives, and to appreciate and admire.

One of the most significant contemporary designative accounts of language is contained in the information processing model, which remains one of the dominant metaphors of cognitive psychology and cognitive neuroscience. In this view, language is one of several ways of processing information; and information is contained in packets or modules that can be coded in various ways and then combined and recombined to create all the varieties of human perception, affect, and thought. Language in the information processing model, as in all designative theories, is conceived as a form of *representation*, a word that compactly conveys the idea that words are labels for pre-existing information. Furthermore, language is transparent to the content of that information.[1] Bucci (1997) offers a sophisticated psychoanalytic version of such a model in her multiple code theory, in which information can be represented in verbal symbolic, nonverbal symbolic, and subsymbolic codes. Dissociation, in this frame of reference, is the dynamically enforced prevention of certain representations coded in one form from being coded in other forms of representation (Bucci, 2003, 2007a, b). Certain information coded subsymbolically or nonverbally, for instance, is dissociated by being dynamically cordoned off from linguistic representation.

In the most simple forms of the designative view, language is no more than a set of labels for the experience that it represents. This simple form of the view is probably the theory of language held implicitly by many, who do not give it a second thought. It is, one might say, the popular or taken-for-granted view of language. But I do not think it is realistic to attribute the simple form of the designative view to any serious student of language and/or cognition.

I turn now to the work of Bucci, since she is perhaps the most prominent psychoanalytic exponent of the designative view. Extending Vygotsky's (1934/1962) signal idea that "word meaning" is the result of binding together two elements, thought and speech, Bucci introduces a concept of her own, "emotional meaning," which is the binding together of not only thought and word, but also emotion. Noting the centrality of affect in psychoanalysis, Bucci invents this triadic version of Vygotsky's two part concept in order to make the information processing metaphor more useful for the scientific study of psychoanalytic concepts and practices.

Bucci encourages us to think about psychoanalysis as the promotion of new experiential organizations, created by linking subsymbolically encoded emotion that has been kept isolated from verbal and nonverbal symbolic modes of representation for unconscious defensive reasons. New links between the subsymbolic mode and symbolic representation allows the representational mind new access to feeling, in the form of "emotional meaning"; and because emotion is now linked with representation, it now becomes possible to know and think about that emotion.

The simplicity and comprehensiveness of the concept of emotional meaning are appealing. During psychoanalytic treatment, certain experience that had been coded only subsymbolically (the subsymbolic is the primary mode in which emotion is registered in the mind) is linked to linguistic representation, and can then be transformed in the ways that words make possible (Bucci, 1997). Attributing to language the capacity to organize and reorganize goes beyond the simplest versions of the designative view.

But despite that, I do not think that Bucci and other information processing theorists can accept the expressivist account of language. The core of the expressivist view is that verbal meaning is not merely representational, but that it *manifests* the person who creates the meaning. (Actually, we will come to see that *all* meaning manifests the person who creates it. But I get ahead of myself.) To use language, that is, is to *express oneself*. We can say that meaning, especially creative meaning, is inseparable from the person who creates it and from the particular language in which it comes to be. The words one chooses, when one is using language creatively, capture not only information but something about one's *being*, so that the meaning in the words is unique to the person speaking them. This kind of significance therefore differs substantially from meaning that pre-exists its linguistic representation. In the expressivist view, language plays a *constitutive* role in the construction of meaning.

Compare this view to Bucci's portrayal of language in the following passages: "While language has multiple levels of form, it operates, in its dominant information processing function, as a sequential, single-channel symbolic device, sending or receiving only one message at a given time" (Bucci, 1998, p. 176). A few sentences later Bucci goes on:

> Language is the medium that is most directly and obviously amenable to intentional control. It is the code that humans invented, the code we use to direct and regulate ourselves, to manipulate others, to communicate, and to lie. Language is the code in which the knowledge of the culture is preserved and transmitted; many—but not all—types of experience may be represented; many types of logical relationships can be expressed. We use language to indicate inclusion into categories and exclusion from them, to negate propositions, and to make generalizations and distinctions, although it is also the case that the symbols of natural language and logic do not precisely correspond. We require language to place events in a time sequence and to develop concepts of past and future. Language is the primary medium of psychoanalysis, although it is not the primary medium of thought, and certainly not of emotion.
>
> (p. 177)

The substance of my disagreement with this second passage is not primarily that it is simply wrong—although, if I understand properly, I must begin by disagreeing with some of its points. For instance, I cannot agree when Bucci says that "language is the medium that is most directly and obviously amenable to intentional control." I think she means that language is *routinely* under intentional control. For an expressivist, however, while we do control language in those instances in which we use it conventionally (when we read a textbook, for example, or chat on a superficial level), we do not control it when we use it creatively (a frequent enough occurrence, as I will explain below), any more than we control our affects. As a matter of fact, according to Merleau-Ponty (1945/1962), affects and the creative use of language have in common their origin in the body.[2] The unbidden quality of language often makes us onlookers at the creations of our most expressive and significant linguistic meanings (D.B. Stern, 1990, 1997, 2015). I can put it no better than I did in 1997: Language is not "passive, docile, or merely categorical. It is instead apocalyptic, intuitive, antic, possessed. Language is no servant; it is disobedient and revelatory. Language is a dervish" (p. 91).

But even someone who favors an expressivist account must admit that language *also* functions as designation. We simply could not get by without the conventional use of language. We often use words as labels for pre-existing meanings. Merleau-Ponty (1945/1962), in describing what he calls empirical speech, quotes approvingly Mallarmé's metaphor that speech of this kind is like the worn and immediately recognized coin placed silently in the hand. Our human world depends on words being used in this way; but this conventional use of language merely counts, or points at, meanings that already exist. Empirical speech cannot birth new meaning. Speech, says Merleau-Ponty (1962), is an "institution," by which he means that we possess "ready-made meanings" for the commonplace matters of the world. These matters arouse in us only "second order thoughts; these in turn are translated into other words which demand from us no real effort of expression and will demand from our hearers no effort of comprehension" (p. 184). In the same way that we depend on conventional linguistic meanings, we also depend upon the generalizations, distinctions, and categorizations that the representational function of language brings into being. And so language is often a code for the representation of experience that is also coded in other forms.

I don't see how anyone could disagree with any of these points. And therefore, as I said, my disagreement with the passage I have quoted from Bucci is not primarily that her account is simply wrong. (But see Note 7.) But I do think that the description is significantly incomplete. No designative theory of which I am aware goes *beyond* the portrayal of language as representation for pre-existing meaning—that is, beyond what Merleau-Ponty describes as the conventional use of language; and it is beyond the conventional use of language that we need to go.

There are many consequences of taking a designative view that I believe are bad for psychoanalysis. I will enumerate what I believe are some of the larger social, political, and even moral issues at the end of this chapter. One of the immediate intellectual and clinical consequences of accepting the designative account, though, would be the demise of the theory of unformulated experience, which would have to be discarded in a world in which unconscious meanings are fully formed. The theory of unformulated experience is thoroughly imbricated with expressivism.

## Psychoanalysis, quantitative empirical research, and language

Most of the researchers who subscribe to the information processing model and other designative theories of language are students of cognitive science. Many are experimental psychologists and cognitive neuroscientists. Some apply the information processing model to other fields, as Bucci applies it to psychoanalysis, to facilitate the quantitative scientific investigation of these other disciplines. It is true that the expressivist interpretation of language does not readily inspire quantitative empirical research. That is natural, since, unlike designative views of language, expressivism was not constructed with the aims of science in mind. *Information* is an objectivist conception, and so its existence, transformations, and the connections between its forms are amenable to study with methods devised for objective investigation. In fact, the concept of information was designed to be studied with such methods; the information model, because of its conception of bits of information that, like Legos, can be combined and recombined to make larger structures, is a prime example of what Bradd Shore (1996) refers to as "modularity schemas," which Shore believes have been a source of modern and postmodern order spanning phenomena as diverse as furniture, language, shopping, corporate organization, food, and television.

> Modularity is a design strategy that breaks complex wholes into elementary units that are understood to be recombinable into a variety of different patterns. A modular orientation to reality views a wide range of phenomena as assemblages, subject to decomposition and

recombination. It values qualities such as flexibility, efficiency, and control.

(p. 118)

*Meaning*, on the other hand, being a subjective phenomenon, and therefore phenomenologically defined, cannot easily be studied by traditional experimental methods. You can point at information; it is objectified; it exists apart from you. Even the information coded by one's own mind can be thought about as separate from oneself, because it has an objective existence. But you cannot create meaning by pointing at it, and it is not objectified; it is experienced in the first person. Meaning is subjective. Because it is the outcome of the continuous interpretive process that is living, and because interpretation is like stepping in the river (never the same river twice), the study of meaning requires the qualitative methods of hermeneutics. Charles Taylor (1985) writes

> Expression is the power of a subject; and expressions manifest things, and hence essentially refer us to subjects for whom these things can be manifest. . . . [W]hat expression manifests can only be made manifest in expression, so that expressive meaning cannot be accounted for independently of expression. If we make expression fundamental, it seems impossible to explain it in terms of something else; but it is itself a subject-related phenomenon, and hence does not allow of an objective science.
>
> (p. 221)

This is why the deviation of expressivist theories of language from the ideals and aims of science is not necessarily a matter of concern to some of us. For us, the validity of psychoanalysis, and especially psychoanalytic practice, does not depend for its verification on quantitative research (Hoffman, 2009). Quantitative research sometimes does, and should, play a role in stimulating psychoanalytic thought; and it does matter that our concepts and practices are consistent with research that we have reason to believe has a validity of its own. We respect science, but a scientific psychoanalysis is not necessarily the ideal for us. A scientific approach makes sense if you think about what Harry Stack Sullivan (1940/1953, 1953) referred to as "problems in living" as psychopathology (although some problems in living, of course, such as psychosis and autism, virtually require such an understanding, at least under some circumstances), because psychopathology is illness, and illness demands specifiable cures. But a scientific approach seems less inevitable or inescapable if you think of problems in living as matters of meaning. Problems of meaning do not demand specifiable cures; they require, instead, an expansion of those meanings, a new grasp of their contexts and significances, the creation of alternatives to them, the growth of a new capacity to unblock them. Does someone who is ashamed of his imperfections need to be "cured" of his shame? Is "cure" really the best way to refer to what is needed by someone with sexual, relationship, or work inhibitions that derive from what they have lived through and what they feel about it? Nor can meaning be thoroughly addressed as learned behavior or cognition, requiring only new learning, the extinction of the old learning, or the demonstration of its irrationality.

The ideal for psychoanalysis held by those of us who understand our field as a matter of meaning has more in common with models provided by the interpretive disciplines than the sciences: the arts and aesthetics, philosophy, the humanities, the interpretive social sciences, and education. Are quantitative scientific methods, for example, the appropriate way to test which theory of art is "correct"? Does the question even make sense? What about philosophy? Should we decide questions of epistemology with quantitative research? The very idea is an oxymoron, since an acceptance of the authority of quantitative research presupposes a particular epistemological commitment.

This is, in fact, exactly the problem encountered by those of us who believe that psychoanalysis is an interpretive, hermeneutic discipline, not a branch of natural science. We frequently face some variety of the challenge to produce scientific evidence for psychoanalytic positions, and the challenge comes not only from those outside our field but often from our psychoanalytic colleagues as well. Frequently there is little or no recognition that the assumptions that shape the demand for scientific verification can themselves be challenged.

Psychoanalysis, then, is an interpretive discipline for those of us who think this way. Its affectively charged meanings and moments cannot be torn away from their subjective origins. This point goes for both kinds of formulated experience, the verbal and the nonverbal, articulations and realizations. All are interpretations. The meanings that arise at any particular time are unique to the very specific purposes that motivated them and the details of the circumstances in which they come into being.

Because these contexts cannot be duplicated, psychoanalytic work cannot be replicated, which is one more reason that the quantitative empirical method, which demands replicability, is not the best means of studying clinical process.

Like the man who spoke prose for 40 years without knowing it, I have always held an expressivist position without having had a name for it. In turn, expressivism, perhaps more than any other part of hermeneutic philosophy, has led me to the interpretivist views I hold about psychoanalysis. And it is these views about psychoanalysis that have most deeply influenced the position I take about the relationship of psychoanalysis and science.[3]

## Information processing and expressivism in psychoanalysis

Do Bucci and other information processing theorists see expressivist accounts as consistent with their understandings of mind? I invite those researchers to offer such an answer themselves, and I hope that the answer reveals common ground. Bucci herself, however, does seem to have answered the question in the negative, assuming that she still believes what she wrote in an influential article from 1985:

> ... the patient comes into the psychoanalytic context with a particular version of his life history—a set of mental representations which it is the job of the treatment to uncover. The *new* version of the narrative can only be effectively constituted as a mental structure by *connecting with the old*, represented largely in nonverbal form in memory. Thus there would be a particular, definable basis for the effectiveness of one narrative over another; this is the directness and strength of its linkage to nonverbal representations stored in memory.
>
> ... [T]hese stored nonverbal representations have a structured and organized form, independent of the language in which they are eventually expressed. The model permits reference to private mental representations, whether conscious or not, as variables in empirically testable, verifiable propositions. The nonobservable variables are defined in terms of their functional relations to observables, using the methodology of the cognitive experimental approach.
>
> (Bucci, 1985, p. 600; italics from the original)

The response of information processing theorists to expressivist accounts of language may depend on the particular researcher or theorist answering the question, of course; but it does seem clear that Bucci, at least, rejects expressivist thinking, preferring a model in which language ideally plays a passive and transparent role in representing nonlinguistic material. In fact, Bucci's perspective, like many others, is inconsistent with the entire rationale for unformulated experience: unconscious experience for her is already there, fully formed; the analyst and the patient do not co-create whatever they make of it, but rather, in a traditional positivist way, they uncover it.

It does seem reasonable to imagine that expressivist accounts of language are problematic for information processing theorists. In expressivist accounts, because novel verbal meanings are inseparable from their authors and from the language used to make them, language cannot be conceptualized as a code for information that exists independently of it. Thoughts cannot be copied by words, or translated into words. Merleau-Ponty (1945/1962) could not be clearer on this point: "It is, indeed, obvious that speech cannot be regarded as a mere clothing for thought, or expression as the translation, into an arbitrary system of symbols, of a meaning already clear to itself" (p. 388). When language is used expressively, meanings and words are inextricable from one another, and they come into being simultaneously. The thought is alive in *these particular words*; other words would not be equivalent and would not suffice. Merleau-Ponty (1964) writes, "Language signifies when instead of copying thought it lets itself be taken apart and put together again by thought. Language bears the meaning of thought as a footprint signifies the movement and effort of a body" (p. 44). When language is used this way, it is the active shaper of meanings, not a passive code transparent to them. The very particular shape of the language is inseparable from its meaning. And so, contrary to the way Bucci puts it, meanings cannot be "independent of the language in which they are eventually expressed." Bits may be fungible; expressive meanings are not. The words we choose matter.

## Expressivist accounts of language

The writers who have most deeply affected my view of language are philosophers: Gadamer, Merleau-Ponty, and Charles Taylor. While the term "expressivism," as far as I know, is used only by Taylor, both

Merleau-Ponty and Gadamer, in their discussions of language, use the words "express" and "expression" just as Taylor does. I offer here a very brief review of Gadamer's and Merleau-Ponty's expressivist accounts of language, followed by a more extensive discussion of Taylor, whose work has been the most useful of the three to my proposition of the unity I have already mentioned between verbal and nonverbal meaning.

### Gadamer's expressivism

Gadamer is not a Romantic. He is less interested in subjectivity than either Taylor or Merleau-Ponty, because for Gadamer, understanding does not grow from one's individual grasp of the object, but instead from a dialogue with the other that reveals the truth that emerges between them. A conversation takes place, and the truth is neither mine nor yours, but ours. The object of understanding may be human or nonhuman, such as a work of art. The conversation that leads to understanding is not predetermined in any way; it can surprise us—and generally, if understanding comes about, it does. And so, for Gadamer, the focus is not on individual psychological processes. He does not emphasize the internal processes of the person trying to understand, but how that person and the object of understanding, which may be another person, eventually manage to create between them through conversation, and then agree on, the nature of what is to be understood.[4]

But while Gadamer does emphasize subjectivity less than expressivists with more Romantic views, his masterwork, *Truth and Method* (1965/2004), first published in German over fifty years ago, makes it clear that he is no objectivist, no child of the Enlightenment. He does not think that anything can be understood from the kind of removed, Cartesian position that objectivism requires, and so he does not favor objectivism in his account of language, i.e., he rejects models of understanding language in which signs are simply linked in predetermined fashion with nonverbal content. In the passage below, Gadamer may sound like a verbal mediation theorist, i.e., someone for whom thought and language are always indivisible, and for whom, therefore, thought is inevitably verbal in nature. (All students of cognition today, agreeing about the value of the large body of literature on nonverbal thinking, agree that the verbal mediation position is outmoded and unviable.) But Gadamer is not that kind of writer. He spent a good deal of his life trying to grasp how we understand art, much of which, like music and painting, is hardly verbal. One understands art not in words but as *manifestation* in a particular medium: ". . . understanding belongs to the encounter with the work of art itself, . . . on the basis of the *mode of being of the work of art itself*" (p. 87).

Gadamer's expressivism, then, is different than that of Merleau-Ponty or Taylor, both of whom more readily accept an everyday role in understanding for the expression of one's idiosyncratic perspective. In fact, for the latter two writers, it seems to be partially the clarity of our personal expressive qualities that determines the degree of success we have in grasping what we are trying to understand. For Gadamer, on the other hand, the process is less personal. In a sense, it is not the individual who tries to express himself through language; it is *experience itself* that becomes present in words, so that the outcome, when understanding finally arrives, has less to do with the particular partners in the conversation (as long as they are collaborating) and more to do with what they are talking about. In one of Gadamer's (1965/2004) statements of his view, he writes that, ". . . experience of itself seeks and finds words that express it" (p. 416). To use language, that is, is not to supply verbal labels for packets of pre-existing meaning, but to create or express meaning. Gadamer arrives at the passage that follows just after pointing out that it is incorrect to think of "the rational construction of an artificial language," a language of simple symbols in which one thing simply stands for another.

> In my view this path leads us away from the nature of language. Language and thinking about things are so bound together that it is an abstraction to conceive of the system of truths as a pregiven system of possibilities of being for which the signifying subject selects corresponding signs. A word is not a sign that one selects, nor is it a sign that one makes or gives to another; it is not an existent thing that one picks up and gives an ideality of meaning in order to make another being visible through it. This is mistaken on both counts . . . Experience is not wordless to begin with, subsequently becoming an object of reflection by being named, by being subsumed under the universality of the word. Rather, experience of itself seeks and finds words that express it. We seek the right word—i.e., the word that really belongs to the thing—so that in it the thing comes into language.
>
> (pp. 416–417)

### Merleau-Ponty's expressivism

Merleau-Ponty's philosophy is phenomenological, heavily influenced by Husserl and Heidegger. His major work is *The Phenomenology of Perception*, his first book, which appeared (in French) in 1945 but was first published in English only in 1962; that book then was followed by a number of others. He was the only widely known phenomenologist of the first half of the 20th century to involve himself with academic psychology, which gives him a particular interest for psychologists, psychiatrists, and psychoanalysts (see, for example, Hoeller, 1993). He mounted a challenge to Descartes's dualistic epistemology, the *cogito*, which holds that the world is defined by our minds, and that mind and world, subject and object, are separate. For Merleau-Ponty, instead, consciousness, the world, and the human body are inter-related and engaged with one another in complex, inextricable ways. Experience is the outcome of these engagements. The *cogito* is replaced by the *body-subject*. One commentator has gone so far as to say that,

> In the field of Western philosophy, Maurice Merleau-Ponty is something like the patron saint of the body . . . [N]one can match the bulk of rigorous, systematic, and persistent argument that Merleau-Ponty provides to prove the body's primacy in human experience and meaning.
>
> (Shusterman, 2004, p. 151)

The function of perception, closely related to the body, was especially crucial for Merleau-Ponty. The heart of knowing was not for him the objectively defined object of the natural sciences and the kind of rational, objective observations correlated with it, made from within the disengaged mind. Knowing or experiencing is instead created by the body and its sensorimotor functions, an expression of the relation of the *body-subject* and the world. All subjectivity emerges from the body and is rooted in that physicality; as a matter of fact, Merleau-Ponty conceives of the body as *incarnate subjectivity*.

> I am my body, at least wholly to the extent that I possess experience, and yet at the same time my body is as it were a "natural" subject, a provisional sketch of my total being. Thus experience of one's own

body runs counter to the reflective procedure which detaches subject and object from one another, and which gives us only the thought about the body, or the body as an idea, and not the experience of the body or the body in reality

(1945/1962, pp. 198–199)

Language, too, emerges from perception and the body, and it does so continuously. Language can be used in a way that is pre-determined, on the basis of habitual, earlier instances of language use (Mallarmé's worn coin in the palm of the hand). But language that matters—language that brings new experience into being—is always a spontaneous, creative response in the present, in which the words used, and the way they are used, remain unformulated until the moment of their emergence. Perception, and thus language, grows from our nonconscious, preconceptual understanding of objects in the world. We understand objects because we are objects ourselves, bodies, part of the same natural order as the objects we perceive. Language is an *expression of our relation* to the world. In the following passage, Merleau-Ponty (1945/1962) contrasts the conventional and creative uses of language, suggesting that creative speech is not a set of labels but is instead inevitably expressive.

It may be said that the body is "the hidden form of being ourself", or on the other hand, that personal existence is the taking up and manifestation of a being in a given situation. If we therefore say that the body expresses existence at every moment, this is the sense in which a word expresses thought . . . [W]e must . . . recognize a primary process of signification in which the thing expressed does not exist apart from the expression . . .

(p. 166)

One more statement of Merleau-Ponty's expressivism (I have cited this statement earlier in this chapter) comes from a discussion in which he has just referred to the "ready-made" or "second order" meanings of empirical speech, words that require "no real effort of expression" and "demand from our hearers no effort of comprehension." In these very common uses of language, the "decisive step of expression" has already been taken. It is that original expression that matters, that opens up the world and changes it:

Our view of man will remain superficial so long as we fail to go back to that origin, so long as we fail to find, beneath the chatter of words, the primordial silence, and as long as we do not describe the action which breaks this silence. The spoken word is a gesture, and its meaning, a world.

[1945/1962, p. 184]

## Charles Taylor: The constitutive properties of language

Taylor, a hermeneutic philosopher, has contributed the most extensive and explicitly relevant discussions of expressivism, and he is the only writer I have come across who has described the history of the controversy between designative and expressivist theories. Actually, it minimizes Taylor's contribution to describe as history his account of the origins of expressivism, because Taylor's contemporary description of expressivism is largely the reason that a coherent history of expressivism became recognizable in the first place.

## Condillac and Herder

I will not attempt to summarize the history of philosophy covered by Taylor. Let me focus on just one episode, one that Taylor himself touches on repeatedly: the reaction to the work of Condillac by Herder, an eighteenth century philosopher who, Taylor tells us, was rescued from relative obscurity by his recognition by Isaiah Berlin as a crucial figure in the study of language. Offering this history is an opportunity to introduce Taylor's views, especially those about the constitutive properties of language. Taylor's expressivism is a natural outgrowth of these views, and I will return to it below.

The episode in question between Condillac and Herder is perhaps the first salvo in the centuries-long argument between those who favor a constitutive/expressivist theory of language and those who prefer designative theories. Taylor calls Herder a "hinge" figure, signifying his role in inaugurating the new view. The following account is drawn from several of Taylor's (1985, 1989, 1991/1995, 1992/1995) papers, although I follow the 1991/1995 paper most closely in discussing Taylor's views of Herder, and I quote from that paper extensively.[5] Taylor's language is itself a fine example of the expressive union of word and meaning. It virtually demands quotation.

The eighteenth century was a time of fascination with origins, such as social evolution. It was natural for an interest in the sources of language to develop. One of the most influential of such theories was that of Condillac, who invented a fable to propose his ideas. Leaning on Locke's designative theory of language, Condillac imagined two children in a desert, expressing themselves by making certain natural cries and gestures. Condillac calls these cries and gestures "natural signs," and he contrasts them with language, which is composed of "instituted signs." The fable is meant to explain how the second kind of sign arose from the first.

Let us say, suggests Condillac, that one child sees the other utter a cry at a moment of distress. The observing child links the cry with the source of distress, and the first word has been instituted. Thereafter, whenever one of the children makes that cry, the other looks about to find the same source of distress. The cry, then, comes to stand for the source of distress. Over many such occasions, the children's vocabulary increases, one word at a time.

In criticizing Condillac's view, Herder claims not only that this depiction of the process of language acquisition is too simple, as we might say today if we were offering a critique of the kind of behaviorist and designative accounts of language proposed by Watson or Skinner. Herder says something more subtle than that. He claims that (in Taylor's words),

> As an account of origins, it presupposes just what we want explained. It takes the relation of signifying for granted, as something that the children already grasp instinctively or that will unproblematically occur to them upon reflection . . . His explanation amounts to saying that words arose because they were already there.
>
> (Taylor, 1991/1995, pp. 80–81)

That is, in Condillac's interpretation of his fable, the words have nothing to do with *formulating the meanings*; the meanings were ready-made, pre-existing, and required only verbal labels, as in what I have already described as designative theories of language.

Taylor goes on to say that this designative view that Herder was attacking continues to exist in today's philosophy, although in a much more subtle and sophisticated form. He singles out Donald Davidson, whose view he characterizes thusly:

> Davidson insists that when I understand you, I can be seen to be applying a theory of the meaning of your utterances, which maps these onto features of the objective world. The descriptive kernel of your utterances maps onto their truth conditions.
>
> (Taylor, 1991/1995, pp. 81–82)

Language, in these terms, is a fairly straightforward matter of representation, as it is for Bucci. Davidson's position, according to Taylor, is not merely that differences in interpretation between two people are probably reflected in differences in how those two people define what to interpret. Instead, claims Taylor, Davidson and others who take similar views make the "much stronger claim that agreement about truth conditions is criterial for agreement in understanding" (1991/1995, p. 82). Taylor is claiming here that, in Davidson's view, understanding should always be present if there is agreement about the link between a word and what it stands for.

If we have the word "etiquette," for example, and we know the phenomena "etiquette" refers to, we should understand the meaning involved. But Taylor says that this is obviously not correct. He invites us to imagine a robot that could make the correct correspondence between words and their referents. There is no way, in Davidson's frame of reference or others like it, to make sense of the fact that such a robot, no matter how exactly it matched word and world, would actually understand nothing. Imagine the robot being outfitted with the word "etiquette" and the correspondence of this word to the phenomena to which it refers. We know without being told that the robot would not understand the meanings involved, which in this case go far beyond word–world correspondences.

But it is interesting to note that it is not necessarily so easy to specify the nature of what the robot would not grasp.

It is whatever the robot is missing, Taylor implies, that Herder believed was also missing from Condillac's account. Whatever it is, it is the same thing that Wittgenstein demonstrates in his discussion of "ostensive definition," in which he shows that, contrary to some opinions, you cannot define a word merely by giving multiple examples of it, or of its use.

Wittgenstein shows that these examples cannot add up to a coherent meaning for the word unless you posit that there is also a linguistic "background" that you consult in considering the collection of examples, a web or network of meanings that lends coherence to the several instances of the meaning. (Taylor [1991/1995] tells us that this image of language as a web, which will come up again in this chapter, comes from Humboldt.)

## Forks on the left and elbows on the table

Imagine having no such linguistic "background," or web of meanings, and being presented with the following collection of actions: opening the door for someone, putting the fork on the left side of the plate, speaking softly in the library, and not singing at the table. Without the background meanings to make them cohere, these examples would remain an arbitrary, and perhaps hilariously arbitrary, assemblage. With the addition of the idea of background, of course, we not only see the sense in the assemblage; we have the sense, sometimes a quite satisfying sense, of what Taylor calls the "rightness" of the meaning.

Signals need to be differentiated from human language, although the capacities to respond to both signals and language are achievements. To know how to respond to a signal is "to learn to apply it appropriately in the furtherance of some non-linguistically-defined purpose or task" (Taylor, 1991/1995, p. 84). The children in Condillac's fable, for instance, learned to apply the cry to the identification of a source of distress.

But in a signal, the relationship between word and what it refers to is unidirectional: the "rightness" of the signal is defined by success at some task. In this case, the correct identification of the source of distress makes the cry the right "word." But the same thing is not true the other way around: understanding and succeeding at the task does not require the correctness of the signal. The "rightness" of the "word," in other words, does not play any role at all in illuminating the children about the meaning of the source of distress. The "rightness" of a signal is only factual; it does not carry the penumbra of meaning that real language does, a penumbra that, because it connects implicitly to the entire linguistic web, including "the circle of the unexpressed" (Lipps, cited by Linge, 1976), cannot fail to participate in creating the meaningfulness of whatever it refers to. The signal, on the other hand, because it is merely a label for meaning that pre-existed it, does not contribute to the meaningfulness of whatever it refers to. It is nothing more than a pointer, Mallarmé's worn coin in the hand.

Taylor wants us to see that the "rightness" of a truly *linguistic* word or expression works in *both* directions: rightness of the words is defined by the task, as is the case for signals; and simultaneously the task is defined by the feeling we have that the words we are using for it are right. We correctly identify the parts of life we understand as etiquette by using the word "etiquette"; and we know what etiquette *is* only because we have the word that identifies it. *Language, that is, has constitutive properties*: it participates in creating the meanings to which it refers. This initial participation of language in the creation of meanings, in other words, is what, later on, allows us to identify and understand what is being referred to when the word is used. I refer the reader back to the example I used in Chapter 3 of a dweller in the Amazon rainforest who had never heard a Viennese waltz, and whose bafflement vanished when his anthropologist interlocutor told him that this strange noise was a new, foreign version of the kind of sounds the forest people made with certain instruments during tribal ceremonies. We can imagine that, thereafter, the Amazonian did the internal, mental equivalent of nodding sagely whenever he heard a Viennese waltz: "Yes!," he would think, perhaps with lingering amazement, but definitely with a sense of linguistic "rightness," "that is *music!*"

This bidirectionality separates language from signals. It is one way to describe what Condillac missed: the cries of the children in his fable, even when they were "instituted," remained mere signals. They did not attain the status of language, because, while the source of distress came to define the significance of the cry, it could not be said, contrary to the case of the word "etiquette," that the cry reciprocally defined the nature of the distress. The relationship remained unidirectional, and the relationship between word and world remained arbitrary. The cry that signified distress could just as well signify anything else. The cry, that is, does not participate in the creation of the meaning of the source of distress, because the meaning pre-existed the cry.

The word "etiquette," on the other hand, *does* participate in the creation of meaning, and what it refers to did *not* pre-exist the word we use for it. The sound of the word "etiquette" is probably arbitrary, a sound that hypothetically could be attached to any meaning (although my own sense is that, probably because I am so familiar with it, it has a sound that seems to belong to its meaning, perhaps because of the onomatopoeic association with "delicate"). But once we have learned the word "etiquette" and its referent, the world looks different than it did before. If someone refers to putting the fork on the left side of the plate, thinking of this action as "etiquette" has Taylor's "irreducible linguistic rightness." We need the word to know the world. *We need the verbal, that is, to know the nonverbal.*

> Consider a gamut of activities, including disinterested scientific description, articulating one's feelings, the evocation of a scene in verse, a novelist's description of character. A metaphor someone coins is right, profound. There is a kind of "getting it right" here . . . Otherwise put, if we want to think of a task or goal which would help to clarify the rightness of words that occur in the human activities just mentioned, it would itself have to be defined in terms like truth, descriptive adequacy, richness of evocation, or something of the sort. We can't define the rightness of the word by the task without defining the task in terms of the rightness of the words.
>
> (1991/1995, p. 84)

## The linguistic dimension

This bidirectional "rightness" is what Taylor calls "the linguistic dimension" of human living. In language, in other words, the relationship between words and meaning is not arbitrary; words and meaning, when used creatively, are inseparable. Language is not straightforwardly representational; it has constitutive properties. This is Taylor's interpretation of what Herder believed was missing from Condillac's story; and it is Taylor's (1991/1995) interpretation of what Herder meant when he claimed that Condillac "presupposes just what we want explained" (p. 80). The sense of irreducible linguistic rightness comes from belonging to a linguistic community and therefore consulting the vibrations of the vast web of language whenever we use words. It is this sense of rightness that is Taylor's (1991/1995) answer (via his imagination of Herder) to Condillac:

> . . . Condillac endows his children from the beginning with the capacity to understand what it means for a word to stand for something,

what it means therefore to talk about something with a word. But *that* is the mysterious thing. Anyone can be taught the meaning of a word, or even guess at it, or even invent one, once they have language. But what is this capacity, which we have and animals don't, to endow sounds with meaning, to grasp them as referring to, and used to talk about, things?

(1991/1995, p. 81; italics from the original)

Herder did try to say what he meant by the special quality language has, and Taylor interprets him in support of Taylor's own sense of the bedrock significance of the linguistic dimension and its corollary, irreducible linguistic rightness.

Herder called his version of the crucial factor "reflection." He used as an example the case of the lamb. Lambs, he pointed out, are for some animals completely irrelevant and therefore unnoticed; but for others lambs are quite relevant as the object of some nonlinguistic purpose (food for the lion, sex for the ram). In neither case—irrelevance or instrumental/instinctual purpose—is there a process of reflection. For Herder, reflection is the capacity to focus on the lamb *without* any such instrumental purpose.[6] Herder imagines that the thing that distinguishes the lamb is its bleating, and that an onomatopoeic imitation of the bleat may have been the first word for lamb. The lamb is *recognized*, in other words, as "the bleating one." Taylor writes:

In other words, in the reflective stance the lamb is first recognized as a lamb; it is first recognized as an object rightly classed as "the bleating one." An issue of rightness arises, which cannot be reduced to success in some life task. This for Herder is inseparable from language. It is defined by the capacity to focus on objects by recognizing them, and thus creates, as it were, a new space around us. Instead of being overcome by the ocean of sensations as they rush by us, we are able to distinguish one wave, and hold it in clear, calm attention. It is this new space of attention, of distance from the immediate instinctual significance of things, that Herder wants to call reflection.

(1991/1995, p. 88)

Herder is often a stand-in for Taylor, a foil allowing Taylor a way to express his own views, and this is nowhere more true than in Taylor's claim that, for Herder, Condillac's ideas about language are a classic form of an "enframing theory." In Condillac's view, language is understood to be composed of elements that preceded the appearance of language in human living: ideas, signs or signals, and their association with one another. Both before the arrival of language and after it, imagination and the association of ideas take place. The only difference, once language is in place, is that the mind is in control. Condillac's theory establishes "the maximal possible continuity between before and after . . . The elements are the same, combination continues, only the direction changes" (Taylor, 1992/1995, p. 102–103).

According to Condillac, then, along with many of the designative theorists who followed him, at some point in human development, language was "added onto" the mind. But the mind did not change in any qualitative sense; it remained more or less the same as it was. This is a view with which Bucci (1997) explicitly agrees: she believes that in the course of evolution language has been spread over the mind like a blanket, adding a separate representational system but not affecting the systems that she believes preceded it:

> . . . the new and powerful representational system of language has been overlaid on a set of other representational systems that were previously in place, but without adequate mechanisms for integration of the systems having been developed.
>
> (Bucci, 1997, p. 321)[7]

Taylor, on the other hand, argues that Herder's "reflection," along with Taylor's own conception of the linguistic dimension, are much more than an enframing theory. The attitude behind "reflection," in fact, is the heart of the reason that Herder was so frustrated by Condillac's argument. Herder (with Taylor agreeing enthusiastically) believes that language was not added on, as in information processing theories, but that it actually changed the human mind in a qualitative way. The linguistic dimension is not one of several alternate codes, but something that human beings live within. It has changed the nature of experiencing. We shall see that this view does nothing to discount the significance of nonverbal meaning, although it does affect the way we understand it. It may also be a good idea to acknowledge at this point that, of course, even after the rise of language, humans maintained objects of fear or desire, and so we still frequently deal with the world outside the linguistic dimension, on the basis of instrumental purposes that do not involve what Herder called reflection.

Recognizing that his view will be discounted by "proponents of chimp language, talking computers, and truth-conditional theories of meaning" (Taylor, 1991/1995, p. 89), for all of whom his objections are liable to seem "gratuitous and puzzling" (p. 89), Taylor tries to understand more closely why those who take a designative view of language feel as they do. He concludes that the crucial factor in irreducible linguistic rightness is what I have already referred to as the background of our action, "something we usually lean on without noticing" (Taylor, 1991/1995, p. 89).

> Language is not an assemblage of separable instruments, which lie as it were transparently to hand, and which can be used to marshal ideas, this use being something we can fully control and oversee. Rather, it is something in the nature of a web, which, to complicate the image, is present as a whole in any one of its parts. To speak is to touch part of the web, and this makes the whole resonate. Because the words we use now only have sense through their place in the whole web, we can never in principle have a clear oversight of the implications of what we say at any moment. Our language is always more than we can encompass; it is in a sense inexhaustible.
>
> (Taylor, 1985, p. 231)

The mistake made in designative theories of language is the obscuring of the continuously resonating background or web by the implicit building of that background into every single sign. In that way, the vibrations of the web of language that are set off by every word we use are made invisible, and the constitutive properties of language are missed. *This* is how people who take a designative view of language can hold their views: the background of language is so thoroughly assumed that it disappears; it is so present that it is absent. We live in it so naturally that we do not see it, the way a fish lives in water.

These ideas are once again reminiscent of Wittgenstein, the author of what is doubtlessly the most thorough and influential account of what we might call "linguistic holism" (Taylor [1991/1995] calls it "the holism of meaning" [p. 93]). According to Wittgenstein, a word has meaning only within an entire lexicon and a context of language practices, which, in their turn, are embedded in a form of life.

## Manifestation: The unity of the verbal and the nonverbal

It is a short step from these arguments to Taylor's recognition of the expressivist qualities of language. In fact, it is a short step to the much broader position Taylor takes that expression actually *constitutes* the linguistic dimension. Let me lay out the case he makes (Taylor, 1991/1995, pp. 92–93).

Language arose in what Taylor calls "an animal form." Those among whom this scheme developed already took instrumental stances toward the objects of their worlds—that is, stances "to things figuring as obstacles, supports, and the like." These stances are "situated," and their contexts are physical. The stances taken by prelinguistic humans were "literally bodily attitudes or actions on or toward objects," stances motivated by some kind of need or want. Reflection, the linguistic dimension, arose as a new stance toward objects, and as such, it could not be "in its origins entirely unconnected to bodily posture or action." And Herder's reflection, too, was situated. But whatever the situated action is that ends up being the embodiment of reflection must differ from earlier actions, because those actions were nonlinguistic. Reflection must be embodied in a *new form* of action, an action that *conveys* reflection, makes it public. Reflection, after all, implies the *knowing* of something, and so it becomes unavoidable that others know, too. To know is to be able to tell.

Part of the linguistic dimension is also the awareness that all reflection is *my* reflection, *my* thought. Language makes it possible for me to know that *I* am the one having the thought. And therefore, a new stance that conveys reflection must also be one that *expresses* reflection. Thus was speech born. Speech, and then the linguistic dimension that it inaugurated, is expressive in its very origins. Anyone who sees the mind as embodied (e.g., Merleau-Ponty, 1945/1962) is drawn to a similar line of argument.

> In order for given words to mean something, to designate their respective objects, we have to be able to speak, that is, give expression to this reflective awareness, because it is only through this expression through speech, that this reflective awareness comes about. A being

who cannot speak cannot have it. We only have it, in contrast to animals, because we talk about things. Expression realizes, and is therefore fundamental.

(Taylor, 1985, p. 229)

## Expressivism and the nonverbal

I have gone to some pains, in Chapter 3, to conceptualize the formulation of nonverbal meaning. I hardly want my interest in expressivist theories of language to obscure that development. Which is to say that Taylor's expressivism would not be useful to me if it were limited to language, because then I might leap out of the frying pan (i.e., an undue privileging of the verbal) only to find myself jumping into the fire (a different view that nevertheless preserves the privileging). Happily, though, Taylor's thought is not limited in that way, nor is that of Gadamer or Merleau-Ponty. Taylor does get to his expressivism via the *route* of language, but he goes on to describe expression in much broader terms, and in a way that encompasses both verbal and nonverbal meaning. He believes (Taylor, 1989) that the appearance of what Herder called reflection was simply the beginning of a way of life in the West that has become widely practiced and accepted since Herder and others began to describe it in the eighteenth century. This way of life, in fact, grows from the same sense of the individual self, with its depth and uniqueness, that eventually spawned psychoanalysis.

But I anticipate myself. For the time being, the important thing is that expression actually *constitutes* the linguistic dimension. Without language, humans did not live within the sense that they had meanings to make and impart. It is that "new space around us" created by the linguistic dimension that freed us from "being overcome by the ocean of sensations as they rush by us." Now, "we are able to distinguish one wave, and hold it in clear, calm attention" (Taylor, 1991/1995, p. 88). This "owning" of experience could not have arisen without the possibility of expressive meaning; to know experience as one's own is to sense its expressive nature and to exist within a new sense of oneself as life's author. The advent of language was just the beginning. Without language, we could not have a sense of agency. The changes wrought when humans entered the linguistic dimension extended far beyond the use of words, into the broader realm of "manifestation."

Language, that is, changed the mind in a much more profound way than merely adding a new form of representation. The advent of language was also the birth of a new *kind* of meaning, a variety of meaning that brought the reflection inaugurated by language to meanings shaped in media far removed from words. Language was not simply a new set of labels; it was the beginning of a new unity of meaning.

Taylor (1985) writes that "something is expressed, when it is embodied in such a way as to be made manifest" (p. 219). Elsewhere (Taylor, 1989) he expands the thought:

> To express something is to make it manifest in a given medium. I express my feelings in my face; I express my thoughts in the words I speak or write. I express my vision of things in some work of art, perhaps a novel or a play. In all these cases we have the notion of making something manifest, and in each case in a medium with certain specific properties.
>
> (p. 374)

And that is not all. The doctrine of expressivism, Taylor (1985) tells us,

> gives a view of language as a range of activities in which we express/realize a certain way of being in the world. And this way of being has many facets. It is not just the reflective awareness by which we recognize things as—, and describe our surroundings; but also that by which we come to have the proper human emotions, and constitute our human relations ... The range of activity is not confined to language in the narrow sense, but rather encompasses the whole gamut of symbolic expressive capacities in which language, narrowly construed, is seen to take its place
>
> (1985, p 234)

We have also seen this idea in the work of Gadamer and Merleau-Ponty: meaning makes manifest the person who creates it. There is every justification in Taylor's version of this conception to expand it even further. Feelings are expressed not only in one's face, but in one's gestures, prosody, and the way one participates in living, one's personal style. An important part of that expressive living is what I described in Chapter 3 as nonverbal meaning, including not only mental content that can rightly be called symbolic but affect states and the procedural meanings that the Boston Group (D.N. Stern et al, 1998) calls implicit relational knowing and that Bucci (1997) describes as subsymbolic.

We are so familiar with the expressive quality of the other's interaction with us that we seldom even notice it explicitly; and of course we are just as ceaselessly expressive from our own side of the interaction. Since the invention of language, all of the meanings we create in life, verbal and nonverbal, are expressive, or at least potentially expressive, whether we are aware of creating them or not, and whether we are aware of their expressive qualities or not.

I suggested in Chapter 3 that we accept, select, and use the potential meanings that we can tolerate (that "feel like me"), and that we do not accept and use meanings that are intolerable to us (that do not "feel like me"). To accept and use is to formulate the unformulated. We accept, and then articulate and realize, those meanings that feel as if they belong to us, that have a quality of "me-ness." I can now come full circle and say the same thing in the language I have introduced in this chapter: the meanings that we *express* or *manifest* are the meanings that "feel like me."

Procedural meanings and states of affect are just as liable as more explicitly symbolic verbal and nonverbal meanings to vary along a scale of perceived "me-ness". Actually, they may be even more amenable to the theory of manifestation than symbolic meanings. Think of the example of the person who is very anxious about sensuality and sexuality, for instance, another example from Chapter 3. In discussing this illustration I suggested that anxiety might prevent this person from being able to flirt, or to grasp and participate in someone else's flirtation with him or her. Flirtation is certainly one of those parts of life that takes place in the realm that we can refer to as implicit relational knowing, or as affect states and procedural meaning. Flirting is something that you do, most of the time, without thinking about it at all. It comes naturally, or it doesn't.

Now, if the procedural meaning that flirting requires does not "feel like me," it is not accepted; and if it is not accepted, it cannot be selected and used in relatedness. If it *does* feel like "me," on the other hand, it *is* used; and the quality of the flirtation will be a personal expression of the flirter.

With Taylor, then, I want to define manifestation as the expressivism we see in theories of language, but now broadened to encompass all forms of meaning. We have seen that the bond between verbal meanings and the words we use to express them is ineluctable. Expressivism, that is, implies language's constitutive properties. In the same way, we now see that *all* meanings are inseparable from the forms of their expression. *All* the media of human experience, that is, have constitutive properties; when meaning is creative and not merely conventional or designative, there is *always* an ineluctable bond between meaning and medium. Just as the words we choose are so often part and parcel of the meanings they convey, so too are gestures, prosody, facial expression, and styles of movement often inseparable from the meanings *they* convey. By "manifestation" I mean to refer to the expressive qualities of *all* meaning. Merleau-Ponty (1945/1962) makes precisely this point:

> There is no fundamental difference between the various modes of expression, and no privileged position to any of them on the alleged ground that it expresses a truth in itself. Speech is as dumb as music, music as eloquent as speech. Expression is everywhere creative, and what is expressed is always inseparable from it.
>
> (p. 391)

Just as we sense that certain well-chosen words have an irreducible rightness, so do we sense that certain nonverbal expressions, such as facial configurations or tone of voice, also have irreducible rightness. We often describe this nonverbal rightness as authenticity or genuineness; and we mean by those words that these expressions, just like the right words, convey exactly what we want to convey. We sense that they are true to our intentions, or to the intentions of the other—although, in fact, we may only grasp our intentions *through* their expression. Our expression and our sense of ourselves are one. And we know, too, when we have been understood, because the other's affective response has that same rightness (Vivona, 2013); we can tell from the details and the whole of the other's response that whatever we have tried to get across has been grasped. The other's response, affecting us deeply, may even help us know more clearly or fully what we expressed in the first place.

We also sense the absence of rightness, again in both our own experience and the response of the other. A slight diminution of naturalness might suggest to us, for example, that we are not quite sure we mean what we are saying, and we might sense the same thing in the response of the other. At other times, we hide our insincerity from ourselves, and avoid observation of any insincerity we sense in the other. To convince ourselves of the naturalness of our expression at such moments is one meaning of what we intend by self-deception.

Should the absence of rightness be considered an expression—a manifestation? No. Despite the fact that such experience can be as informative as the presence of rightness, the absence of rightness is not expressive. Expression is something that we grasp directly, according to Taylor. "Something is manifest when it is available for all to see. It is not manifest when there are just signs of its presence, from which we can infer that it is there . . ." (1985, p. 219). Your car parked outside your office, which tells me that you are there, is not an expression, for instance. A facial expression does constitute a manifestation, though, because it manifests feeling directly. On the other hand, a tic, says Taylor, is not expressive, because its meaning is not conveyed by its form. The meaning must be inferred, as I infer your presence in your office from your car parked out front. A tic is a signal, not a linguistic sign.

We are usually no more able to specify exactly why our own or the other's emotional responses have a rightness about them than we are able to describe why certain words are precisely right. They just are. Irreducible linguistic rightness is what makes great writing, and irreducible nonverbal (procedural) rightness is what makes great acting, and other arts, too. Sometimes great painting, for instance, is due not only to the success of the artist's image but also to our sense of the authenticity of the gesture that actualized the artist's intention. Merleau-Ponty (1964), for instance, movingly describes a slow-motion film of Matisse in the act of painting, vivifying for us the act of creation as expressive activity. Unsurprisingly (because it is as much Merleau-Ponty's view as it is Taylor's), and in agreement with what I am calling manifestation, Merleau-Ponty ends his loving gloss of the master at work by pointing out that it is the expressive quality of the painting that makes it "no different" than "truly expressive speech."[8] Taylor makes the same point:

> . . . [W]e cannot draw a boundary around the language of prose in the narrow sense, and divide it off from those other symbolic-expressive creations of man: poetry, music, art, dance, etc. If we think of language as essentially used to say something *about* something, then prose is indeed in a category of its own. But once one takes language as being expressive in this way, that is, where the expression constitutes what it expresses, then talking *about* is just one of the provinces

constituted by language; the constitution of human emotion is another, and in this some uses of prose are akin to some uses of poetry, music, and art.

(1985, p. 233; italics from the original)

## Manifestation and unconscious process

*To whom* are meanings expressive? *Who sees* the ways we manifest ourselves? The most conventional use of expression is public, of course: our meanings are expressively meaningful to others. They hear the thoughts we formulate in words, but they also hear, see, and feel much more than that; they are presented with the expressions of our affective life. Now, the interesting thing here is that we may express parts of life to others that we do not see in ourselves; and of course they may also express to us meanings that remain hidden to them. Psychoanalysts see things about their patients that their patients cannot themselves see; and patients, too, make observations of their analysts of things invisible to them.

We think most easily of expression going on in this way—that is, between people; but expression also takes place within us, from one part to another. We learn about our own feelings via our expressions of them in what we generally call our "inner lives." We know our natures by articulating and realizing what we find within ourselves. We observe and sense one self-state from within another.[9] We express ourselves to ourselves. In the meantime, we are expressing a somewhat different picture of our natures to others.

What about, though, those meanings that we seem to express, but that we remain unaware of? What about, for instance, the expression of fear that flits across one's face clearly enough to be seen by the other, but without fear registering in one's own mind? Or a quaver in one's voice that is not reflected in one's feelings, and that is registered by the other, but that one does not hear oneself? Or the regularities in our dealings with others that those others see much more clearly than we do ourselves? What about, in other words, all those observations we can make of the other that we cannot make of ourselves? Should we consider these phenomena to be manifestations? Are they expressions of the person who manifests them?

To answer this question requires us to add a level of complexity to the argument that Taylor, Merleau-Ponty, and Gadamer advance in these matters. What we must add is the fragmentation of the self (or the fact of unconsciousness, if we use that model instead). If personhood were homogenous, if there were no internal differentiations, if the mind had no alien part—if, that is, there were no unconscious—then all expression would derive from a single source, and we would have little choice but to consider a facial expression we display without being aware of it to be the same as the facial tic Taylor used as an example of a piece of conduct that is actually inference rather than expression. That is, if there were no unconscious, our sense of "me-ness" would always have to be criterial for the ascription of expression.

But in psychoanalysis, of course, we take unconscious processes for granted. My own preference is to think about unconscious processes in terms of dissociation and the fragmented, multiple self (Stern, 1997, 2010a); but for the purpose of the point I am making at the moment, any conception of unconsciousness will do. In psychoanalysis, in other words, we can conceive of a straightforward emotional expression that is divorced from conscious intention, and that is nevertheless unquestionably a manifestation of the person whose expression it is. Dreams are one example that leap to mind; symptoms are another. As a matter of fact, psychoanalysis depends on such disavowed expressions: without them, there would be no hints of the mysteries of the inner life.

## Designation and manifestation: A dialectic

A designative meaning correlates a symbol with some piece of the world, and this correlation can, at least in principle, be objectively studied. The correlation is always the same; the meaning is always the same. Context does not affect it, or affects it very little. Expressive meaning, on the other hand, is all about context. We cannot even say that context is "embedded" in expressive meaning. That way of putting the matter is insufficient, because it suggests that context merely influences meaning, and we are talking about something more than influence. Context *is part of* expressive meaning. That is what it means to say that expressive meaning is constitutive. Taylor (1985) puts the point in the form of a rhetorical question: "What is it that we see in things when we understand them as [linguistic] signs that we do not when we fail to apprehend them as such, but just as the furniture of a non-expressive universe?" (p. 218; word in parentheses added).

It will be no secret, if you have read this far, that expressive meaning interests me much more than designative meaning. That attitude is in some ways unfair to designative meaning. It would be unrealistic not to recognize that designative meaning is the most frequent kind of meaning in human life. Most of the time, we are not creating new meaning, but doing what we need to do to keep on keeping on—and familiar, designative meanings are the medium of keeping-on.

In fact, if we were to be strictly accurate, we should really describe more subtly the two kinds of linguistic theories I have called designative and expressivist: we should refer to designative/expressivist theories and expressivist/designative theories, the order of the terms indicating the degrees of emphasis in the respective theories on the alternative forms of meaning. No doubt most designative theories preserve some place for expressive meaning. An excellent example does not leap to mind here, but it seems likely that such an example exists. But I am quite sure that there is a significant place in expressivist theories for designative meaning. I have tried to make this point here and there in this chapter, but I think it needs to be made explicitly and emphatically, because my preference for expressivism is otherwise likely to obscure the reader's awareness that I recognize designative meaning at all.

Expressivism is important when we are creating new meanings; it is new meanings that are closely tied to our status as their authors. A poem, a painting, a dance could not have been created by anyone other than their makers, and this fact is generally hard to miss.[10] The same thing is true of new thoughts and feelings and implicit relational knowing, especially when the appearance of these meanings is accompanied by a sense of surprise (see Stern, 1990).

But there are many moments, of course, and perhaps even aspects of most moments, in which the meanings it makes most sense to create are meanings that are familiar because they have been made many, many times before. Familiarity, that is, while it can serve unconscious defensive purposes when we insist on maintaining it (Sullivan, 1940/1953, 1953, 1956; Schachtel, 1959; Stern, 1983, 1997; Chapter 3), is also absolutely necessary to day-to-day living. If a substantial part of our experience were not composed of, and given easy expression by, familiar perceptions, thoughts, and feelings, we would be so endlessly fascinated with trivial tasks that nothing else would ever be accomplished. Furthermore, and perhaps even more to the point, we must admit that familiar meanings were themselves new and expressive once, and serve as both the raw materials of new meaning and the ground of possibility against which the continuous unfolding of newly expressive meaning takes place. Merleau-Ponty (1945/1962), writing here about speech but intending his point to apply to all media, makes the point this way:

> This is why we have been led to distinguish between a secondary speech which renders a thought already acquired, and an originating speech that brings it into existence. . . . Now all words which have become mere signs for a univocal thought have been able to do so because they have first functioned as originating words, and we can still remember with what richness they appeared to be endowed, and how they were like a landscape new to us, while we were engaged in "acquiring" them, and while they still fulfilled the primordial function of expression. . . . We are invited to discern beneath thinking which basks in its acquisitions, and offers merely a resting place in the unending process of expression, another thought which is struggling to establish itself, and succeeds only by bending the resources of constituted language to some fresh usage.
>
> (p. 389)

Familiarity makes up the ground against which novel perceptions, thoughts, and feelings can register. Familiar meanings are also the materials that expression bends to new purpose. Old meanings, that is, make new ones possible. (Gadamer makes a closely related point when he says that preconceptions, or what he calls prejudices, are the ground of being. They are the source of novelty just as surely as they are, when used differently, novelty's prevention.) Familiar meanings, of course, are liable to be designative ones, the kind of meanings that Taylor dismisses as "the furniture of a non-expressive universe." But we need our furniture!

And so we should think of expressive meanings and designative ones as the two aspects of a dialectic. When we create novel expressive meanings, designative meanings are either in the background, serving as the ground for our expressive figures, or are actually being reformulated as part of the process of new expression. And when we compose meanings we have composed many times before—designative meanings—the possibility of expressive reformulation of those meanings is always there in the background. The potential for new expressive meaning, that is, if the context is right (i.e., if the interpersonal field brings the possibility to relevance), is actualized only because of the potential that is implicit in conventional, designative meaning but has not yet been tapped. Experience is so complicated, actually, that it is probably most accurate to say that there are various different sets of foreground and background meanings active in any particular moment, each set with its own relations between designative and expressive meaning.

## Why does expressivism matter?

What should psychoanalysis and psychoanalytic psychotherapy be?

If unconscious meanings are understood to pre-exist their discovery, if we believe they are already nonverbally coded and merely await a link to the verbal register, then they are capable of objective definition, and both the theory and the practice of psychoanalysis can be objective sciences. If that is the way the world is, perhaps psychoanalysis *ought* to be an objective science. Perhaps, if we think about human problems as objectively identifiable psychopathology, and if we therefore consider psychoanalysis and psychoanalytic psychotherapy to be, first and foremost, cures or remedies, quantitative empirical research would actually be the best way for us to proceed. In that case, we might eventually be able to answer these questions: How can we identify correctly the meanings that exist in the unconscious (or belatedly connect them to the verbal representational system)? What unconscious meanings are *really there* in the human mind? What criteria tell us when our interpretations are correct?

And most of all: What is the correct way to do psychoanalysis? That is, if the revelation of objectively defined unconscious contents were to be the criterion of therapeutic efficacy, then it ought to be just as feasible to specify how psychoanalysis and psychoanalytic psychotherapy should be conducted as it is to describe how to carry out any other task that has an objectively measurable outcome. How should the analyst or therapist actually behave? Once this last question is answered, it ought to be possible to develop manualized treatments to regularize the application of technique.[11]

All of this and more follows, it seems to me, from the position that meaning is primarily designative, the belief that unconscious meaning is already there in our minds, with its corollary that language and other media are transparent to the meanings encoded in them.

But these consequences do not follow from the expressivist view. From that perspective, unconscious meaning is potential meaning, unformulated; and it therefore cannot simply be revealed. It remains to be created, although of course the formulated meaning must respect whatever reality constraints are relevant in each particular instance (Stern, 1997, pp. 29–30). Because unconscious experience is possibility, it does not have an objective existence, and because the context of creation is always built into the process of formulating new meaning, it makes no sense to refer to the "correct" identification of unconscious meanings. Nor can we establish criteria for the "accuracy" of an interpretation, which also means that we have no such criteria to use in making judgments about the correctness of the analyst's behavior. Interpretation itself, as a matter of fact, ceases to be the way the analyst conceptualizes his method, because for the analyst to believe he can interpret suggests that he knows, or at least can hypothetically know, what is there in the patient's mind—because the unconscious has definable contents.

In the model defined by expressivism and unformulated experience, analysts do not and cannot know such a thing, any more than they have that kind of privileged access to the contents of their own minds. One upshot of all this is that expressivism and unformulated experience quite definitely do not encourage us to believe that the theory and practice of psychoanalysis can be objective sciences. More important, we are encouraged to believe that they should not be objective sciences. As I said earlier in this chapter, and can now repeat with what I hope is even greater justification, our field should be more closely allied to the arts and the humanities than to the natural sciences. Any psychoanalyst who holds views anchored in expressivist views and unformulated experience is also liable to disagree with views in which the analyst, on the basis of theory, is credited with knowledge about the contents of the patient's unconscious.

If the purpose of what we offer is not the treatment of a disease or the correction of a developmental history damaged in objectively verifiable ways, and if what we try to give our patients is not even really the remedy for a pre-existing problem, how should we envision what we do?

Expressivism does offer us something here, something like a moral path. If we take seriously that our lives are a kind of continuous expression, that we are always in the process of manifesting ourselves, then we are implicitly acknowledging the significance of the task of individuation or the growth of the self, a task that psychoanalysis has had a great deal to say about over the years. (My own favorite exponent of this view is Ernest Schachtel [1959].)

To champion individuation, though, is not to deny that psychoanalysis offers the more medically defined kinds of relief I mentioned—cure, correction, and remedy. Of course, we all know that we do offer this latter kind of relief. But if we work toward the accomplishment of individuation and freedom, however we define those qualities, most of the time we will also be doing what we can to achieve the other kinds of relief. While individuation and the freedom to experience one's own mind are not intended as remedies, they do tend to bring remediation with them.

Individuation as a goal for clinical psychoanalysis might seem problematic for those who, like me, advocate a theory of the self as multiple. Doesn't individuation imply the growth of the *individual* self?

There is no reason that this must be so. Even those of us who think of the self as multiple have a conception of *the person*, after all. For a theorist of the multiple self, individuation is the manifestation of *all* parts of subjectivity—not only the self-states that make up "me," but even those that begin in dissociation, or "not-me." One of the most clinically significant ways to think of therapeutic action is as the expansion of the self: "not-me," that is, becomes part of "me." Adaptation to demand ceases to be the most desirable way to live. Thought and feeling become free and spontaneous. These goals are entirely consistent with the thinking about manifestation that I have presented in this chapter, and it is one way of describing individuation. It is also consistent with therapeutic action as the growth of mind: that is, to individuate is to be increasingly capable of formulating experience. A greater and greater proportion of unformulated experience can be accommodated within the self: articulated or realized, accepted and used.

To accept that our lives continuously manifest us is to agree that it is important *how* we manifest ourselves. Obstacles to our freedom in this regard, especially the obstacles we supply for ourselves, ought to be deconstructed in psychoanalysis, and opportunities for the fullest kind of expression of whatever potential we bring with us into the world ought to be welcomed. If we leaven our respect for individual growth with the recognition of the value of community, this kind of growth need not result in the kind of worship at the altar of individualism that has been roundly, and rightly, criticized in the literature of social criticism over the last decades.

I offer a last quotation from Taylor (1989), one that reinforces the claims I have made for individuation. "What is new," he writes, referring to our recognition of the differences between us that manifestation reveals,

> is the idea that this really makes a difference to how we're called on to live. The differences are not just unimportant variations within the same basic human nature; or else moral differences between good and bad individuals. Rather they entail that each one of us has an original path which we ought to tread; they lay the obligation on each of us to live up to our originality
>
> (p. 375)

That path we ought to tread does not lead only through the choices we make in our everyday lives. Like those choices, the choices clinicians make among theories also grow from a sense of what is most emotionally and esthetically compelling to us, and what we believe is most important in living—that is, our ideals. Theories in our field are therefore statements of values, not best judged by whether they are right or wrong. Every theory worth its salt—and in my view there are many that are worth their salt—is right in important respects. None of them is simply wrong. Each theory is, rather, a path to be followed or turned away from, the expression of certain esthetic values and a certain kind of morality and ethics; and so esthetic, moral, and ethical consequences are inevitably associated with our theoretical and clinical choices (Stern, 2012a). We should weigh those consequences, and we should be willing to argue for our conclusions. We should understand our theoretical and clinical choices as particularly significant expressions of who we are. Our theories manifest us.

This point is not limited to explicit theories; our implicit theories—all those unformulated principles of clinical practice that so often determine what we do with our patients (Sandler, 1983; Canestri, 2006; Canestri et al, 2006)—also manifest us. Just like explicit theories, implicit theories are paths by which we select the moral and ethical consequences to which we commit ourselves, and to which we devote our professional lives (Stern, 2012a).

The way we understand language, including the relation of the verbal and the nonverbal, is one of those paths of meaning. I suspect that, without giving the matter a great deal of explicit consideration, most of us tend to think of linguistic issues as matters of fact, to be decided in some empirical, objectivistic way. But that is no more the way we should select a theory of language and the nonverbal than it is the way we should choose theories of psychoanalysis or the values that inform our daily living. Moreover, as I hope I have demonstrated, our theories of language and the nonverbal help to determine our larger views of the clinical process. I hope this book has made a convincing case for the view that the way we understand language should not be decided by so-called objective "evidence," but by a careful consideration of which view is most compelling to us and leads to the clinical consequences we believe are most important to accomplish.

## A last word

The interpersonal field is simultaneously the impetus for new expressive meaning and the context within which it is born. It is the field that, in opening to new relational possibilities, allows the mind new freedom; and it is also the field, when it is frozen and constricted, that prevents the actualization of those same possibilities and freedoms. When the field allows it, expressive meaning arises spontaneously, as circumstances, internal and external, call for it. An equivalent expression: when the field allows it, states of being or self move spontaneously in and out of awareness, as matters at hand, internal and external, make them more and less relevant.

When we say something new, or we bring to the analytic relatedness a new procedural meaning—that is, when what we mean is not merely what Merleau-Ponty refers to as "ready-made" or "second order"—we are not bringing into the known world meanings that had already existed in the unconscious part of the mind, as worthy and interesting an accomplishment as that would be. We are not, in my view, revealing unconscious fantasy (Stern, 2010b, 2014). We are instead creating something from materials that have been unformulated, something that has not existed before. New meanings, once they have been formulated, forever transform the web of language, so that what can be said, felt, known, and meant are each just a little different than they were.

That, by itself, would be enough to justify the work of psychoanalysts and psychotherapists; but we are doing more than that. When something new is manifested in the clinical situation, it is not only the capacity for thought and feeling that is affected, however significant we all agree the growth of the mind is in our work. We are, in addition to that, expanding the very possibilities of being. We are affecting what life can become, and we are doing so not only for the present moment but also for the moments that have yet to arrive; and not only for ourselves but also for many others we have not yet encountered.

What do I mean by saying that the possibilities for the being of others are affected by the new meanings we create in psychoanalysis and psychotherapy? I mean this: New expressive meanings, after the analytic sessions in which they come about, proliferate into the future, changing not only the lives of the patient and analyst who create them, but other lives, too, via the multiplying number of interpersonal fields of which these new meanings become part. Each of us affects many more lives than our own, and new meanings created in psychoanalysis and psychotherapy therefore do not and cannot exist in isolation from the rest of life. The new possibilities for living created in the clinical process eventually reverberate, via human interaction, in the lives of others.

With every new formulation, the invisible, unformulated proto-meanings—the unknown, the unsaid, the unseen, the unfelt—that surround, contextualize, and contain new expressive meanings, and without which new meanings could not exist, change just as significantly as the new meanings themselves. The effect of creating a new formulation, in other words, is not limited to the expansion of meaning we can sense directly; creating a new formulation also reconfigures foreground and background, known and unknown, expressed and inexpressible. (I think back to Chapter 2 here, and the case of Robert, in which I made this point.) We are used to paying attention to the significance of what is articulated and realized in the analytic process. But it is not only the meanings that come into the light that affect experience; the shape of the darkness matters, too. We have some control over the new meanings we make (although in most important respects they are unbidden [Stern, 1990, 2013c]). But we have even less conscious influence on the infinity of the unsaid. That part of our worlds falls together, by itself, around new expressive meanings, the way that darkness fills out the space beyond the lamplight. Our lack of conscious, purposeful influence on this background experience does not detract from its sizable and largely invisible influence on us. The continuous creation of the unformulated context of experience may be just as significant in the construction of our lives as the more visible meanings we articulate and realize. We pay very little attention to this profound, dialectical outcome of clinical process.

What I have described in these last paragraphs takes place, as far as I am concerned, as a result of the one thing I most hope to have conveyed in this book: All meanings, inside psychoanalysis and outside it, fall within the broad bounds of the linguistic, so that even when words are not our medium, we expand the possibilities of being from within language, not from outside it.

## Notes

1 It is a commonplace in contemporary cognitive science that certain kinds of experience, such as certain portions of emotional experience and procedural meaning, either cannot be represented in words at all, or can be represented only partially or inconsistently. I am excluding such experience from the generalization that meaning is transparent to language in the designative view.

2   If we therefore say that the body expresses existence at every moment, this is in the sense in which a word expresses thought. Anterior to conventional means of expression, which reveal my thoughts to others only because already, for both myself and them, meanings are provided for each sign, and which in this sense do not give rise to genuine communication at all, we must, as we shall see, recognize a primary process of signification in which the thing expressed does not exist apart from the expression, and in which the signs themselves induce their significance externally. In this way the body expresses total existence, not because it is an external accompaniment to that existence, but because existence realizes itself in the body. This incarnate significance is the central phenomenon of which body and mind, sign and significance are abstract moments.

(Merleau-Ponty, 1945/1962, p. 166)

3 For a closely related argument against the information processing metaphor (but in academic psychology, not psychoanalysis), and its replacement by an interpretive approach centered on the creation of meaning, see Bruner's (1990) now-classic text, *Acts of Meaning*.

4 The agreement Gadamer is referring to here is specifically limited to agreement regarding the nature of what is to be understood. I want to make sure that Gadamer is not misunderstood to mean that the conversational partners must come to agreement in their views. That is not what he wants to say, nor is it the meaning I have intended when I have used this part of Gadamer's argument (e.g., Stern, 2013b). I have been misinterpreted (Ferro & Civitarese, 2013), though, in this way.

5 After I wrote this part of the text, Taylor (2016) published a book-length account of his work on language. That most recent reference contains much

of the same material that I have used in the text in describing expressivism, and specifically the account of the key issue about language that separated the views of Condillac and Herder.

6   In psychoanalysis, a similar distinction has been made by Schachtel (1959), who wrote about autocentric perception and allocentric perception. In autocentric perception, one perceives the object according to the needs we hope it will alleviate; the perception is instrumental in that sense. In allocentric perception there is no intrusion of need, so that the object is perceived in and for itself. It is examined from all angles, in all dimensions, and so is revealed much more fully than the object can be grasped in autocentric perception. Schachtel goes on to expand this observation, describing two "attitudes" we take toward life and one another: the autocentric attitude and the allocentric attitude.

7   I quoted the sentence in the text, which is the first sentence of a paragraph, because it substantiates the point made in the text about the way Bucci views language. But I also want to quote the remainder of this paragraph, because it illustrates rather starkly the difference in attitudes and aesthetics about language between expressivists and at least one person who prefers the designative view. Where Gadamer, Merleau-Ponty, and Taylor find passion, elegance, and expressive power in the language of everyday subjectivity, Bucci sees clumsiness, brute force, primitiveness, inefficiency, and limited capacity and application:

> From the viewpoint of communicating subjective experience, including emotion, it seems somewhat premature, even misguided, in the grand, evolutionary scheme of things, to have inserted a powerful new system without having also provided a satisfactory means by which connections to other representational formats can be made. Language has the feel of a first-generation computing device—a breakthrough that is very exciting, potentially enormously useful, but expensive, cumbersome, slow and difficult to operate, limited in its application, vulnerable to misuse, and bearing significant risks. It is powerful enough, even in its present primitive form, to drive out other systems, but is perhaps destined to be replaced soon (in the evolutionary order) by better designed and more effective symbolic representational modes.
>
> (Bucci, 1997, p. 321)

8       Matisse, set within a man's time and vision, looked at the still open whole of his work in progress and brought his brush toward the line which called for it in order that the painting might finally be that which it was in the process of becoming. By a simple gesture he resolved the problem which in retrospect seemed to imply an infinite number of data (as the hand in the iron filings, according to Bergson, achieves in a single stroke the arrangement which will make a place for it). Everything happened in the human world of perception and gesture; and the camera

gives us a fascinating version of the event only by making us believe that the painter's hand operated in the physical world where an infinity of options is possible. And yet, Matisse's hand did hesitate. Consequently, there was a choice, and the chosen line was chosen in such a way as to observe, scattered out over the painting, twenty conditions which were unformulated and even informulable for any one but Matisse, since they were only defined and imposed by the intention of executing this painting which did not yet exist.

The case is no different for all truly expressive speech . . .

(Merleau-Ponty, 1964, pp. 45–46)

9  Elsewhere I have referred to this as internal or imaginative witnessing (D.B. Stern, 2009, 2012b), and have argued that such witnessing of oneself goes on routinely.
10  That does not mean, incidentally, that creative productions should necessarily be experienced and analyzed primarily in terms of the psychologies of their authors. It is undeniable, I think, that creative works can (and should) be understood as expressions of their authors. But these works, once made, hold their own conversations with those who view or read them, as Gadamer spends much of his work telling us. And that means that our relationships with creative works are with the works themselves, not with those who made them. But that is a story for a different day.
11  Hoffman (2009) has taken up these issues in a recent article. For a symposium discussion of the issues brought up by Hoffman's article, see Safran (2013), Cushman (2013), Stern (2013d), Fonagy (2013), Strenger (2013).

# A comparison of the roles of the verbal and the nonverbal in the theory of unformulated experience and the work of The Boston Change Process Study Group

The views of the nonverbal I present in Chapter 3 are related to the work of the Boston Change Process Study Group (BCPSG), writers and clinicians whose views are similar to mine in some respects and different in others. Both the similarities and the differences between us are significant enough to deserve detailed consideration. But to include such a consideration in the text would have the effect of interrupting and distracting from my own argument, and so I have decided to present the relevant points in this appendix, which can either be read independently or during a brief hiatus in the reading of Chapter 3. (I have indicated in that chapter where this material becomes most relevant.) I first take up the BCPSG concept of "implicit relational knowing," and then proceed to other and broader points of comparison between my work and theirs.

## Implicit relational knowing and realization

The nonverbal realizations we use in negotiating relatedness constitute a procedural (in Bucci's terms, subsymbolic) form of knowing, described by the Boston Change Process Study Group's (D.N. Stern, et al 1998) influential conceptualization of "implicit relational knowing":

> Procedural knowledge of relationships ... is implicit, operating outside both focal attention and conscious verbal experience. This knowledge is represented non-symbolically in the form of what we will call *implicit relational knowing* ... There is [a kind of procedural knowledge] that concerns knowing about interpersonal and intersubjective relations, i.e. how 'to be with' someone ([D.N.] Stern, 1985, 1995). For instance, the infant comes to know early in life what forms of affectionate approaches the parent will welcome or turn away, as

described in the attachment literature (Lyons-Ruth, 1991) . . . Such *knowings* integrate affect, cognition, and behavioural/interactive dimensions.

(D.N. Stern, et al., 1998, p. 904; italics from the original)

Implicit relational knowing is very similar to what I mean by the kind of nonverbal, procedural realizations that we use in negotiating relatedness. However, there is also an important difference between BCPSG's conception of nonverbal procedural meaning and mine. For me, nonverbal realizations are outcomes of a process of formulation, and this process of formulation adds a dynamic element not present in the BCPSG conception. That is, unformulated experience—verbal or nonverbal—may be maintained indefinitely in its unformulated state for unconscious defensive reasons; it can be formulated only if the meaning is not too threatening— if, in the words I have already used in the text, it feels enough "like me" to be "accepted" and "used." (I give the words in quotation marks particular meanings in Chapter 3.) Bromberg (2006, pp. 153–202) would describe this state as "safe but not too safe."

Implicit relational knowing, on the other hand, is an exclusively affective, cognitive, perceptual, and behavioral conception—and BCPSG intends it to be. That is, while the idea is meant to explicate the shape and form of experience, it is not intended to have a motivational or volitional aspect in the traditional psychoanalytic sense. Even when implicit relational knowing takes place outside awareness, which it very often does, it is not *dynamically* unconscious. Precisely because it is implicit, it exists in only one state; it does not exist in the two dynamically meaningful states I describe as formulated and unformulated. For me, procedural knowing can be dissociated, just as other forms of psychic life can be. BCPSG does not envision that possibility.

I believe that the Boston Group would agree to differentiate their work from mine on this basis. Daniel Stern (2004), for instance, seems to agree with my assessment when he writes that,

Implicit relational knowing is non conscious; it is not unconscious in the sense of repressed. Rather, it has never, as yet, needed to be put into words and may never need to be. It is non conscious in the sense of never becoming reflectively conscious.

(p. 242)

## A broader comparison of dissociative enactment and the work of BCPSG

While BCPSG and I seem to agree on this particular difference between us, BCPSG has described what they consider to be another difference between their work and mine that I consider inaccurate. They (BCPSG, 2013) argue that, while they portray the therapeutic relationship as a continuous nonlinear process, punctuated by notable episodes, or "now moments" (D.N. Stern, et al, 1998), I present what I call "enactment" as if it does not grow from a context that has continuity over time. They argue that my work distorts our understanding of the analytic relationship by making it seem as if enactments pop up out of nowhere, rather than growing from interactive, procedural processes that may have been taking place, invisibly, over a significant period of time (BCPSG, 2013):

> From a nonlinear dynamics perspective, these exchanges may have been occurring beneath a threshold of organizational complexity at which small quantitative increases eventuate in qualitative discontinuities and the development of new levels.
>
> (BCPSG, 2013, p. 734)

Actually, though, the point of view BCPSG takes on this issue is very much the same as my own. *Of course* enactments grow out of interactive processes, quite realistically portrayed as procedural, that may have been going on for quite some time. I have simply chosen a different emphasis than BCPSG: they have focused on the therapeutic relationship as a continuous, nonlinear process, while I have selected for explication the moments of crisis that grow out of this continuous, nonlinear process.[1] For them to claim otherwise strikes me as a rhetorical exercise, not an actual difference between what they and I believe.

My emphasis (D.B. Stern, 2010a, 2015) begins with a definition of "enactment" as "the interpersonalization of dissociation" (D.B. Stern, 2004). I mean by this phrase that, when the interpersonal field shifts in such a way that "not-me" (that dissociated part of subjectivity that cannot be tolerated—that does not feel like "me") threatens to enter awareness, triggering a crisis of identity ("I am what I *cannot, must not,* be"), the unacceptable aspect of identity is attributed to the other person in the interpersonal field. One then treats that other person as if they were the intolerable aspect of oneself. One might act (without awareness, of course) in a way that could be described something like this (just for example): "*I'm* not hateful. *You* are." Or, "*I'm* not greedy. *You* are." This account is obviously reminiscent of projective identification. I will not take up the similarities and differences here, but the interested reader can consult a brief comparison between the two views that I have published elsewhere (D.B. Stern 2010a, pp. 17–18).

In the literature on the subject of enactment, it is common to approach the issue with a broader lens than I use. In those accounts, mutual enactment is understood to be the unconscious part of the interpersonal field—that is, the unconscious events and meanings of both analyst and patient, and particularly those events and meanings that take place in, or are expressed through, conduct. I have not taken that perspective, though— because I have wanted to preserve a specific meaning for the term "enactment." I fear that the more general definition, that broader lens used by so many of my colleagues, would eventually result in the loss of the term's usefulness, since of course all conduct has unconscious meanings.

But despite taking this view, I have argued that ongoing relatedness is the ground from which the seed of dissociative enactment sprouts, and in which it often grows for a significant period of time before flowering as a part of the relationship that requires explicit clinical attention. I have made this point repeatedly. Here is one general statement of the position:

> If we [were to] think of enactment as unconscious participation in relatedness, [we might be led to] take the position that *all* interactions are enactments, or have enactive qualities, even those interactions in which both participants' perceptions of ongoing interaction are relatively unobstructed. I have not adopted that way of defining enactment, however, because the phenomenon would then have to be understood as omnipresent. We would never cease enactment; and in this way the term would lose any specific meaning. And so, despite my acceptance that all interaction does indeed have unconscious aspects, I prefer to restrict the use of the term "enactment" to the interpersonalization of dissociation.
>
> (D.B. Stern, 2010a, p. 16; italics from the original)

Here is another example of a passage (D.B. Stern, 2003) that contradicts the understanding of my work offered by BCPSG. In this passage, I am discussing an emotionally intense mutual enactment (intensely emotional for both me and the patient) that was eventually breached by the work done by the patient and me (and especially the patient) on a dream she had.

> What happened in response to Hannah's interpretation of her dream was not as simple, then, as the resumption of my analytic capacity or Hannah's to be a collaborative analysand. Hannah's offer of collaboration, as surprising as it was to me, grew from both a conscious and an unconscious context. Though I could not sense these contexts, no doubt I was as central as she was in their development. That is the nature of many of the surprises that occur in psychoanalysis, in fact: surprise is the feeling we have when an event in the relationship takes place in a way that feels out of the blue, devoid of context.
>
> (D.B. Stern, 2003, p. 763)

Of course the point of saying that these events *feel* out of the blue is that they are *not* out of the blue at all. They grow from context, often invisible context. Even when the events seem sudden, like tipping points— perhaps reflecting the nonlinear re-organization of the field in response to a disturbance of its equilibrium (that is, in my terms, a shift in the configuration of the field created by the interactive conduct of the two participants)—these events emerge from a system with a long-term, complex, and nonlinear organization.

Here is another example, this time from a recent article:

> I hope it goes without saying that it was the relatedness George and I had made between us over a long period of time that allowed these events to take place. In the end what happened was really very simple, even if what led up to it was not. As is most often the case in analytic work, the moments of greatest impact are shaped by, and take their significance from, the context of the relationship in which they take place. At any earlier time in the treatment, it would have been worse than useless for me to suggest to George that maybe he could imagine that I wanted to come back. It would have been either Pollyannism on my part, or intellectualization.
>
> (D.B. Stern, 2017, pp. 510–511)

I present one final example here, just to nail down the point. In this lengthy passage (D.B. Stern, 2013c), after having described one particular clinical episode, I speculate about the nonconscious (and necessarily nonverbal and procedural) interaction that may have led up to the incident and affectively contextualized it. It would be hard to understand this account, it seems to me, in any other way than an affirmation of enactment as a *particular kind of event within the broader, procedural analytic relationship.* Because of the length of the passage, I present it in a note.[2] Those readers interested in further substantiation of the point can turn to it.

Frankly, the claim by BCPSG that I present a decontextualized view of enactment seems tendentious to me. It is hard to understand how this criticism makes sense about the work of someone who describes the primary object of his own thinking as "Emergent properties of the interpersonal field" (D.B. Stern, 2015). I have great respect for, and interest in, the work of BCPSG. As I have said, we differ over the importance of the dynamic perspective in psychoanalysis, and over matters of language; but I also think that their conceptualization of therapeutic relatedness overlaps with mine in many important respects.

There does exist another major difference between our bodies of work that I have not yet described, though, and this difference is perhaps the most important one.

## A difference in the consequences of changes in the field

This major difference revolves around our respective conceptions of the analytic field.

BCPSG (2010) lays little emphasis on verbal-reflective understanding. Therapeutic action, for them, has to do with shifts in procedural knowing—implicit relational knowing—that take place as a result of affectively charged events in the therapeutic relationship. Change takes place not by thinking, at least not by thinking in the conventional sense, but by doing (in both affect and conduct), and by the feeling that lies behind doing and that comes about as the doing shifts. They take the position that the verbal-reflective understanding of these shifts in relatedness is usually not terribly important, and that, in fact, language is not necessarily even up to the task of representing them. The interpersonal field, for BCPSG, is important only in and of itself. Certain key changes in the field are themselves the changes that matter.

I, on the other hand, am not so willing to de-emphasize verbal-reflective knowing and understanding, as I am sure is clear from what I have said in the text. The creation of verbal-reflective understanding retains a crucial significance in my understanding of therapeutic action. What I try to say in the text is that the realization of nonverbal meaning is absolutely necessary, but not sufficient.

Benjamin (2017, Chapter 5) takes issue with the argument by BCPSG (2013) that the effects of the analyst's enactive participation should be dealt with implicitly and procedurally. She makes a compelling case, with which I agree, for an alternative based in her own theory of recognition and the Third: the analyst's acknowledgment of responsibility for their (sometimes hurtful) involvement in the enactment, an accompanying verbal symbolization of the nature of the interaction, and perhaps a mutually constructed description of the way the interaction grows from, and is embedded, in the patient's history. Rather than breaking into "being with," says Benjamin, as BCPSG would have it, the symbolic processing of enactments (i.e., knowing them in words) can have the effect of reinforcing the most important aspects of implicit relational knowing:

> The procedural meaning of reconstructing our action together or co-creating a metaphor to express our understanding is that we create a container together . . . (D)ialogic engagement fosters a form of mutual containing in which emotions become communication that moves the other. In this movement . . . symbolization manifests as intersubjective process, a form of recognition between self and other. Procedure matches content. The movement of shared reflection and feeling elicits other self-states who enter the play.
>
> (Benjamin, 2017, p. 178)

The contribution of symbolization, that is, is hardly limited to the semantic value of what is said. Symbolization can also contribute to the expansion of relatedness.

Like Benjamin and other writers such as Loewald (1978) and Vivona (2003, 2006, 2012, 2013), I have greater confidence in the value of the representational capacity of language than does BCPSG. Daniel Stern (1985), arguably the greatest influence on the Boston Group, took the view for decades that language, while irreplaceable, of course, was also often a source of experiential constriction and loss of meaning. Stern felt keenly that language was simply inadequate to a great deal of nonverbal meaning, and that trying to force procedural meaning into words was to court intellectualization and to leave the healing qualities of relatedness behind. This is a position with which I have some sympathy, as I hope is clear from the text–but for me, because of my interest in the constitutive properties of language, it is only part of the story.

For Daniel Stern, language is a set of labels for experience, as it is for Bucci (see especially Note 7 in Chapter 4). In these views, the limits of language tend to be emphasized. There is an emphasis on the failure of language to represent adequately the complexity of human interaction and the inner world—a lack of range, depth, subtlety, and flexibility. For Daniel Stern, language is not the constitutive, formative, generative influence I have tried to present it to be (and describe in greatest detail in Chapter 4). For him, the nonverbal world is the "real" source of meaning. Language is merely a tool to bring the nonverbal into view and perhaps to think about it; and language is adequate only to the extent that it can represent and express those meanings.

For the hermeneutic writers who inspire me, on the other hand, language not only carves up the undifferentiated world into the pieces we experience as meaningful; language also creates its own kind of "real" meaning. It is no more reasonable to decry language for not being adequate to the representation of nonverbal meanings than it is to find nonverbal symbolic representation wanting because it is unable to represent verbal-reflective meanings!

In my account, the interpersonal field is important in and of itself, as it is for BCPSG. But it is also important as a kind of gatekeeper of mind. Remember that the interpersonal field is the key factor determining which meanings are formulated, accepted and used in the spontaneous creation of living. And keep in mind that these meanings are both verbal and nonverbal.

And so, whereas BCPSG and I agree that clinical attention is best focused on the field and its changes and frozen, constricted places, our views diverge on the significance of changes in the field. For BCPSG, the significance of changes in relatedness is limited to the changes themselves—which take place in the nonverbal, procedural realm. That is no small matter, of course, and no small part of my own conception of the aims of psychotherapy and psychoanalysis. But for me, the positive effects of thawing frozen parts of the field, a process not limited to work with dissociative enactments but present in analytic relatedness every day (D.B. Stern, 2013c), are not confined to procedural changes. Breaches of dissociations, and the resolution of enactments those breaches make possible, have the effect of expanding the range, depth, and freedom of thought. The creation of greater freedom in the field has a direct impact on the nonverbal, yes, both procedural and symbolic; but the effect is just as great on the verbal. As the field between them becomes more flexible and spontaneous, what each person can experience in verbal terms is expanded, too, in just the same way as is the nonverbal. Keep in mind that, from the perspective of unformulated experience, the nature of *all* the experience that each person can have in the other's presence—verbal as well as nonverbal—depends on the particular configuration of the interpersonal field. Successful work with enactments, then, despite the fact that such work begins with events in the realm of the procedural— the "new perception"—leads to greater relational freedom and the liberation of the capacity of the mind to create spontaneous, unbidden experience, including verbally mediated thought (see especially D.B. Stern, 2013c).

## Notes

1   For a useful presentation of the difference between these two kinds of approaches to enactment, see Bass (2003).

2   In retrospect, I can speculate about the patterns of relatedness that were functioning to constrict the experience that was possible between William and me. Given what I have told you already, you can no doubt imagine easily enough that William worried that his need of me would be burdensome. I believe that he often did his best, from one moment to the next, and without awareness, to give me the sense that he wanted or needed very little from the relatedness between us. And yet, of course, he did; that is, he wanted something important from me and he conveyed to me that he did, although in ways that usually allowed him to keep from himself the significance of what he was doing. I have already mentioned that sometimes he was mildly annoyed with me when he sensed my own interests, even if the evidence was as minor as my wish to share with him a funny moment.

   Looking back in time, it seems likely to me that, feeling William's worry about burdening me or being disappointed in me, I responded with a certain caution, hoping (in a way that I did not formulate) to avoid the outcomes that would have let him down, annoyed him, or shamed him by making him feel like a burden to me. This was all quite subtle, if I am right to construct our history this way; and it resulted in a certain tightness or awkwardness (though "awkwardness" feels like too strong a word) around my nurture and concern for William. That tightness, in turn, would have made William feel just a bit tighter about these things himself, resulting in a kind of subtly inhibited quality in the atmosphere. The possibility of William's shame was, I believe, ever present. All of this (again, if I am right) was obscured by a seamless quality in our dealings with one another, a quality that, by allowing us to keep these issues blunted or dampened, protected both of us from direct exposure to our subtle awkwardness with one another.

When I think back on it I feel that, for a few weeks prior to the episode I have recounted, I had a certain anticipatory awareness of all of this, a kind of orienting toward it, the way a flower turns to the sun. Without having found any words to describe it, or even explicitly noticing it—and certainly without having explicitly reflected on it—I was sensing certain affective snags and chafings related to the tightness I have described. In a less than conscious way, I was playing with these snags, noting them and giving them increasingly free rein to gambol about in my mind. I think I worked myself into a slightly different relation to these aspects of our relationship, so that when I spoke to William about calling me on the phone, I spoke from a state in which I was more relaxed about these issues between us than I had been. I think the impact of my less inhibited state registered on William. I think he might have felt, rightly, that when I spoke I was just giving voice to a spontaneous thought. He could have taken this impression from my tone of voice or my relaxed informality. The very spontaneity of the remark, in fact, probably contributed to the way it moved William. He could tell, I speculate, that what I said came from my wish to comfort him and not from a technical prescription—although it would be precisely my contention that the point here is that these two kinds of response can be, and in this case were, indistinguishable. But of course, like me, William put none of these events or understandings into words prior to our later discussion of them.

As a consequence of this expansion of relational freedom and the changes in the interpersonal field that fell into place as a result, we each became spontaneously capable, in the presence of the other, of unbidden experience we had not been capable of having before. I had the urge to tell him he should have called me, and he could be moved by it; and then, later on, I had the unbidden thought about his abandonment in the hospital; and again he could respond to it and allow himself the spontaneous experience of being witnessed. William's response to me was just as much the result of a new relational freedom as my responses were: that is, the fact that I could offer William an experience of witnessing did not necessarily mean that he would be able to accept it.

(D.B. Stern, 2013c, pp. 23–25)

# References

Atlas, G. & Aron, L. (2017). *Dramatic Dialogue: Contemporary Clinical Practice*. New York & London: Routledge.

Baranger, M. & Baranger, W. (1961–1962/2008). The analytic situation as a dynamic field. *International Journal of Psychoanalysis*, 89: 795–826. (Original work published 1961–1962 in Spanish. This is a translation of the 1969 revision of the original article.)

Baranger, M. & Baranger, W. (2009). *The Work of Confluence: Listening and Working and Interpreting in the Analytic Field*, ed. L.G. Fiorini. London: Karnac.

Baranger, M., Baranger, W. & Mom, J.M. (1983). Process and non-process in analytic work. In: *The Work of Confluence: Listening and Interpreting in the Psychoanalytic Field*, ed. L. G. Fiorini. London: Karnac, 2008, pp. 63–88.

Bass, A. (2003). "E" enactments in psychoanalysis. *Psychoanalytic Dialogues*, 13: 657–675.

Beebe, B. & Lachmann, F. (2002). *Infant Research and Adult Treatment: Co-constructing Interactions*. Hillsdale, NJ: The Analytic Press.

Beebe, B. & Lachmann, F. (2013). *The Origins of Attachment: Infant Research and Adult Treatment*. New York and London: Routledge.

Benjamin, J. (1988). *The Bonds of Love*. New York: Pantheon.

Benjamin, J. (1995). *Like Subjects, Love Objects*. New Haven, CT: Yale University Press.

Benjamin, J. (1998). *The Shadow of the Other*. New York & London: Routledge.

Benjamin, J. (2004/2017). Beyond doer and done to: An intersubjective view of thirdness. In: *Beyond Doer and Done To: Recognition Theory, Intersubjectivity, and the Third*. New York and London: Routledge, pp. 21–48.

Benjamin, J. (2017). *Beyond Doer and Done To: Recognition Theory, Intersubjectivity, and the Third*. New York and London: Routledge.

Berger, P.L. & Luckmann, T. (1966). *The Social Construction of Reality: A Treatise in the Sociology of Knowledge*. Garden City, NY: Anchor Books.

Bion, W.R. (1962/1977). *Learning From Experience*. In: *Seven Servants: Four Works by Wilfred R. Bion*. New York: Jason Aronson, pp. 1–111.

Bion, W.R (1965). *Transformations*. London: Heinemann.

Bion, W.R. (1970). *Attention and Interpretation*. London: Tavistock.

Black, M.J. (2003). Enactment: Analytic musings on energy, language, and personal growth. *Psychoanalytic Dialogues*, 13(5): 633–655

Blass, R. (2017). Reflections on Klein's radical notion of phantasy and its implications for analytic practice. *International Journal of Psychoanalysis*, 98: 841–859.

Bollas, C. (1987). *The Shadow of the Object: Psychoanalysis of the Unthought Known*. New York: Columbia University Press.

Bonovitz, C. (2009). Looking back, looking forward: A reexamination of Benjamin Wolstein's *interlock* and the emergence of intersubjectivity. *International. Journal of Psychoanalysis*, 90: 463–485

Boston Change Process Study Group (2007). The foundational level of psychodynamic meaning: Implicit process in relation to conflict, defense and the dynamic unconscious. *International Journal of Psychoanalysis*, 88: 843–860.

Boston Change Process Study Group (2008). Forms of relational meaning: Issues in the relations between the implicit and the reflective-verbal domains. *Psychoanalytic Dialogues*, 18: 125–148.

Boston Change Process Study Group (2010). *Change in Psychotherapy: A Unifying Paradigm*. New York: W. W. Norton & Co.

Boston Change Process Study Group (2013). Enactment and the emergence of new relational organization. *Journal of the American Psychoanalytic Association*, 61: 727–749.

Botella, C. & Botella, S. (2005). *The Work of Psychic Figurability*. Hove, UK and New York: Brunner/Routledge.

Bromberg, P. M. (1998). *Standing in the Spaces: Essays on Clinical Process, Trauma, and Dissociation*. Hillsdale, NJ: The Analytic Press.

Bromberg, P.M. (2000). Potholes on the royal road: Or is it an abyss? *Contemporary Psychoanalysis*, 36: 5–28.

Bromberg, P.M. (2003/2006). Something wicked this way comes: Where psychoanalysis, cognitive science, and neuroscience overlap. In *Awakening the Dreamer: Clinical Journeys*. Mahwah, NJ: The Analytic Press, pp. 174–202.

Bromberg, P. M. (2006). *Awakening the Dreamer: Clinical Journeys*. Hillsdale, NJ: The Analytic Press.

Bromberg, P. M. (2008) "Mentalize THIS!": Dissociation, enactment, and clinical process. In *Mind to Mind: Infant Research, Neuroscience, and Psychoanalysis*, ed. E. Jurist, A. Slade & S. Bergner. New York: Other Press, pp. 414–434.

Bromberg, P. M. (2009) Truth, human relatedness, and the analytic process: An interpersonal/relational perspective. *International Journal of Psychoanalysis*, 90: 347–361.

Bromberg, P.M. (2011). *The Shadow of the Tsunami: And the Growth of the Relational Mind*. New York and London: Routledge.

Bowie, M. (1991). *Lacan*. Cambridge, MA: Harvard University Press.

Bruner, J. (1990). *Acts of Meaning*. Cambridge, MA: Harvard University Press.

Bucci, W. (1985). Dual coding: A cognitive model for psychoanalytic research. *Journal of the American Psychoanalytic Association*, 33: 571–607.

Bucci, W. (1997). *Psychoanalysis and Cognitive Science: A Multiple Code Theory*. New York: Guilford Press.

Bucci, W. (2003). Varieties of dissociative experiences: A multiple code account and a discussion of Bromberg's case of William. *Psychoanalytic Psychology*, 20: 542–557.

Bucci, W. (2007a). Dissociation from the perspective of multiple code theory, Part I. *Contemporary Psychoanalysis*, 43(2): 165–184.

Bucci, W. (2007b). Dissociation from the perspective of multiple code theory, Part II. *Contemporary Psychoanalysis*, 43(3): 305–326.

Canestri, J. (2006). Implicit understanding of clinical material beyond theory. In: *Psychoanalysis: From Practice to Theory*, ed. J. Canestri. London: John Wiley & Sons, pp. 13–28.

Canestri, J., Bohleber, W., Denis, P. & Fonagy, P. (2006), The map of private (implicit, preconscious) theories in clinical practice. In: *Psychoanalysis: From Practice to Theory*, ed. J. Canestri. London: John Wiley & Sons, pp. 29–43.

Cardinal, M. (1984). *The Words to Say It*. Cambridge, MA: VanVactor and Goodheart.

Cushman, P. (2013). Because the rock will not read the article: A discussion of Jeremy D. Safran's critique of Irwin Z. Hoffman's "Doublethinking our way to scientific legitimacy". *Psychoanalytic Dialogues*, 23: 211–224

Damasio, A. (1999). *The Feeling of What Happens: Body and Emotion in the Making of Consciousness*. New York: Houghton Mifflin Harcourt.

Davies, J.M. (2004). Whose bad objects are we anyway? Repetition and our elusive love affair with evil. *Psychoanalytic Dialogues*, 14(6): 711–732.

Dyess, C. & Dean, T. (2000). Gender: The impossibility of meaning. *Psychoanalytic Dialogues*, 10(5): 735–756

Dyller, I. (2014). Language in the analytic hour: Clinical discussion of Harris, Kirshner, and Spivak. *Journal of the American Psychoanalytic Association*, 62(6): 1075–1080.

Ehrenberg, D.B. (1992). *The Intimate Edge: Extending the Reach of Psycho-analytic Interaction*. New York: Norton.

Ferro, A. & Civitarese, G. (2013). Analysts in search of an author: Voltaire or Artemisia Gentileschi? Commentary on 'Field Theory in Psychoanalysis, Part II: Bionian Field Theory and Contemporary Interpersonal/Relational Psychoanalysis' by Donnel B. Stern. *Psychoanalytic Dialogues*, 23: 646–653.

Fingarette, H. (1963). *The Self in Transformation*. New York: Basic Books.

Fingarette, H. (1969). *Self-deception*. London: Routledge and Kegan-Paul.

Fink, B. (1995). *The Lacanian Subject: Between Language and Jouissance*. Princeton NJ: Princeton University Press.

Fink, B. (1999). *A Clinical Introduction to Lacanian Psychoanalysis: Theory and Technique*. Cambridge, MA: Harvard University Press.

Foehl, J. (2014). A phenomenology of depth. *Psychoanalytic Dialogues*, 24: 289–303.

Fonagy, P. (1991), Thinking about thinking: Some clinical and theoretical considerations in the treatment of a borderline patient. *International Journal of Psychoanalysis*, 72: 639–656.

Fonagy, P. (1995). Playing with reality: The development of Psychic reality and its malfunction in borderline personalities. *International Journal of Psychoanalysis*, 76: 39–44.

Fonagy, P. (2012). Does it matter if there is a nonverbal period of development? On the infant's understanding the social world and its implications for psychoanalytic therapy. *Journal of the American Psychoanalytic Association*, 60: 287–296.

Fonagy, P. (2013). There is room for even more doublethink: The perilous status of psychoanalytic research. *Psychoanalytic Dialogues*, 23: 116–122.

Fonagy, P. & Moran, G.S. (1991). Understanding psychic change in child psychoanalysis. *International Journal of Psychoanalysis*, 72: 15–22.

Fonagy P., Moran, G. S. & Target, M. (1993). Aggression and the psychological self. *International Journal of Psychoanalysis*, 74: 471–485.

Fonagy, P. & Target, M. (1995). Understanding the violent patient: The use of the body and the role of the father. *International Journal of Psychoanalysis*, 76: 487–501.

Fonagy, P. & Target, M. (1996). Playing with reality: I. Theory of mind and the normal development of psychic reality. *International Journal of Psychoanalysis*, 77: 217–33.

Fonagy P. & Target, M. (2000). Playing with reality: III. The persistence of dual psychic reality in borderline patients. *International Journal of Psychoanalysis*, 81: 853–873.

Fonagy, P. & Target, M. (2007). Playing with reality: IV. A theory of external reality rooted in intersubjectivity. *International Journal of Psychoanalysis*, 88: 913–937.

Fonagy, P., Gergely, G., Jurist, E. & Target, M. (2002), *Affect Regulation, Mentalization, and the Development of the Self*. New York: Other Press.

Foucault, M. (1980). *Power/Knowledge*, ed. C. Gordon. New York: Pantheon.

Freud, S. (1895). Project for a scientific psychology. *The Standard Edition of the Complete Psychological Works of Sigmund Freud, Volume I (1886–1899): Pre-Psycho-Analytic Publications and Unpublished Drafts*. London: Hogarth, pp. 281–391.

Freud, S. (1900). The Interpretation of Dreams. *The Standard Edition of the Complete Psychological Works of Sigmund Freud, Volume IV*. London: Hogarth, pp. ix–627

Freud, S. (1901). The Psychopathology of Everyday Life. *The Standard Edition of the Complete Psychological Works of Sigmund Freud, Volume VI (1901): The Psychopathology of Everyday Life*. London: Hogarth, pp. vii–296.

Freud, S. (1911). Formulations on the two principles of mental functioning. *The Standard Edition of the Complete Psychological Works of Sigmund Freud, Volume XII (1911–1913): The Case of Schreber, Papers on Technique and Other Works*. London: Hogarth, pp. 213–226.

Freud, S. (1912). The dynamics of transference. *The Standard Edition of the Complete Psychological Works of Sigmund Freud, Volume XII (1911–1913): The Case of Schreber, Papers on Technique and Other Works*. London: Hogarth, pp. 97–108.

Freud, S. (1913). On beginning the treatment (Further recommendations on the technique of psycho-Analysis I). *The Standard Edition of the Complete Psychological Works of Sigmund Freud, Volume XII (1911–1913): The Case of Schreber, Papers on Technique and Other Works*. London: Hogarth, pp. 121–144

Freud, S. (1914). Remembering, repeating and working-through (Further recommendations on the technique of psycho-Analysis II). *The Standard Edition of the Complete Psychological Works of Sigmund Freud, Volume XII (1911–1913): The Case of Schreber, Papers on Technique and Other Works*. London: Hogarth, pp. 145–156.

Freud, S. (1915a). Repression. *The Standard Edition of the Complete Psychological Works of Sigmund Freud, Volume XIV (1914–1916): On the History of the Psycho-Analytic Movement, Papers on Metapsychology and Other Works*. London: Hogarth, 141–158.

Freud, S. (1915b). The Unconscious. *The Standard Edition of the Complete Psychological Works of Sigmund Freud, Volume XIV (1914–1916): On the History of the Psycho-Analytic Movement, Papers on Metapsychology and Other Works*. London: Hogarth, pp. 159–215

Freud, S. (1937). Constructions in analysis. *The Standard Edition of the Complete Psychological Works of Sigmund Freud, Volume XXIII (1937–1939): Moses and Monotheism, An Outline of Psycho-Analysis and Other Works*. London: Hogarth, pp. 255–270.

Fromm-Reichmann, F. (1955). *Principles of Intensive Psychotherapy*. Chicago: University of Chicago Press.

Gadamer, H.-G. (1965/2004). *Truth and Method*, revised translation, by J. Weinsheimer & D. G. Marshall, from the 2nd edition in German. London: Continuum.

Ghent, E. (1990). Masochism, submission, surrender: Masochism as a perversion of surrender. *Contemporary Psychoanalysis* 26: 108–135.

Goodman, N. (1978). *Ways of Worldmaking*. Indianapolis, IN: Hackett Publishing Company.

Green, A. (1975). The analyst, symbolization, and absence in the analytic setting. *International Journal of Psychoanalysis*, 56: 1–22.

Green, A. (1986). The dead mother. In: *On private madness*. London: The Hogarth Press, pp. 142–173.

Green, A. (1999). *The Work of the Negative*, trans. A. Weller. London: Free Association Books.

Greenberg, J. (1996). Psychoanalytic words and psychoanalytic acts: A brief history. *Contemporary Psychoanalysis*, 32: 195–213.

Grotstein, J.S. (2007). Bion's discovery of zero: ("no-thing"). In: *A Beam of Intense Darkness: Wilfred Bion's Legacy to Psychoanalysis*. London: Karnac Books, pp. 114–129.

Harris, A. (2014). Curative speech: Symbol, body, dialogue. *Journal of the American Psychoanalytic Association*, 62: 1029–1045.

Heidegger, M. (1959/1971). The nature of language. In: *On the Way to Language*, trans. P. D. Hertz. New York: Harper and Row, pp. 55–108.

Hirsch, I. (2014). *The Interpersonal Tradition: The Origins of Psychoanalytic Subjectivity*. New York and London: Routledge.

Hoeller, K. (1993). *Merleau-Ponty and Psychology*. Atlantic Highlands, NJ: Humanities Press.

Hoffman, I.Z. (1983). The patient as the interpreter of the analyst's experience. *Contemporary Psychoanalysis*, 19: 389–422.

Hoffman, I.Z. (1998). *Ritual and Spontaneity in the Psychoanalytic Process: A Dialectical–Constructivist View*. Hillsdale, NJ: The Analytic Press.

Hoffman, I.Z. (2009). Doublethinking our way to "scientific" legitimacy: The desiccation of human experience. *Journal of the American Psychoanalytic Association*, 57(5): 1043–1069.

Homer, S. (2006). *Jacques Lacan*. London and New York: Routledge.

James, W. (1890). *Principles of Psychology*. New York: Henry Holt.

Kirshner, L. (2014). Raids on the unsayable: Talk in psychoanalysis. *Journal of the American Psychoanalytic Association*, 62(6): 1047–1061.

Knausgaard, K.O. (2012). *My Struggle, Book 1*, trans. D. Bartlett. New York: Farrar, Straus & Giroux.

Lacan, J. (1949/2004). The mirror stage as formative of the *I* function as revealed in psychoanalytic experience. In *Ecrits: A Selection*, trans. B. Fink, H. Fink, & R. Grigg. New York: Norton, pp. 75–81.

Lacan, J. (1953/2004). The function and field of speech and language in psychoanalysis. In *Ecrits: A Selection*, trans. B. Fink, H. Fink, & R. Grigg. New York: Norton, pp. 31–106.

Lacan, J. (1977/2004). *Ecrits: A Selection*, trans. B. Fink, H. Fink, & R. Grigg. New York: Norton.

Lachmann, F. & Beebe, B. (1996). Three principles of salience in the patient–analyst interaction. *Psychoanalytic Psychology*, 13: 1–22.

LaFarge, L. (2014). Psychoanalytic controversy: How and why unconscious phantasy and transference are the defining features of analytic practice. *International Journal of Psychoanalysis*, 95: 1265–1278.

Langer, S. (1942). *Philosophy in a New Key; A Study in the Symbolism of Reason, Rite, and Art*. Cambridge, MA: Harvard University Press.

Laplanche, J. (2011). *Freud and the Sexual: Essays 2000–2006*, trans. J. House, J. Fletcher & N. Ray. New York: The Unconscious in Translation.

Lecours, S. & Bouchard, M. (1997). Dimensions of mentalisation: Outlining levels of psychic transformation. *International Journal of Psychoanalysis*, 78: 855–875.

Levenson, E.A. (1972/2005). The fallacy of understanding. In: *The Fallacy of Understanding & The Ambiguity of Change*. New York and Hove, UK: Routledge.

Levenson, E. A. (1979). Language and healing. In: *The Purloined Self*, Second Edition, ed. A. Slomowitz. New York and London: Routledge, 2017.

Levenson, E.A. (1983/2005). The ambiguity of change: The fallacy of understanding. In: *The Fallacy of Understanding & The Ambiguity of Change*. New York and Hove, UK: Routledge.

Levenson, E.A. (1991/2016). *The Purloined Self: The Interpersonal Perspective in Psychoanalysis*, ed. A. Slomowitz. New York and London: Routledge.

Levenson, E.A. (1992). Shoot the messenger—Interpersonal aspects of the analyst's interpretations. *Contemporary Psychoanalysis*, 29: 383–396

Levenson, E.A. (2017). *Interpersonal Psychoanalysis and the Enigma of Consciousness*, ed. A. Slomowitz. New York and London: Routledge.

Levine, H.B., Reed, G.S. & Scarfone, D. (eds.) (2013). *Unrepresented States and the Construction of Meaning: Clinical and Theoretical Contributions*. London: Karnac.

Liberman, D. (1974). Verbalization and unconscious phantasies. *Contemporary Psychoanalysis*, 10: 41–55.

Linge, D.E. (1976). Editor's introduction. In: *Philosophical Hermeneutics* ed. D.E. Linge. Berkeley, CA: University of California Press, pp. xi–lviii

Litowitz, B.E. (2011). From dyad to dialogue: Language and the early relationship in American psychoanalytic theory. *Journal of the American Psychoanalytic Association*, 59: 483–507

Litowitz, B. (2014). Coming to terms with intersubjectivity: Keeping language in mind. *Journal of the American Psychoanalytic Association* 62: 295–312.

Loewald, H. (1978). Primary process, secondary process, and language. In: *The Essential Loewald: Collected Papers and Monographs*. Hagerstown, MD: University Publishing Group, pp. 178–204.

Lombardi, R. (2015). *Formless Infinity: Clinical Explorations of Matte-Blanco and Bion*. London and New York: Routledge.

Lombardi, R. (2016). *Body–Mind Dissociation in Psychoanalysis: Development After Bion*. New York and London: Routledge.

Lyons-Ruth, K. (1991). Rapprochement or approchement: Mahler's theory reconsidered from the vantage point of recent research on early attachment relationships. *Psychoanalytic Psychology*, 8: 1–23.

Lyons-Ruth, K. & Boston Change Process Study Group (2001). The emergence of new experiences: Relational improvisation, recognition process, and non-linear change in psychoanalytic therapy. *Psychologist-Psychoanalyst:*

*Newsletter of the Division of Psychoanalytic Psychology of the American Psychological Association*, 21: 13–17.

Matte-Blanco, I. (1988). *Thinking, Feeling, and Being: Clinical Reflections on the Fundamental Antinomy of Human Beings and the World*. London & New York: Routledge.

Mead, G.H. (1934). *Mind, Self, and Society*. Chicago, IL: University of Chicago Press.

Merleau-Ponty, M. (1945/1962). *The Phenomenology of Perception*, trans. C. Smith. New York: Routledge & Kegan Paul.

Merleau-Ponty, M. (1964). *Signs*. Evanston, IL: Northwestern University Press.

Mitchell, S.A. (1988). *Relational Concepts in Psychoanalysis*: *An Integration*. Cambridge, MA: Harvard University Press.

Mitchell, S.A. (1993). *Hope and Dread in Psychoanalysis*. New York: Basic Books.

Mitchell, S.A. (1997). *Influence and Autonomy in Psychoanalysis*. Hillsdale, NJ: The Analytic Press.

Mitchell, S.A. (2000). *Relationality*. Hillsdale, NJ: The Analytic Press.

Mooney, T. (2017). *The Bourgeois Gentleman*, by Jean Baptiste Moliére. http://moliere-in english.com/2007/scripts/bourgeois/index.html

Ogden, T.H (1994). *Subjects of Analysis*. New York: Aronson.

Ogden, T.H. (1997). Some thoughts on the use of language in psychoanalysis. *Psychoanalytic Dialogues*, 7(1): 1–21.

Ogden, T.H. (1998). A question of voice in poetry and psychoanalysis. *Psychoanalytic Quarterly* 67: 426–448.

Ogden, T.H. (1999). 'The music of what happens' in poetry and psychoanalysis. *International Journal of Psycho-Analysis*, 80: 979–994.

Ogden, T.H. (2016). On language and truth in psychoanalysis. *Psychoanalytic Quarterly* 85: 411–426.

Paivio, A. (1971). *Imagery and Verbal Processes*. New York: Holt, Rinehart, and Winston.

Paivio, A (1986). *Mental Representations: A Dual Coding Approach*. New York and Oxford: Oxford University Press.

Pizer, S.A. (2000). *Building Bridges: Negotiation of Paradox in Psychoanalysis*. Hillsdale, NJ: The Analytic Press.

Reis, B. (2007). Sensing and (analytic) sensibilities: Some thoughts following Eyal Rozmarin's "An Other in psychoanalysis." *Contemporary Psychoanalysis*, 43: 374–385.

Safran, J.D. (2012). Doublethinking or dialectical thinking: A critical appreciation of Hoffman's "Doublethinking" critique. *Psychoanalytic Dialogues*, 22: 710–720.

Sander, L.W. (2002). Thinking differently: Principles of process in living systems and the specificity of being known. *Psychoanalytic Dialogues*, 12: 11–42.

Sandler, J. (1983). Reflections on some relations between psychoanalytic concepts and psychoanalytic practice. *International Journal of Psycho-Analysis*, 64: 35–45.

Sapir, E.A. (1941). *Language: An Introduction the Study of Speech*. New York: Harcourt Harvest.

Sarraute, N. (1939). *Tropisms*, trans. M. Jolas. New York: Braziller.

Sauvayre, P. & Hunyadi, O. (2018). An introductory Lacivanian idiolect: Notes on the unconscious. Paper presented at the William Alanson White Institute, New York, New York, Feb. 23, 2018. Unpublished.

Schachtel, E. (1959). *Metamorphosis: On the Conflict of Human Development and the Psychology of Creativity*. New York: Basic Books.

Schafer, R. (1976). *A New Language for Psychoanalysis*. New Haven, CT: Yale University Press.

Searles, H.F. (1965). *Collected Papers on Schizophrenia and Related Subjects*. New York: International Universities Press.

Segal, H. (1957). Notes on symbol formation. *International Journal of Psychoanalysis*, 38: 391–397.

Shore, B. (1998). *Culture in Mind: Cognition, Culture, and the Problem of Meaning*. New York: Oxford University Press.

Shusterman, R. (2004). The silent, limping body of philosophy. In: *The Cambridge Companion to Merleau-Ponty*, ed. M.B.N. Hansen & T. Carman. Cambridge, UK: Cambridge University Press, pp. 151–180.

Slavin, M.O. & Kriegman, D. (1998). Why the analyst needs to change: Toward a theory of conflict, negotiation, and mutual influence in the therapeutic process. *Psychoanalytic Dialogues*, 8: 247–284.

Slochower, J. (2006). *Psychoanalytic Collisions*. New York & London: Routledge.

Spivak, A. (2014). The interpretive process: The power of "mere" words. *Journal of the American Psychoanalytic Association*, 62: 1063–1073.

Stern, D.B. (1983) Unformulated experience: From familiar chaos to creative disorder. *Contemporary Psychoanalysis*, 19: 71–99.

Stern, D.B. (1985). Some controversies regarding constructivism and psychoanalysis. *Contemporary Psychoanalysis*, 21: 201–208.

Stern, D.B. (1989). The analyst's unformulated experience of the patient. *Contemporary Psychoanalysis*, 25: 1–33.

Stern, D.B. (1990). Courting surprise: Unbidden perceptions in clinical practice. *Contemporary Psychoanalysis*, 26: 452–478.

Stern, D.B. (1991). A philosophy for the embedded analyst: Gadamer's hermeneutics and the social paradigm of psychoanalysis. *Contemporary Psychoanalysis*, 27: 51–80.

Stern, D.B. (1992). Commentary on constructivism in clinical psychoanalysis. *Psychoanalytic Dialogues*, 2: 331–363.

Stern, D.B. (1996). Dissociation and constructivism. *Psychoanalytic Dialogues*, 6: 251–266. Reprinted in: *Memories of Sexual Betrayal*, ed. R. Gartner. New York: Jason Aronson, pp. 77–93.

Stern, D.B. (1997). *Unformulated Experience: From Dissociation to Imagination in Psychoanalysis*. New York and London: Routledge.

Stern, D.B. (2003). The fusion of horizons: Dissociation, enactment, and understanding. *Psychoanalytic Dialogues*, 13: 843–873.

Stern, D.B. (2004). The eye sees itself: Dissociation, enactment, and the achievement of conflict. *Contemporary Psychoanalysis*, 40: 197–237.

Stern, D.B. (2009). Partners in thought: A clinical process theory of narrative. *Psychoanalytic Quarterly*, 78: 701–731.

Stern, D.B. (2010a). *Partners in Thought: Working with Unformulated Experience, Dissociation, and Enactment*. New York and London: Routledge.

Stern, D.B. (2010b). Unconscious fantasy versus unconscious relatedness: Comparing interpersonal/relational and Freudian approaches to clinical practice. *Contemporary Psychoanalysis*, 46: 101–111.

Stern, D.B. (2012a). Implicit theories of technique and the values that inspire them. *Psychoanalytic Inquiry*, 32: 33–49.

Stern, D.B. (2012b). Witnessing across time: Accessing the present from the past and the past from the present. *Psychoanalytic Quarterly*, 81: 53–81.

Stern, D.B. (2013a). Field theory in psychoanalysis, Part I: Harry Stack Sullivan and Madeleine and Willy Baranger. *Psychoanalytic Dialogues*, 23: 487–501.

Stern, D.B. (2013b). Field theory in psychoanalysis, Part II: Bionian field theory and contemporary interpersonal/relational psychoanalysis. *Psychoanalytic Dialogues*, 23: 630–645.

Stern, D.B. (2013c). Relational freedom and therapeutic action. *Journal of the American Psychoanalytic Association*, 61: 227–255.

Stern, D.B. (2013d). Psychotherapy is an emergent process: In favor of acknowledging hermeneutics and against the privileging of systematic empirical research. *Psychoanalytic Dialogues*, 23: 102–115.

Stern, D.B. (2014). A response to LaFarge. *International Journal of Psychoanalysis*, 95: 1283–1297.

Stern, D.B. (2015). *Relational Freedom: Emergent Properties of the Interpersonal Field*. New York and London: Routledge.

Stern, D.B. (2017). Unformulated experience, dissociation, and *Nachträglichkeit*. *Journal of Analytical Psychology*, 62: 501–525.

Stern, D.N. (1985). *The Interpersonal World of the Infant: A View from Psychoanalysis and Developmental Psychology*. New York: Basic Books.

Stern, D.N. (1992). The 'pre-narrative envelope': An alternative view of 'unconscious phantasy' in infancy. *Bulletin of the Anna Freud Centre*, 15: 291–318.

Stern, D.N. (1995). *The Motherhood Constellation*. New York: Basic Books.

Stern, D.N., Sander, L.W., Nahum, J.P., Harrison, A.M., Lyons-Ruth, K., Morgan, A.C., Bruschweilerstern, N. & Tronick, E.Z. (1998). Non-interpretive mechanisms in psychoanalytic therapy: The 'something more' Than Interpretation. *International Journal of Psycho-Analysis*, 79: 903–921.

Stern, D.N. (2004). *The Present Moment in Psychotherapy and Everyday Life.* New York: Norton.

Stolorow, R.D. & Atwood, G. (1992). *Contexts of Being.* Hillsdale, NJ: Analytic Press.

Strenger, C. (2013). Why psychoanalysis must not discard science and human nature. *Psychoanalytic Dialogues,* 23: 197–210.

Sullivan, H.S. (1940/1953). *Conceptions of Modern Psychiatry.* New York: Norton.

Sullivan, H.S. (1950/1971). The illusion of personal individuality. In: *The Fusion of Psychiatry and Social Science.* New York: Norton, 1971, pp. 198–226.

Sullivan, H.S. (1953). *The Interpersonal Theory of Psychiatry.* New York: Norton.

Sullivan, H.S. (1956). Selective inattention. In: *Clinical Studies in Psychiatry,* eds H.S. Perry, M.I. Gawel & M. Gibbon. New York: Norton, pp. 38–76.

Target, M. & Fonagy, P. (1996). Playing with reality: II. The development of psychic reality from a theoretical perspective. *International Journal of Psychoanalysis,* 77: 459–479

Tauber, E.S. & Green, M.R. (1959). *Prelogical Experience: An Inquiry into Dreams and Other Creative Processes.* New York: Basic Books.

Taylor, C. (1971/1985). Interpretation and the sciences of man. In: *Philosophy and the Human Sciences: Philosophical Papers, Volume 2.* Cambridge, UK: Cambridge University Press, pp. 15–57.

Taylor, C. (1975). *Hegel.* Cambridge, UK: Cambridge University Press.

Taylor, C. (1985). Language and human nature. In: *Human Agency and Language: Philosophical Papers, Volume 1.* Cambridge, UK: Cambridge University Press, pp. 215–247.

Taylor, C. (1989). *Sources of the Self: The Making of the Modern Identity.* Cambridge, MA: Harvard University Press.

Taylor, C. (1991/1995). The importance of Herder. In: *Philosophical Arguments.* Cambridge, MA: Harvard University Press, pp. 79–99.

Taylor, C. (1992/1995). Heidegger, language, and ecology. In: *Philosophical Arguments.* Cambridge, MA: Harvard University Press, pp. 100–126.

Taylor, C. (1995). *Philosophical Arguments.* Cambridge, MA: Harvard University Press.

Taylor, C. (2016). *The Language Animal: The Full Shape of the Human Linguistic Capacity.* Cambridge, MA: Harvard University Press.

Trevarthen, C. (1979). Communication and cooperation in early infancy: A description of primary intersubjectivity. In: *Before Speech: The Beginning of Interpersonal Communication,* ed. M. Bullowa. New York: Cambridge University Press.

Tronick, E.Z. (2007). *The Neuro-Behavioral and Social-Emotional Development of Infants and Children.* New York: Norton.

Tublin, S. (2011). Discipline and freedom in relational technique. *Contemporary Psychoanalysis,* 47: 519–546.

Valéry, P. (1952). The course in poetics: First lesson, trans. J. Matthews. In: *The Creative Process*, ed. B. Ghiselin. Berkeley, CA: University of California Press, pp. 92–106.

Vivona, J.M. (2003). Embracing figures of speech: The transformative potential of spoken language. *Psychoanalytic Psychology*, 20: 52–66.

Vivona, J.M. (2006). From developmental metaphor to developmental model: The shrinking role of language in the talking cure. *Journal of the American Psychoanalytic Association*, 54:877–902.

Vivona, J.M. (2009a). Embodied language in neuroscience and psychoanalysis. *Journal of the American Psychoanalytic Association*, 57: 1327–1360.

Vivona, J.M. (2009b). Leaping from brain to mind: A critique of mirror neuron explanations of countertransference. *Journal of the American Psychoanalytic Association*, 57: 525–550.

Vivona, J.M. (2012). Is there a nonverbal period of development? *Journal of the American Psychoanalytic Association*, 60: 231–265.

Vivona, J.M. (2013). Psychoanalysis as poetry. *Journal of the American Psychoanalytic Association*, 61: 1109–1137.

Vivona, J.M. (2014). Speech as the confluence of words, body, and relationship: Discussion of Harris, Kirshner, and Spivak. *Journal of the American Psychoanalytic Association*, 62(6): 1081–1086.

Vygotsky, L. (1934/1962). *Thought and Language*. Cambridge, MA: MIT Press.

Wachtel, P.L. (2003). The surface and the depths: The metaphor of depth in psychoanalysis and the ways in which it can mislead. *Contemporary Psychoanalysis*, 39: 5–26.

Wachtel, P.L. (2014a). Depth, perception, and action: Past, present, and future. *Psychoanalytic Dialogues*, 24: 332–340.

Wachtel, P.L. (2014b). *Cyclical Psychodynamics and the Contextual Self: The Inner World, the Intimate World, and the World of Culture and Society*. New York and London: Routledge.

Wachtel, P.L. (2017). The relationality of everyday life: The unfinished journey of relational psychoanalysis. *Psychoanalytic Dialogues*, 27: 503–521.

Waintrater, R. (2012). Intersubjectivity and French psychoanalysis: A misunderstanding? *Studies in Gender and Sexuality*, 13: 295–302.

Wake, N. (2011). *Private Practices: Harry Stack Sullivan, the Science of Homosexuality, and American Liberalism*. New Brunswick, NJ: Rutgers University Press.

Whorf, B.L. (1956). *Language, Thought, and Reality: Selected Writings of Benjamin Lee Whorf*. Cambridge, MA: MIT Press.

Wordsworth, W. (1850). *The Prelude 1850*, ed. W. Jonson. Columbia, SC: CreateSpace Independent Publishing Platform, 2014.

Zeddies, T. (2002). More than just words: A hermeneutic view of language in psychoanalysis. *Psychoanalytic Psychology*, 19: 3–23.

# Index